MW00685778

GANDHI'S ECONOMIC THOUGHT

Do Gandhi's economic writings deal with the problems of the real world, or merely describe a dream of utopia?

Mohandas Karamchand Gandhi was not an academic but the charismatic leader of the Indian national movement. He was inspired by a vision of *swaraj* (self-government), which, for him, meant not just freedom from colonial rule but the achievement of self-reliance and self-respect by the villagers who make up most of India's population. His economics was a part of this vision.

This volume examines Gandhi's economic theories in areas that include:

* consumption behaviour;
* industrialisation, technology and the scale of production;
* trusteeship and industrial relations;
* work and leisure; and
* education as human capital.

This is a clearly written and well-researched study of Gandhi's *economic* thoughts that will be of interest not only to economists and social scientists, but also to anyone interested in Gandhi.

Ajit K. Dasgupta was educated at Presidency College, Calcutta, and Magdalene College, Cambridge. He has taught economics at universities in India, Britain, Canada, Australia and New Zealand and is an Emeritus Professor of the University of Otago. He is the author of *A History of Indian Economic Thought*.

ROUTLEDGE STUDIES IN THE HISTORY OF ECONOMICS

GANDHI'S ECONOMIC THOUGHT

Ajit K. Dasgupta

London and New York

First published 1996
by Routledge
11 New Fetter Lane, London EC4P 4EE

Simultaneously published in the USA and Canada
by Routledge
29 West 35th Street, New York, NY 10001

©1996 Ajit K. Dasgupta

Typeset in Garamond by Routledge
Printed and bound in Great Britain by
TJ Press Ltd, Padstow, Cornwall

British Library Cataloguing in Publication Data
A catalogue record for this book is available from the British Library

Library of Congress Cataloguing in Publication Data
Dasgupta, Ajit Kumar.
Gandhi's economic thought / Ajit K. Dasgupta
p. cm.—(Routledge studies in the history of economics)
Includes bibliographical references and index.
1. Gandhi, Mahatma, 1869–1948 — Views on economics.
2. Gandhi, Mahatma, 1869–1948 — Political and social views.
3. Economics – India. I.—Title. II. Series.
HB126.I43G394 1996
330.1—dc20 96–10733
CIP

ISBN 0–415–11430–6

To Sipra with love

CONTENTS

CONTENTS

ACKNOWLEDGEMENTS

I have benefited by discussion with, or comments from, Bina Agarwal, D. P. Chaudhri, Sipra Dasgupta, Danielle Pender and Joe Wallis.

I am grateful to Jeanne Skinner, who prepared the manuscript for the press with care, skill and patience, and to Rujbir Kaur Pabla, who helped with the proof-reading.

1

INTRODUCTION

That Mohandas Karamchand Gandhi (1869–1948) is one of the outstanding moral and political thinkers of our times is accepted world-wide. But was he an economist? Anjaria writes: 'When the history of economic thought in India in recent times comes to be written Gandhi's name will certainly occupy a place of honour in it.'[1] But he hastened to add: 'It does not matter in this context whether we call Gandhi an economist or not; that is, partly at any rate, a question of definition of terms.'[2] A study of Gandhi's economic ideas must in some way come to grips with this question.

Gandhi was much farther off the mainstream of economics than other Indian nationalist economists, such as Ranade, had been. Machinery is a 'grand yet awful invention',[3] 'the law of supply and demand is a devilish law',[4] 'tractors and chemical fertilisers will spell ruin for India'.[5] It is for opinions such as these that Gandhi as an economist is usually remembered. Even a sympathetic reader may find it difficult to take such statements seriously.

Some of the methodological issues that arise in an analysis of Gandhi's economic ideas are discussed in this chapter, which is organised in four sections. The first section addresses the question of whether Gandhi's economics is purely utopian. The second section examines the place of religion in Gandhi's world view. The subsequent section considers Gandhi's views on the inter-relationship of economics and ethics; and the nature of Gandhi's ethical theory is discussed in the final section.

1

UTOPIA AND REALITY IN GANDHIAN ECONOMICS

A question that will occur to a careful reader of Gandhi's economic writings is whether they describe simply a dream of utopia or are meant to deal with problems of the real world.

In describing the content of his economic vision Gandhi draws an analogy with Euclid. 'Euclid has defined a straight line as having no breadth, but no one has yet succeeded in drawing such a line and no one ever will.'[6] But this is consistent with either interpretation. It could mean that, like the straight line 'which cannot be drawn', the Gandhian model relates to an ideal economic order where people could well be motivated quite differently from those in any society that we know of. However, it could also mean that 'something like' a straight line can be drawn, and in economics as in geometry the postulational method can help in achieving clarity in thought and in solving real-life problems, for 'we must have a proper picture of what we want, before we can have something approaching it'.[7] Both versions contain elements of truth. Gandhi was not an academic but the charismatic leader of the Indian national movement. He was inspired by a vision of *swaraj* (self-government) which, for him, meant not just freedom from colonial rule but the achievement of self-reliance, and self-respect, by the villagers who make up most of India's population. His economics was a part of this vision.

Thus, Gandhi was trying to describe an economic ideal to strive for rather than simply an economic plan to implement. To that extent his economics was utopian. However, 'utopian' can also refer to something 'impractical' or even 'impossible'. Gandhi's economic thought was not 'utopian' in that sense. It was certainly meant to apply to an actual society, that of rural India in particular. It would still apply only to a few selected aspects of that society while neglecting others, but that is true of *all* economic models. The case for this 'pragmatic' view of Gandhian economics appears more plausible if we remember the context of his writings.

Most of them appeared in daily newspapers or weekly journals, *Young India* (in English), *Navajivan* (in Gujrati), and *Harijan* (in Hindi), and were addressed to a mass audience whose attention he tried to capture by making his points short and sharp. In this he succeeded, and as a journalist, especially during the 1920s and 1930s, he exercised considerable influence. Also, his writings were produced and published in the heat of political battle.

2

Yet another argument in favour of this interpretation is that Gandhi regarded his conclusions on economic policy as only provisional. Thus, in his preface to *Hind Swaraj*, he described the views expressed there as 'mine, yet not mine'.[8] They were his only in the sense that he hoped to act according to them. However, if his views proved to be wrong he would have no hesitation in rejecting them.[9] Gandhi's American biographer, Louis Fischer, notes this provisional aspect of Gandhi's ideas: he was always thinking aloud: 'He did not attempt to express his ideas in a finished form. You heard not only his words but also his thoughts. You could, therefore, follow him as he moved to a conclusion.'[10] In the same spirit he came to admit that some of the things he had earlier condemned, e.g. railways, motor cars and machinery could in certain circumstances confer benefits too, and that they should not be prohibited altogether. Appropriate restrictions on their use could perhaps provide adequate safeguards against misuse.[11]

Writings on Gandhian economics have usually focused attention on the specific policies that he proposed: opposition to modern manufacturing production based on the use of machinery, advocacy of village industries, in particular, the spinning wheel, and boycott of foreign goods. It is with policies such as these that Gandhi's name is associated. On our argument proper understanding of his views requires a rather different emphasis. The structure of his arguments, the assumptions he made, and the principles of conduct to which he appealed, must be regarded as of central importance. It is these, I believe, that make his specific policy proposals comprehensible, not the other way round. I thus agree with Anjaria[12] that 'Gandhism is not just a series of disjointed maxims of policy or a catalogue of urgent reforms and remedial measures',[13] and with Nanda that 'What is called Gandhism is ... only a distinctive attitude to society and politics rather than an ideology; a particular ethical standpoint rather than fixed formulae or a definitive system.'[14] What, then, made his attitude distinctive?

GANDHI'S RELIGION

I shall examine first the common view that the distinctive element in Gandhi's attitude to politics, economics and society came from his religious world outlook. Gandhi's speeches and writings are indeed replete with a religious terminology which became a kind of 'signature tune' and has been called his saintly idiom. That idiom has received much attention. What has been missed is that expressions of

dislike of organised religion and detestation of religious fundamentalism of all brands occur no less frequently in his published works.
Gandhi was highly sceptical about the value of religious rites and
ceremonies, with the sole exception of the public prayer meeting,
which he turned into a means of educating the public on political
economic and moral issues. The basic element of a religious outlook is
concern with 'the other world'. Gandhi did not share this concern.
'You need not think of the world beyond. If you can do your duty here
the "beyond" will take care of itself.'[15]

Also, he held religion to be an essentially personal matter, something 'between oneself and one's God'.[16] He suggested that there
might, in effect, be as many religions as there were persons, and was
fond of pointing out that religious persecution was as ancient as
religion itself.[17] None of these attitudes is characteristic of a truly
religious world outlook. As Morris-Jones has noted, Gandhi had 'little
intellectual interest in, or capacity for handling, religious or metaphysical ideas'.[18]

Nevertheless, there *was* a sense in which religion was important in
shaping Gandhi's ideas: religions provided some criteria of right and
wrong and could help in framing rules of conduct in one's daily life.
But religion in this sense was indistinguishable from ethics. And
indeed Gandhi did not distinguish between them. 'For me morals,
ethics and religion are convertible terms.'[19] What their 'convertibility'
implied comes out if we look at Gandhi's attitude to individual
religions.

Gandhi professed to be a devout Hindu and often chided his
countrymen for failing to live up to the high moral norms of their own
past. He was adamant, however, that the norms themselves could not
be derived from tradition, custom or religious text. 'It is good to swim
in the waters of tradition but to sink in them was suicide.'[20] Likewise,
Hinduism was hemmed in by many old customs, some of which were
good but the rest were to be condemned. Gandhi's condemnation
extended not only to bad customs but even to religious texts. He
insisted that his belief in Hindu scriptures did not require him to
accept every word and every verse as divinely inspired and he declined
to be bound by any interpretation, however learned, if it was
'repugnant to reason or moral sense'.[21]

Even the Veda, regarded by Hindus as the holiest texts of all
because they represented the word of God, were not exempt: 'no
matter what is credited with Vedic origin if it is repugnant to the

moral sense it must be summarily rejected as contrary to the spirit of the Veda, and perhaps *what is more* as contrary to fundamental ethics'.[22]

Because he found many such passages in the Hindu scriptures, he called for the scriptures to be revised. An authoritative body, he suggested, should be set up:

> that would revise all that passes under the name of scriptures, expurgate all the texts that have no moral values or are contrary to the fundamentals of religion and morality, and present such an edition for the guidance of Hindus.[23]

This suggestion did not meet with a favourable response! Gandhi had great respect, too, for religions other than his own and quoted from the Bible or the Koran to make a point, almost as frequently as he quoted from the *Bhagavadgita*, but they too were subject to the judgement of reason. 'I reject any religious doctrine that does not appeal to reason and is in conflict with morality.'[24] Accordingly he insisted that even the teachings of the Holy Koran cannot be exempt from criticism. 'After all we have no other guide but our reason to tell us what may be regarded as revealed and what may not be.'[25]

The claims of divine revelation, therefore, remained subject to those of human reason. Thus for example for certain offences such as adultery, stoning to death was the prescribed punishment in Islamic law but Gandhi found it to be an inhuman practice, which 'cannot be defended on the mere ground of its mention in the Koran'.[26]

Gandhi often mentions his debt to the teachings of Jesus and in particular to the Sermon on the Mount. It was his *teachings*, however, that appealed. The orthodox Christian belief that Jesus was the only begotten son of God appeared to Gandhi to be a claim to monopoly which was contrary to reason. It was also irrelevant in considering the validity of Jesus's teachings on how to lead a good life. For this reason Gandhi described himself as a rebel against orthodox Christianity and its interpretation of the life of Jesus.

Recounting the history of Christianity Gandhi also points out that Jesus was an Asiatic whose message was delivered through many media and 'when it had the backing of a Roman emperor it became an imperialist faith as it remains to this day'.[27] The role of Christianity, and Christian missionaries, in the establishment and maintenance of European imperialism in Afro-Asian countries receives marked attention in Gandhi's writings.

Gandhi had great respect, too, for the Jain and Buddhist faiths, mainly because they gave a central place to *ahimsa* and preached compassion not only for all humankind but for all living creatures; but he criticised the mechanical and negative way in which these doctrines were being applied by present-day Jains and Buddhists. On Jain practices in contemporary India, he comments: 'Where the doctrine of compassion is followed in action, it seems to be limited to feeding ants and preventing people from catching fish.'[28]

I conclude this part of my discussion by expressing agreement with Morris-Jones that Gandhi's world outlook was *not* a religious one.

> Religion is said to have played a great part in his life. Yet his attachment to religion is limited ... it is his ethical emphasis and the lack of a developed doctrinal system which enabled Gandhi to remain throughout an eclectic in religion.[29]

It is Gandhi's 'ethical emphasis' and its relevance for his economic ideas that I shall discuss next.

ECONOMICS AND ETHICS

What really differentiates Gandhi's approach to economic issues from the mainstream tradition is his extraordinary emphasis on the ethical aspect of economic behaviour. Indeed, he believed that economic and ethical considerations were inseparable. Replying to the poet Tagore who had reproached him for mixing these up, Gandhi wrote: 'I must confess that I do not draw a sharp or any distinction between economics and ethics.'[30]

They could, he said, be considered in isolation, as indeed they usually were, but for conclusions derived from economic analysis to be valid or relevant they should not. It is *because* standard economic analysis failed to take ethical considerations into account, suggested Gandhi, that economics itself had become largely irrelevant for either understanding behaviour or prescribing policy. For this reason he likens the economics that disregards moral and sentimental considerations to 'wax works that being life-like still lack the life of the living flesh. At every crucial moment these new fangled economic laws have broken down in practice'.[31]

Because ethical considerations were closely bound up with economic ones, it was not legitimate to regard ethical influences simply as disturbing factors that 'prevented economic laws from having free play'.[32] It was not reasonable to abstract from them even as a first approximation. Nevertheless Gandhi never gave up a belief in the vital importance of economic considerations for the life of individuals and

6

nations nor in the possibility that a less narrowly focused and more relevant economics *could* be developed.

Gandhi insisted that the relationship between economics and ethics works both ways. While economic concepts were laden with ethical implications, ethics too must descend from the clouds and become 'good economics'. Ethics, Gandhi is saying, is not simply an exercise for philosophers, a convenient handle for sharpening their wits on the logic of extremes. It must be relevant to the ordinary business of life where one's options are limited by resource constraints. Ethics by its very nature is an enterprise for the worldly, a guide to the perplexed; and its answers, to be credible, need to be economically viable. 'No person in the world has found it possible to maintain something which is a source of constant economic loss.'[33]

If religion and morality appeared to be at odds with economics, something had to give. The conflict could be due to the economic interest taking the form of unmitigated selfishness which does not care for the welfare of others. This is the case that critics of free market economics usually have in mind. But denunciations of economics from a religious or moral point of view, such as the one Gandhi himself had made in *Hind Swaraj*, could be irresponsible, too, '(in other words) if a religion cuts at the very fundamentals of economics it is not a true religion but only a delusion.'[34]

Trying to carry out ethically good policies by methods involving continuing economic loss was futile. Viable methods of financing projects had to be found. This helps explain why Gandhi, who worked all his life for the cause of protecting animals, and cows in particular, regarded schemes for conducting tanneries on sound economic lines as essential for the cause to succeed. That required exploring possibilities of profitable export, utilising by-products, and putting bones, hides and intestines of cows to practical use.[35] Similar reasoning explains why Gandhi strongly opposed a proposal that cotton spinners should also be encouraged to weave, for he believed that this involved economic disadvantage. 'Whatever is basically harmful on economic grounds is also certainly harmful from the religious point of view. Untainted wealth can never be opposed to religion.'[36]

GANDHI AND ETHICAL THEORY

Gandhi's approach to economic issues was explicitly based on ethical considerations. His understanding of the nature of ethical enquiry is therefore important for a study of his economic thought. For this purpose it is useful to distinguish between three leading schools of ethics, namely utilitarianism, consequentialism and deontology, in so far as they bear on issues relating to choice.[37]

Broadly speaking consequentialism is the view that in order to determine whether a particular choice is the right choice for an agent to make, one must look at the consequences of the choice for the world at large, and only at these. Utilitarianism, an ethical doctrine with which economics has been closely associated, may be defined as that particular form of consequentialism in which the only consequences that matter are those bearing on the utilities of human beings, utility being understood either in the sense of pleasure/happiness (as in Bentham and J. S. Mill) or preference − satisfaction (as in modern economic theory).

Both consequentialism and utilitarianism are 'teleological' theories, the word 'teleological' being derived from 'telos', which in Greek means end or purpose. While teleological theories differ among themselves they agree in asserting that the rightness of an action depends upon the goodness of its effects and only on these.

Deontological theories, by contrast, see the rightness of an action as being intrinsic to the action itself. To determine whether an action is right it is not required that we must examine the consequences of doing it. An action could be right simply because it satisfies accepted moral rules, or corresponds to moral intuition, or fulfils the obligations incumbent on the agent and so on, regardless of its good or bad effects. To which school, if any, does Gandhi belong?

Gandhi refers to utilitarianism as the 'doctrine of the greatest happiness of the greatest number', a phrase first used by Jeremy Bentham, the founding father of utilitarian philosophy. According to Gandhi the doctrine has two main features. First, it holds that 'in order to achieve the supposed good of 51 per cent the interest of the 49 per cent may be or rather should be sacrificed'.[38] Second, the theory is solely concerned with *economic* happiness, that is, with that part of individuals' happiness which arises from material prosperity. Gandhi supposes utilitarianism to be the dominant ethical doctrine in Western countries and sums it up as follows:

People in the west generally hold that it is man's duty to promote the happiness-prosperity that is of the greatest number. Happiness is taken to mean material happiness exclusively, that is economic prosperity. If in the pursuit of this happiness, moral laws are violated, it does not matter much. Again, as the object is the happiness of the greatest number, people in the west do not believe it to be wrong if it is secured, at the cost of the minority. The consequences of this attitude are in evidence in all western countries.[39]

Gandhi has two points to make: that one should be concerned with the good of *all* rather than just with those of a majority; and that one should not be *exclusively* concerned with material prosperity but also with the moral aspect of actions.

Now, Gandhi's first point arises from a misunderstanding of utilitarian doctrine. Strictly speaking, 'the greatest happiness of the greatest number', a phrase introduced by Bentham, in his *Fragment on Government* in 1776, is self-contradictory: for maximisation to be meaningful there should be one maximand, not two. Bentham later came to realise this himself, and pointed out that distributing a minority of 2,000 men as slaves among the majority of 2,001 could promote the happiness of the greatest number but not the greatest aggregate happiness. Accordingly he dropped the reference to number and used instead 'the greatest happiness'.[40] According to utilitarianism, it is greatest happiness *in the aggregate* that a moral agent should try to achieve by an appropriate choice of actions. Now aggregate happiness achieved in a particular state of affairs may not be a proper measure of its goodness, but that was already covered by Gandhi's *second* point.

Despite his mistake about what utilitarianism actually states, critical remarks on utilitarianism scattered throughout Gandhi's writings suggest that he may have been pointing to a genuine difficulty with that doctrine. Taking aggregate happiness as the maximand still does not address the question of how that aggregate is distributed among individuals. As Scheffter notes, a major criticism of classical utilitarianism is that it 'will require us to ignore the misery of a few people and concentrate instead on increasing the pleasures of the many simply in order to maximise aggregate satisfaction'.[41] Gandhi's abiding concern with the welfare of minorities points in the same direction.

Gandhi's second point, that there is more to human welfare then pleasure or happiness or preference-satisfaction, is a recurrent theme in his economic writings. Moral consequences of actions, he urged, mattered a great deal. I shall return to this point towards the end of this section in connection with Gandhi's doctrine of the unity of ends and means.

Gandhi rejected utilitarianism. He saw ethical norms as shaping economic behaviour. He described truth as God, and his pronouncements on the central importance of personal autonomy, human dignity and respect for the individual have a distinctly Kantian flavour. For these reasons he is commonly seen as a deontologist. But the differences between the Gandhian and the deontological view of choice are more basic than their similarities.

First, Gandhi did not accept the central tenet of deontological moral theory – that certain actions are right *per se*, irrespective of their consequences. Gandhi, too, extolled the virtues of some kinds of action – keeping promises, honouring vows, helping neighbours and friends, doing one's job conscientiously, treating people as equals, fighting for the oppressed and so on. To do such actions was one's human duty. But he did not claim that they were right simply by virtue of being the kinds of actions they were. Instead he sought to justify such actions in terms of their contribution to a broader purpose – the service of humankind. To assess that contribution one had to look at consequences. Thus, for example, if the ruler did his duty, by acting as the trustee of his people, the people would flourish and the ruler survive. If mill workers did *not* do their duty, 'anarchy and chaos' would be the result,[42] and so on.

A second difference between Gandhi and the deontologists relates to the importance of motives. In assessing the rightness of an action deontologists tend to place a great deal of weight on the nature of the motive with which the action was performed. Some motives, they believe, count as being morally superior to others and actions based on them have some merit whatever the outcome. Gandhi too did not regard motive as irrelevant: 'It is not enough that an act done by us is itself good; it should have been done with the intention to do good.'[43] On the other hand, if an action helped to bring about a morally bad outcome he would not accept the pureness of the motive as a mitigating factor. For this reason he condemned acts of 'misplaced benevolence'. To this category belonged such apparently charitable deeds as providing free meals to the able-bodied poor without requiring them to render some honest work in return; giving alms to professional beggars, which, he proposed, should be made punishable by law; foreign aid, which undermined incentives to work and save; and doles for the unemployed unaccompanied by stringent conditions such as the obligation to accept work, if provided (see Chapter 2, especially pages 30–35). It was their consequences, and above all the erosion of self-respect by recipients of 'charity', that made such policies morally bad in Gandhi's estimation. That they might have been inspired by the purest of motives made no difference to this judgement.

Finally, Gandhi, unlike most deontologists, was greatly concerned with the problem of a conflict arising *between* one moral principle and another. Deontologists claim that certain actions are right as such. The claim rests ultimately on the 'categorical' character of certain moral obligations, requirements and principles. An action which satisfies them is right, one which violates them is wrong, irrespective of any other result. But what if one moral obligation incumbent on the agent is in conflict with another? This, Gandhi believed, was usually the case in choosing between actions. All basic principles of conduct can be derived from Truth. 'But life is not so simple. It is not possible to enunciate one grand principle and leave the rest to follow of itself.'[44]

That life is not 'a straight line' and that one cannot arrive at the right choices by applying an over-riding moral principle in terms of which every alternative can be assessed, are persistent themes in Gandhi's works.[45] On the contrary, even the simplest choices in life usually involve a number of *different* moral principles. This would not much matter if there was a well-established hierarchy among the various principles or if the relationship between them was always one of complementarity rather than substitution, but Gandhi did not believe this was the case. Life, he states, 'is a bundle of duties, very often conflicting. And one is called upon continually to make one's choice between one duty and another'.[46]

The deontological prescription for choice, namely that an agent's actions must not violate certain 'absolute moral side-constraints',[47] was therefore impracticable, for satisfying one constraint may *require* violating another. Practical ethics, according to Gandhi, was a matter not of absolute but of relative *dharma*. 'Relative *dharma* does not proceed on a straight path, like a railway track. It has on the contrary to make its way through a dense forest where there is not even a sense of direction.'[48]

Looking at consequences of actions helps us in finding a direction. One could always appeal to 'absolute' principles, that is truth and *ahimsa*, which was the way to achieving truth, but determining what constituted truth or *ahimsa* in any particular instance always required estimating results and working out trade-offs. Here is an example;

I am a member of an institution which holds a few acres of land whose crops are in imminent peril from monkeys. I believe in

11

the sacredness of all life and hence I regard it as a breach of *ahimsa* to inflict any injury on the monkeys. But I do not hesitate to instigate and direct an attack on the monkeys in order to save the crops.[49]

Here the benefits from saving the crops were judged to outweigh the moral loss involved in doing injury to the monkeys.

Similarly, Gandhi's commitment to *ahimsa* did not stop him from becoming an early advocate of voluntary euthanasia and under certain circumstances even of 'involuntary euthanasia'. He expressed approval of the action of an actress who had shot her husband to save him from a painful death by cancer.

I wouldn't see any sin in ending the life of the husband who was lingering in pain and to whom no relief could be given even by careful nursing. If, however, the husband is conscious his wishes should be ascertained. If he wishes to live despite the pain, he should be allowed to live.[50]

Again it is to consequences that he looks rather than to absolute principles such as the sacredness of life. Gandhi's ethical position is consequentialist. It is, however, sufficiently flexible to be able to accommodate the core concern of deontological ethics – that certain moral ends are so very important that they must be treated as non-negotiable. There are two elements in Gandhi's ethical theory that enable this to be done. First, in respect of their ethical significance, he refused to draw any sharp distinction between means and ends, between actions and outcomes. Moral consequences attached to both so the means require to be justified as such, without reference to the ends they are designed to achieve. Second, he believed that some consequences could be morally good or bad to an extent greater than any that could be measured. This allows consequences to be *infinitely* good or bad.

Together these imply that certain actions – such as treating a fellow human being as an untouchable – could have an infinite degree of morally evil consequence attached to them. Such actions therefore cannot be right actions for an agent to perform. In this respect, Gandhi's consequentialism thus merges into deontology.

2

PREFERENCE, UTILITY AND WELFARE

INTRODUCTION

Gandhi's commitment to the proposition that 'ultimately, it is the individual who is the unit'[1] inevitably led him to an individualist, rather than a collectivist, view of society's welfare. It was individuals, rather than caste, class, tribe, race or state, who mattered: 'if the individual ceases to count, what is left of society?'[2] Social choice which was dictatorial or imposed could not properly be regarded as choice at all and *satyagraha* in the form of non-violent non-cooperation always remained a valid option. Considerations relating to individuals' preferences and welfare were therefore in Gandhi's view of crucial importance not only in determining consumers' choices on goods and services but also for making judgements about social and economic institutions and policies. In this matter, Gandhi's view is entirely in line with the thrust of modern economic theory which, unlike sociology or political science, places the individual at the centre.

There is, however, another element in Gandhi's world view where he parts company with standard economics. This is his conviction that one's behaviour as an economic agent cannot be isolated from one's behaviour as an autonomous moral agent. Economic analysis that seeks either to promote understanding of behaviour or provide guidance for policy must therefore find a place for ethical considerations. From this point of view the concept of preference that is most relevant for economic analysis is not individual preference as such but rather individual preference modified by reflection, corrected by knowledge and experience and regulated by ethical principles. It is this normative concept of preference, which I shall call 'ethical preference', that lies at the heart of the Gandhian approach to economic theory.

13

The concept of ethical preference follows logically from Gandhi's insistence on the inter-relationship between economics and ethics, a point which I discussed in the previous chapter. Here I should like to point out that Gandhi's approach to the notions of preference and welfare nicely illustrates the distinction drawn by Barry between want-regarding and ideal-regarding principles. Want-regarding principles

> take as given the wants people happen to have and concentrate attention entirely on the extent to which a certain policy will alter the overall amount of want-satisfaction or on the way in which the policy will affect the distribution among people of opportunities for satisfying wants.[3]

Principles that are *not* want-regarding in this sense are defined by Barry as ideal-regarding. These include principles which suppose the satisfaction of some types of want-satisfaction to be without any value at all, those which state that it would actually be better if certain wants were *not* satisfied and those which attribute value to things other than want-satisfaction, for example to people's characters, beliefs or overall life-styles.[4] Standard economic analysis, at least implicitly, accepts the want-regarding principle, which Gandhi rejects.

This chapter is organised as follows: the present section serves as an introduction; the following section discusses Gandhi's theory of the limitation of wants; and the third, his concept of *swadeshi*. The fourth section deals with Gandhi's views on altruism and charity; and the fifth with his views on work and leisure. The chapter concludes with a few remarks on Gandhi's approach.

THE LIMITATION OF WANTS

Gandhi's ideas on preference, choice and welfare can be regarded as particular applications of his general concept of ethical preference. The application that I shall consider first is his doctrine of the limitation of wants, a typically Gandhian contribution to normative economics. In essence it argues that an individuals' welfare is best achieved not, as economic theory suggests, by attempting to maximise the satisfaction of a multiplicity of desires subject only to the prevailing budget constraint, but rather by reflecting on one's desires and trying to choose between them. The claim is supported by arguments bearing on the relationships between desire, satisfaction, happiness and welfare. While economic theory has often regarded

14

these concepts as closely related and sometimes even as synonymous, Gandhi's thesis rests on the argument that they are quite distinct.

First, not all kinds of happiness contribute to human welfare. That drink or drugs can make people happy for a while is not, for example, a relevant consideration for policy.[5] Second, satisfying desires need not necessarily contribute to happiness. Primarily this is because an individual's desires for goods and services do not form a fixed set such that their satisfaction would make the individual happy: 'We notice that the mind is a restless bird; the more it gets the more it wants and still remains unsatisfied. The more we indulge our passions the more unbridled they become.'[6]

Multiplying one's daily wants in unreflective fashion merely makes a person subject to an unending sequence of desires. Such a process does not lead an individual to any sustainable steady-state consumption path. Those who are part of a mad rush to multiply wants, thinking that this will add to their real substance, are mistaken. On the contrary, self-indulgence and the ceaseless multiplication of wants hamper one's growth because they are erosive of contentment, personal autonomy, self-respect and peace of mind. And it is from these that one's long-run happiness can be found, not just from obtaining what one likes at the moment. This is a theme that occurs throughout Gandhi's writings. He wrote in 1909: 'Contentment is happiness. Who has ever known any happiness other than this? Every other kind of happiness is but a mirage. The nearer we approach it, the further it recedes.'[7]

And here is Gandhi making the same point in 1942:

Man's happiness really lies in contentment. He who is dis-contented, however much he possesses, becomes a slave to his desires. And there is really no slavery equal to that of his desires.... And what is true for the individual is true for society.[8]

On both occasions it is clear from the context that Gandhi was not telling the poor to be content with poverty but rather telling the rich that uncontrolled self-indulgence could not make one happy. Gandhi himself was quite conscious about who his targets were, and denied allegations that he was interested only in spiritual uplift, not in raising material standards for the common man. 'In my own way I have tried – more than perhaps any other man – to increase the level of material resources of the average man in India.'[9] This is a point to which I shall return later in this chapter.

15

Gandhi argued that individuals do not have to follow their existing desires blindly but could, if they wished, control, regulate or modify them after due reflection and, where necessary, the acquisition of relevant information. This, he suggested, could be achieved more easily if individuals came to formulate their preferences in terms of characteristics of commodities rather than simply in terms of commodities as such. In choosing items of daily necessity, such as foodstuffs, this was both a natural and a convenient way to proceed. The nutritive content of food items, how easily they could be combined to form a balanced diet, digestibility and ease of cooking should, he stated, count as relevant characteristics, as well as their appeal to the palate. 'Neem leaves ought not to be shunned simply on account of their bitter taste, their efficacy is well-known.'[10]

For the same reason, he decries 'preferring bone-white sugar to rich brown *gur* and pale white bread to rich brown bran-bread' and calls this mistaking the shadow for the substance.[11] He remained optimistic, however, that with education, and perhaps some help and advice from knowledgable people, individuals would be quite willing to modify their preferences in the right direction. 'There may be some who burden their diet with useless articles and many whose diet is badly deficient in vitamins. You have to introduce the right kind of diet to them.'[12]

Gandhi looked on rural development as consisting in large measure of changing individuals' preferences in this fashion. Individuals may be impelled towards unlimited wants not only by their own desires but also by the prevailing social ethos. In modern Western society, states Gandhi, the basis of culture or civilisation is understood to be the multiplication of all one's wants.

> If you have one room you will desire to have two rooms, three rooms, the more the merrier. And similarly you will want to have as much furniture as you can put in your house, and so on endlessly. And the more you possess the better culture you represent or some such thing![13]

There is an echo here of Tolstoy whom Gandhi has described as a mentor:

> Today I obtain a coat and goloshes, tomorrow a watch and chair, after tomorrow a sofa and lamp, then carpets in the sitting-room and velvet clothes, then race-horses and pictures in gilt frames, till finally I fall ill from my excessive labours and die.[14]

Yet another reason why trying to maximise desire-satisfaction may not make an individual or a society happy has to do with the means required to achieve such an outcome. The process of trying to satisfy an ever-expanding multitude of wants, argues Gandhi, has its own costs. In particular, it requires the extensive use of machinery, which he strenuously opposed (see Chapter 4).

Typically a country pursuing the quest will be 'made hideous by the smoke and the din of mill chimneys and factories' and its roadways,

> traversed by rushing engines dragging numerous cars crowded with men mostly who know not what they are after, who are often absent-minded and whose tempers do not improve by being uncomfortably packed like sardines in boxes and finding themselves in the midst of utter strangers who would oust them if they could and whom they would in their turn oust similarly.[15]

Besides, in a country where every household had a car, 'there would be very little room left for walking'.[16] Such things, observes Gandhi, are held to be symbol of material progress but, 'they add not an atom to our happiness'.[17] Deliberate restriction of material desires by individuals by means of 'the utmost effort'[18] offers a more rational solution.

Another argument in favour of limiting wants turns on the adverse *moral* consequences of economic growth. As we have seen, at the heart of the Gandhian approach to economic issues is the belief that ethical and economic considerations are inseparable. The objective must be to bring about improvements in both the economic and the moral well-being of individuals, and thereby of society. But material progress can itself affect moral standards. These 'externalities' must be taken into account in the overall reckoning and a balance struck. Sometimes they could be of a positive kind. This is likely to be the case when there is mass poverty.

Millions of people in India live on only one meal a day. 'They say that before we can think or talk of their moral welfare, we must satisfy their daily wants. With these, they say, material progress spells moral progress.'[19] Gandhi agrees with 'them' but, he argues, what is true of thirty million is not necessarily true of the universe. Indeed, such a deduction would be 'ludicrously absurd' for 'hard cases make bad law'.

> No one has ever suggested that grinding pauperism can lead to anything else than moral degradation. Every human being has a right to live and therefore to find the wherewithal to feed himself and where necessary to clothe and house himself.[20]

That, however, was not the issue. 'The only statement', suggests Gandhi, 'that has to be examined is whether it can be laid down as a law of universal application that material advancement means moral progress.'[21] His answer is that it cannot: both at the level of individuals and societies, there are too many examples to the contrary. In general, Gandhi believes that material affluence beyond a point not only does not imply but actively hinders moral progress. Gandhi does not discuss whether, or how, one could determine just *where* the point was located but he was convinced that it does exist. For this reason when discussing comparative standards of living of different societies Gandhi always asked questions about moral as well as economic aspects. Neither literacy nor wealth *per se*, without a moral backing, had any attraction for him as a 'social indicator'.[22] To a correspondent who had pointed out Japan's achievements in terms of material progress and the level of literacy, Gandhi responded: 'And why are you so enamoured of the material progress of Japan? I do not know whether the material has gone side by side with the moral progress.'[23]

There are echoes here of Ruskin, who wrote in *Unto This Last*:

> It is impossible to conclude, of any given mass of acquired wealth, merely by the fact of its existence, whether it signifies good or evil to the nation in the midst of which it exists. Its real value depends on the moral sign attached to it.

The limitation of wants appeared to be a way of avoiding adverse effects of material progress.

Whichever of these various justifications of the doctrine of limitation of wants one takes as primary, they have one thing in common, namely that such limitation is not intended as a glorification of austerity but rather as an exercise in the optimisation of overall individual welfare. In taking up such a position Gandhi anticipated a basic theme of the recent literature against economic growth. Indeed he was one of the first writers to argue explicitly and in a systematic way that non-economic aspects of welfare are important and that a single-minded pursuit of the maximum satisfaction of material wants might not lead to the best of all possible worlds. In developing this thesis Gandhi was influenced by Ruskin and Tolstoy but he had a far more positive and practical approach than either.

Doctrines calling for a limitation of wants can easily be construed as an attempt at ideological justification of the status quo and sometimes such may indeed be their purpose. When, for example, St. Augustine and his followers developed the theory of the reorientation and

18

limitation of wants as a way of dealing with the scarcity of resources they often combined this with an explicit appeal to the poor to remain content with their lot.

Gandhi did not. On the contrary he often called on poor and exploited people *not* to remain content with what they had. Noting that industrial labourers in India were dissatisfied with their lot, Gandhi stated that they had ample justification for being dissatisfied.[24] In assessing the interpretative significance of Gandhi's doctrine of the limitation of wants the question of *what* things wants should be limited to is, therefore, of considerable importance. Gandhi's views on this appear to have changed over time.

In some of his early writings he appeals to the principle of what he calls satisfying one's 'natural wants'. Each person should be able to satisfy all natural wants and no more. These are conceived as minimal, or basic, needs. 'One should make do with the fewest possible articles of food, and in the smallest possible quantity . . . no more than what is absolutely necessary to pay the body its hire.'[25]

However, natural wants will vary from one individual to another depending on metabolism. If one person has a weak digestion and so requires only a quarter pound of flour for his bread and another needs a pound, the former's natural want will be correspondingly lower. Natural wants also vary with climate. 'Fiery whisky in the north of the British Isles may be a necessity, it renders an Indian unfit for work or society. Fur coats in Scotland are indispensable, they will be an intolerable burden in India.'[26]

Some natural wants, according to Gandhi, could only be specified at the village, rather than the individual, level. To this category belong transport and sanitation:

> The roads should be so scrupulously clean in this land of crores of barefooted pedestrians that nobody need hesitate in walking or even sleeping in the streets. The lanes should be macadamised and have gutters for letting out water. The temples and mosques should be kept so beautifully clean that the visitors should feel an air of tranquil holiness about them. The village should as far as possible, be full of shady trees and fruit trees in and around them. It should have a *dharamshala*, a school and a small dispensary. Washing and privy arrangements should be such as may not contaminate the air, water and roads of the village.[27]

But even in the case of goods and services of this kind the observed level of demand did not necessarily indicate the quantum of real need, for demand itself could be determined by supply.

> Wherever there is a hospital it is bound to be filled up with patients. From this it should not be concluded that it would be a great boon to the villages if there were seven lakh hospitals in seven lakh villages.[28]

Elsewhere, especially in his later writings, Gandhi appears to take a rather broader view of 'basic needs'. The proliferation of material wants is still rejected as a goal. One's aim should rather be their restriction consistent with comfort, which is less narrowly interpreted than natural want. Typical of this broader outlook are passages such as the following;

> If by abundance you mean everyone having plenty to eat and drink and to clothe himself with, enough to keep his mind trained and educated, I should be satisfied. But I should not like to pack more stuff in my belly than I can digest and more things than I can ever usefully use. But neither do I want poverty, penury, misery, dirt and dust in India.[29]

And again, 'Everyone must have balanced diet, a decent house to live in, facilities for the education of one's children and adequate medical relief.'[30] For the same reason, spinners' wages should be adequate for ensuring 'wholesome and nutritious food, necessary clothing, comfortable houses and other amenities necessary for a happy home'. The tiller of the soil should have a 'sufficiency of fresh, pure milk and oil, fish, eggs and meat if he is a non-vegetarian, adequate but not fine clothing (what would fine clothes, for instance, avail him if he is ill-nourished and underfed?)'[31] facilities for sanitation, comfortable housing, clean drinking water, dirt-free roads and a sense of participation in decisions that affect his daily life.

Half a century after Gandhi's death, the bill of goods that he prescribed as a minimum is still not one that the average household of most third world countries is in a position to consume. The actual consumption of both rural and urban poor falls far short of the limits to wants that Gandhi set. On the other hand, the affluent, and even many of those not so affluent, are often engaged in a frantic display of luxury consumption in a way that Gandhi had supposed to be peculiarly 'Western'. In this perspective the limitation of wants can be seen as a means of reducing rather than condoning inequality.

This aspect of Gandhi's doctrine of the limitation of wants comes out clearly in some of his later writings, for example, in his statement that while he did not want to taboo everything above and beyond the bare necessities, 'they must come after the essential needs of the poor are satisfied. First things must come first'.[32]

ETHICAL PREFERENCES AND SWADESHI

Gandhi's concept of ethical preferences also provided the moral basis of the Swadeshi Movement, which I shall discuss next. The word *swadeshi* means indigenous or home-grown.

The Swadeshi Movement was a mass movement undertaken by the Indian National Congress under Gandhi's leadership to encourage people, especially those living in cities, to develop the habit of consuming Indian rather than foreign products, and products of village industry rather than mill-made products. They were urged in particular to wear *khaddar* (clothing woven from yarn spun by villagers using the *charkha*, or spinning wheel). During the 1930s the Swadeshi Movement became widespread in some parts of India. It is generally regarded both as an important chapter in the political history of the Indian national movement and as part of the legacy of Gandhi. My concern, however, is not with that history but rather with Swadeshi regarded as an instance of the principle of ethical preferences which Gandhi tried to establish. Gandhi himself stressed that Swadeshi was not to be seen simply as a political expedient designed to weaken the hold of Lancashire on the Indian market for textiles and thereby embarrass the British rulers. It had to be justified in terms of fundamental moral principles. The principle that he invoked most often for this purpose was that of neighbourhood. Gandhi defined *swadeshi* as 'a principle which is broken when one professes to serve those who are more remote in preference to those who are near'.[33] A teaching that is shared by all humankind, states Gandhi, and one that is common to all religions alike, is that one must be kind and attentive to one's neighbours. The duty of helping one's neighbours is at the core of the ethics of Swadeshi. While, it is true, we have duties to all humankind the duties we owe to all segments of it are not of equal importance. There is a hierarchy of duties based on the degree of proximity. Proximity is the decisive element in forming ties in terms both of closeness of feeling and knowledge of circumstances: 'Our capacity for service is limited by our knowledge of the world in which we live.'[34] Accordingly, we must start with service to our neighbours. 'An individual's service to his country and humanity consisted in

21

serving his neighbours.'[35] One could not starve one's neighbour and claim to serve one's distant cousin in the North Pole for one must not serve one's distant neighbour at the expense of the nearest.[36] This was not only the teaching of religion but also the foundation of 'true and humane economics'.[37] Gandhi saw no contradiction between the principle of *swadeshi*, interpreted in terms of neighbourhood, and that of rendering service to all humanity, which he also upheld.

Asked if a man can serve his immediate neighbours and yet serve the whole of humanity, Gandhi replied that he can, provided the service to neighbours was not itself exploitative of others. The neighbour himself would in turn serve his neighbours and in this way the chain of service would be extended to include the world, rather than shut it out.[38]

For the same reason, the principle of neighbourhood, according to Gandhi, was neither metaphysical nor too philosophical for comprehension, but just good commonsense, for 'if you love your neighbour as thyself, he will do likewise with you',[39] and both would gain thereby.

The neighbourhood principle was not confined to the choice of commodity-bundles but applied quite generally to the choice of states of affairs: 'when you demand *swaraj*, you do not want *swaraj* for yourself alone but for your neighbour too'.[40] It was the choice of commodities, however, that formed the primary concern of the Swadeshi Movement.

The neighbourhood principle has a direct consequence for the interpretation of ethical preferences in terms of Swadeshi, namely that whenever local products are available they should be preferred to their imported counterparts. Whether the latter were imports from foreign countries or from other regions of the same country made no difference. From around 1919 onwards Gandhi spelt out this moral imperative of local buying in much detail and using numerous specific examples: 'And so long as the Godhra farmers and weavers could supply the wants of the Godhra citizens, the latter had no right to go outside Godhra and support (say) the Bombay farmers and weavers.'[41]

A few years later, addressing people of his own home town (Porbander), he is repeating this argument in almost identical words, but using another set of examples:

> Is it right that instead of getting stone from Ranavav, you should order your requirements from Italy? How can you afford to order your cloth or ghee from Calcutta in preference to the cloth

woven in your own villages and the ghee made from the milk of your own cows and buffaloes?[42]

By consuming cloth or ghee 'imported' from Calcutta rather than those made locally, the people of Porbander were being chained with fetters. Likewise 'if Bengal will live her natural and free life without exploiting the rest of India or the world outside, she must manufacture her cloth in her own villages as she grows her corn there'.[43]

As between countries the neighbourhood principle translates as patriotism. An individual's preference ordering over commodity-bundles should therefore be guided by patriotism. 'The law of each country's progress demands on the part of its inhabitants preference for their own products and manufacturers.'[44]

Accordingly, for Indians there is a moral obligation to use products made in India whenever they can get them, even though these may be inferior to their foreign counterparts.

> There are several Swadeshi things on the market which are in danger of disappearance for want of patronage. They may not be up to the mark. It is up to us to use them and require the makers to improve them whenever improvement is possible.[45]

Gandhi does not, however, explain how consumers continuing to use a product could at the same time 'require the makers to improve them'. He mentions a number of goods belonging to this category. India produces a sufficient quantity of leather. It is therefore a duty on the part of an Indian consumer to wear shoes made of Indian leather in preference to foreign leather shoes, even if they are comparatively dearer and of an inferior quality . For the same reason products of Indian textile, sugar or rice mills 'must be preferred to the corresponding foreign products'.[46] *Swadeshi* items should not be discarded in favour of 'better or cheaper foreign things', for comparisons of price or quality are not relevant for the kind of consumer's choice Gandhi is talking about, but patriotism is. 'We attend flag-hoisting ceremonies and are proud of our national flag. Let me tell you that our pride has no meaning if you do not like things made in India and hanker after foreign ones.'[47]

If, on the other hand, a particular commodity is *not*, or cannot easily be made in India, the argument ceases to apply. Accordingly, while Gandhi regards it as a sin to import wheat from Australia on the score of its superior quality, he would not rule out importing oatmeal from Scotland, for oats are not grown in India. 'I buy useful healthy literature from every part of the world. I buy surgical instruments from England, pins and pencils from Austria and watches from Switzerland.'[48]

For the same reason, he asserts: 'All British goods do not harm us. Some goods such as English books we need for our intellectual or spiritual benefit.'[49]

While upholding the principle of 'patriotic preference', Gandhi was at pains to bring out that the spirit of *swadeshi* was not vindictive. Exclusion of foreign goods was not intended as a punishment, it was a necessity of national existence.[50] Nor was it narrow or parochial, 'for I buy from every part of the world what is needed for my growth'.[51] But by the same token: 'I refuse to buy from anybody anything, however nice or beautiful, if it interferes with my growth or injures those whom nature has made my first care.'[52]

Not all foreign things, therefore, were to be excluded but only *certain* foreign things, especially foreign cloth. Gandhi attached considerable moral importance to this distinction: 'If the emphasis were on all foreign things, it would be racial, parochial and wicked. The emphasis is on all foreign cloth. The restriction makes all the difference in the world.'[53]

Equally, the ethics of *swadeshi* required that the exclusion should not be targeted at British cloth only. It applied just as much, say, to the import of cloth from Japan, which was rapidly increasing during the 1930s. 'How can I take a single yard of Japanese cloth, however fine and artistic it may be? It is as poison to us, for it means starvation of the poor people of India.'[54]

Gandhi's doctrine that buying local products was a moral imperative had protectionist implications, but Gandhi had no particular allegiance to free trade. In response to an interviewer's comment that no country was free from foreign competition, Gandhi observed that on the contrary each sovereign nation tried to protect its infant industries by bounties and tariffs, and pointed to the sugar industry in Germany which had developed under a prohibitive tariff wall.[55] However, the exercise of ethical preferences by consumers was, he claimed, a better solution because it was voluntary and hence was in correspondence with the principle of non-violence, and was more likely to benefit the poor. 'India cannot wait for a protective tariff and protection will not reduce the cost of clothing. Secondly, mere protection will not benefit the starving millions.'[56]

Consumption behaviour that corresponded to the principle of ethical preferences, far from destroying the economic benefits flowing from foreign trade, would conduce to the healthy growth of nations and so promote both material and moral progress.

> That economics is untrue which ignores or disregards moral values. The extension of the law of non-violence in the domain of economics means nothing less than introduction of moral values as a factor to be considered in regulating international commerce.[57]

Nor, Gandhi claimed, would his approach to foreign trade lead to anarchy: 'There will be nations that will want to interchange with others because they cannot produce certain things. They will certainly depend on other nations for them, but the nations that will provide for them should not exploit them.'[58]

While the argument applies in principle to all home-grown products, Gandhi singles out the products of village industry for special attention. Within that category *khaddar* claims pride of place. Indeed, the Swadeshi Movement came to be regarded primarily as a means of encouraging consumers to wear *khaddar*. Accordingly, people, especially townspeople, were asked to buy *khaddar* in preference to mill-made cloth and to boycott foreign cloth altogether.

Gandhi's identification of the Swadeshi Movement with village industry, and with hand-spinning in particular, was based on a twofold argument: that the urban population of India owed a special moral duty towards the villages; and that this duty would be best discharged by providing a market for village products and above all for hand-spun cloth. The first part of the argument is a logical consequence of the principles of neighbourhood (there are few towns or cities in India that are not surrounded by villages) and patriotism (most Indians are villagers). Gandhi sought to strengthen it further by introducing yet another moral principle, that of historical justice. Both economic and moral standards in the villages had declined through long neglect. City people as a whole were partly to blame. 'The poor villagers are exploited by the foreign government and also by their own countrymen, the city-dwellers. They produce the food and go hungry. They produce milk and their children have to go without it.'[59]

Reparation had to be made: 'We are guilty of a grievous wrong against the villagers and the only way in which we can expiate it is by encouraging them to revive their lost industries and arts by assuring them of a ready market.'[60]

This solution was entirely feasible, provided that city people came to accept their moral responsibility. 'We have to be rural-minded and think of our necessities and the necessities of our household in terms of rural-mindedness . . . it is in consonance with the true economics of our country.'[61] Gandhi saw himself as an exponent of this 'true economics'. 'A link has been built to bridge the yawning gulf between the cities and villages. We have only to cross this bridge. Patronising village industries will constitute the crossing of the bridge.'[62] Gandhi emphasised that this was not a matter of charity. As he saw it, he was proposing a 'purely commercial proposition'.[63] All that was required was the exercise of ethical preferences when choosing one's consumption bundle.

The second part of the argument seeks to justify the use of hand-spun cloth as the appropriate means of repaying the debt that city people owe to the villagers, and is based on standard economic reasoning. Spinning was a solution for rural unemployment. The whole scheme of *khadi*, according to Gandhi, rested upon the supposition that these were millions of poor people in India who had no work during at least four months of the year. On Gandhi's reckoning, around three-quarters of the population of India belonged to this category. Because agricultural work was seasonal, they remained idle for a third of the year or more. This, Gandhi believed, was the principal cause of their endemic poverty. Even in a normal year their life was lived on the border-line of starvation. If there was crop-failure or famine, the extent of involuntary unemployment became much greater and many of them died of hunger and disease.[64] For the semi-starved but partially employed millions, spinning provided a means of part-time employment as well as an insurance against famine.[65] Thus Gandhi saw spinning primarily as a supplementary industry for agriculture rather than as a means of employment for village artisans.[66]

Why, one might ask, choose spinning rather than some other subsidiary occupation for agricultural workers? Gandhi's answer to this was strictly pragmatic. Spinning had long been practised by villagers in the past. It required only a very simple and low-cost implement and little technical knowledge or skill. It could be learned easily, did not require too much attention, could be done at odd moments and, for these reasons, was suitable as part-time employment for masses of rural people. Neither cattle breeding nor weaving, which had been suggested as possible alternatives to spinning as a supple-ment to agriculture, enjoyed these advantages even though they were more remunerative.[67]

26

Spinning was 'the easiest, the cheapest and the best'.[68] It was the most economic means of 'putting money into the pockets of the largest number of villagers with the minimum of capital outlay and organisational effort'.[69] The test of *swadeshi* 'was not the universality of the use of an article which goes under the name of *swadeshi* but the universality of participation in the production or manufacturing of such article'.[70] Judged by this test spinning had a potential unmatched by other contenders.

That cotton spinning was a specific remedy for agricultural unemployment also implied that it was not recommended for universal adoption. It was not, for example, meant for individuals who already had more remunerative employment, such as urban workers in textile mills.[71] It could not work in a district or region which did not have large numbers of people with idle hours at their disposal.[72] Gandhi neither contemplated nor advised the abandonment of a single, healthy, life-giving industrial activity for the sake of hand spinning.[73] On one occasion, he found that a number of women had been spinning who were not without occupation or means of making a living. 'Perhaps they spin in response to our appeal and because they realise it is for the good of the country.'[74] Nevertheless, Gandhi remained firm in his resolve that their spinning should stop, for the *charkha* movement had not been conceived with such people in mind but only for able-bodied people who were idle for want of work.[75] The operative principle was quite clear: if there were no crises of semi-unemployed people there would be no room for the spinning wheel.[76]

Gandhi's preoccupation with the need to find a subsidiary occupation for farmers can be understood properly only if certain other considerations are kept in mind. The first is his view that the possibility of bringing about improvements in agricultural production itself was very limited. Because an extremely high percentage of cultivable land in India was already under cultivation, there was little scope for increasing the agricultural area. Also, if agriculture was to provide the sole means of livelihood, one acre was commonly estimated to be the minimum viable area for supporting a household.

According to Gandhi's calculations this amount of land was more than was generally available in many parts of the country. With increasing pressure of population on the land the situation was likely to worsen, rather than improve. 'The small holdings daily getting smaller, the custom of fragmenting farms, must even make mere agriculture, in spite of improvements, a poor remedy for driving away her poverty.'[77]

27

To a number of nationalist economists, including Gandhi's own political mentor, G. K. Gokhale, improving the productivity of land already under cultivation did, however, appear to be a promising solution. Towards this end they advocated concerted efforts, especially by the government, to expand irrigation facilities so as to make farmers less dependent on the vagaries of rainfall, and also to encourage them to adopt higher-yielding varieties of crops and improved agricultural practices. Gandhi did not take up this line of argument because to the end he remained unconvinced that a high and sustainable growth in labour productivity in agriculture could be achieved without large-scale mechanisation of agriculture, which he strongly opposed (see Chapter 4).

The limitation of wants and *swadeshi* both rest ultimately on the concept of ethical preferences. People should seek not simply to maximise satisfaction of self-interested desires subject only to a budget constraint, but to achieve the long-run goals both of individual welfare and of helping others.

If by and large people's actual preferences were the same as ethical preferences as a result of reflection, debate or social agreement all would be well. Such need not, however, be the case and if it is not, the implications of the ethical preference approach are not clear. This is a difficulty that arises in all ideal-regarding theories, including Gandhi's. If Gandhian economics were taken as relating only to an ideal economic order, the difference would not much matter. However, that is not my reading. Gandhi himself was much concerned about the difference between the actual preferences of urban Indians, especially in the matter of clothing, and what he thought their ethical preferences should be. He was not, however, entirely consistent in his analysis. In his more optimistic moments he appears to believe that a 'true and national taste for *khaddar*' (i.e. an ethical preference) already exists in a latent form and hence that market demand is likely to lag only briefly behind supply. At other times he argues that tastes are not something given, but change with consumption and that the use of *khaddar* itself 'revolutionises our tastes'.[78]

Sometimes he suggests that all one has to do is to 'revive the national taste for *khaddar* and you will find every village a busy hive',[79] but in the same breath he notes that 'as it is the resources of the *khaddar* organisation are strained to the utmost in order to create a market for the article'.[80] Often he seems unsure: '*khaddar* has yet to become popular and universal',[81] or even despondent: '*Khadi* has not . . . caught the fancy of the people.'[82]

A great difficulty was the absence of a ready market for *khaddar*. 'I confess that it cannot for the time being compete with mill-cloth.'[83] After an initial spurt the demand for *khaddar* failed to show any dramatic rise. Unsold stocks began to accumulate in parts of the country where efforts to increase production of handspun cloth in the villages had been a success. Gandhi's conclusion was that *khadi* needed 'a great deal of propaganda'.[84] After all, that was how all goods were sold. Textile mills 'have their own agencies and peculiar methods for advertising their wares'.[85] In his presidential address to the Indian National Congress in November 1924, Gandhi criticised the proposition, 'that supply follows demand'. Demand for manufactured goods such as mill cloth was, he claimed, often artificially and deliberately created by producers by such devices as advertisement and even selling below cost in order to drive out competitors and capture the market. In his writings during the next few years, Gandhi often returned to this theme. 'The capitalist may for capturing the market sell his calico for nothing. The manufacturer whose only capital is labour cannot afford to do so.'[86]

Appropriate means of persuasion were necessary to encourage the consumption of *khaddar*. Under Gandhi's leadership, advertising campaigns were undertaken by the Congress and its agencies in favour of *khaddar*. Wearing it was made a condition of membership of Congress. Answering criticisms that this was an infringement of the freedom of choice, Gandhi argued:

> For those who are within the Congress to have the option of using mill-spun is to kill the *khaddar* industry. *Khaddar* needs all the protection that can be given to it before it can produce an impression upon the market.[87]

Exhibitions of village handicrafts were arranged throughout India to provide information to townspeople. Gandhi himself addressed mass meetings and wrote in the press in favour of wearing *khaddar*, for which he declared himself to be a salesman. 'We are in the same position as the trader who day and night plans for an increase in his business. We are the salesmen of *swaraj*.'[88]

The urban middle classes were particularly targeted. Acknowledging that *khaddar* was 'yet to become popular and universal', Gandhi argued that it could only become so if 'the thinking portion of India' would make a start. 'They must therefore restrict their use of cloth to *khaddar* only. Our mills need no patronage from us. Their goods are popular enough . . . *khaddar*, which has to find a market must command preference among enlightened men.'[89]

That remained the favoured strategy, with 'the buying middle class at the one end and the manufacturing poor class at the other'.[90] Some attempts were also made to increase efficiency in production and marketing and improve the quality of the product. Much to Gandhi's disappointment, none of these measures succeeded in bridging the gap between ethical preferences and market demand. At an early stage of his campaign for *khaddar* Gandhi wrote somewhat wistfully about Queen Elizabeth I, who had prohibited the import of soft cloth from Holland, who herself wore coarse cloth woven 'in her own dear England' and 'imposed that obligation upon the whole of that nation'.[91] Gandhi did not however aspire to such an option for himself. Sales talk was permissible, force never was. 'We do not want to spread *khadi* through coercion. We want to do our work by changing people's sense of values and habits.'[92] But this was not enough for his cause to succeed. Towards the end, Gandhi seems to have realised this himself: 'Mill-made cloth is said to be much cheaper than *khadi* and has a variety of colour, design and finish that *khadi* does not possess.'[93]

For this reason, even after all his efforts, the limit of the patronage for *khaddar* appeared to have been reached. 'It may be that in the prosecution of our search we may find, as some suggest we shall, that *khadi* can never become an economic proposition.'[94] It never did.

ALTRUISM AND CHARITY

'Altruism' literally means being concerned for the welfare of others, as opposed to egoism, which refers to being concerned solely for oneself. There is a so-called theory of 'ethical egoism' which tells us that we have no reason to promote the welfare of others, unless that happens to promote our own welfare. The possibility that one can, or should, sometimes sacrifice one's own interest for the sake of others, is thus excluded. The assumption of self-interested preferences which underlies standard economic analysis reflects the influence of ethical egoism on economic thought.[95] By contrast, ethics, as the word is normally construed, takes being concerned for others, and not solely for oneself, as its starting point. Gandhi's view of ethics certainly belongs to this category. As we have seen, his concept of ethical preference turns on being concerned with the welfare of other human beings, the poor and the exploited, villagers, fellow countrymen and so on.

Altruism and self-interest are both acceptable as reasons for action in Gandhi's moral world and he believed that maintaining a proper balance between them was conducive to social progress. He did *not* regard the two as incompatible. 'What benevolence would not teach them today, selfishness would teach them tomorrow. Experience shows that altruism and self-interest can be blended in trade.'[96] One *could* serve both God and Mammon: 'It is a grave delusion to say that one cannot preserve truth while earning wealth.'[97] That self-interest and altruism could be combined was just as true for the macroeconomic as for the individual level. 'There is no doubt that a union of dharma and artha is possible for an individual, the society and the nation.'[98] Gandhi's approach to economic policy was inspired by this principle. For example, he wanted improvements in urban transport and sanitation to be financed not solely by rates but by contributions from the wealthy who stood to gain much from such improvement. Gandhi points out that:

> if a good road is constructed in a city the value of the buildings appreciates. If the roads in Ahmedabad are widened and kept clean the adjoining land will rise in value. In addition to this, there is an economic gain which follows from improved health of the people and the resulting increase in their vitality and lifespan.[99]

If wealthy businessmen of the city are persuaded that they have much to gain by such improvements they might be prepared to make financial contributions towards bringing them about, for they would secure a happy blending of self-interest and benevolence. By the same token the accumulation of garbage in the streets involves loss to employers. 'The fact that there is an economic loss in preserving this filth is something which should be understood by the wealthy citizens of Ahmedabad. Because, diseases spread fast owing to uncleanliness and lead to loss of manpower.'[100]

Again, Gandhi is appealing to the self-interest of businessmen and not only to their social conscience, for here their self-interest and the public interest point in the same direction. In the same spirit Gandhi insisted that *khadi* shops should not run at a loss but should yield a reasonable rate of return: on one occasion he indicated 10 per cent as a reasonable rate. He also disapproved of a tendency he had observed not to accept any remuneration for service performed in the national cause:

> every labourer is worthy of his hire. No country can produce thousands of unpaid whole-time workers. We must therefore

develop an atmosphere in which a patriot would consider it an honour to serve the country and to accept an allowance for such service.[101]

He was not prepared to lay down any precise guideline on what the trade-off between self-interest on one hand and compassion or altruism on the other should be. 'Everyone fixes a limit for himself.'[102] Nevertheless, his message was clear: people should try to be less self-interested and more altruistic.

Altruism itself may be interpreted in a variety of ways. Running through all of Gandhi's writings bearing on this topic is a distinction between what may be described as self-regarding (or 'warm-glow') altruism on the one hand and other-regarding (or 'consequentialist') altruism on the other. An instance of the former is giving alms to a beggar, which makes the donor feel good and so increases his utility, whether or not it actually brings about an improvement in the recipient's welfare. The latter involves examining such consequences and taking action accordingly. Gandhi condemned the former type of action as a form of self-indulgence not deserving the name of altruism at all and for this reason opposed most forms of action commonly described as charitable. In an early piece of writing,[103] Gandhi quotes in full a well-known passage from the New Testament (I Corinthians 13) which extols the virtue of charity. However, Gandhi interprets the passage in his own way, taking it to mean that charitable action need not represent a virtue at all. He takes his cue from two particular statements which suggest that the practice of charity must itself satisfy some other norms in order to qualify as 'true charity'. These are: 'And though I bestow all my goods to feed the poor and though I give my body to be burned, and have not charity it profiteth me nothing.' And: 'Charity vaunteth not itself, is not puffed up, doth not behave itself unseemly.'

Gandhi, too, did not believe that charity in the sense of 'bestowing all my goods to feed the poor' was necessarily a virtue. 'There is no reason to believe', he stated 'that charity *per se* is meritorious.'[104] In order to judge whether a particular charitable action is good or bad one must look at its expected effects on recipients, donors and society at large. The effects that Gandhi was most concerned with were those on the incentive to work of recipients of charity, and he found the idea of giving free meals to a poor but healthy person who had not worked for them in some honest way particularly abhorrent. Giving free meals to the poor had long been an honoured Hindu custom. It was known as *sadavarta.* Some European authors had written in praise of this custom, arguing that Indians had developed a system of feeding the poor which was voluntary and self-organised and provided an alternative to the state-run workhouse. Gandhi did not agree. The system, he maintained, had done no good to India.

> Could there be any merit in feeding people in this manner? To me it appeared to be a mere sin committed through thoughtlessness and ignorance, even though the sentiment behind it may be of the purest nature.[105]

Gandhi was convinced that such charity actually contributes to poverty, idleness, hypocrisy and crime because if food is available without effort those who are habitually lazy remain idle and become poorer.[106] Hence philanthropic businessmen in contemporary India who sought to acquire religions merit by practising charity in this way were actually committing grievous wrong.

During a visit to Calcutta, Gandhi came across the sight of hundreds of hungry people being provided with free meals as an act of private charity by a philanthropic businessman. The sight appeared to him 'neither ennobling nor honourable'. Gandhi denounced the organisers: 'They did not know what they were doing. They were ignorant of the irreparable harm they were doing to India by this misplaced benevolence.'[107]

Gandhi's principal reason for calling such benevolence misplaced is that the people being fed were capable of work. None of the men and women who were being fed were physically incapacitated for work. They had just as strong arms and legs as anyone. And Gandhi believed that the organisers of such charity were simply wrong in thinking that there was any merit in feeding people who could work for a living. Such misplaced charity added nothing to the wealth of the country, whether material or spiritual, and was really a form of self-indulgence by donors. For the same reason he exhorted the millionaires of Bombay *not* to give all their money to the poor.

> If the Parsi millionaires gave all their money to the poor of this country their sufferings would not cease for did they want to keep these cores of persons dependent on their *sadavartas* or did they want to make them self-dependent?[108]

In Gandhi's view the able-bodied poor should have no 'free lunch'. Depending upon others for one's basic necessities was a habit which once acquired was extremely difficult to throw off. 'By their own efforts, by their own work these people should earn their livelihood and get their clothing.'[109] Philanthropists who really wanted to help could do so by opening institutions where meals would be given under clean, healthy surroundings to men and women who would have to perform some work in return for being fed. The most appropriate type of work for this purpose, according to Gandhi, was spinning but people should be free to choose any other work which was both useful and feasible. But the rule should be: no labour, no meal.

There was an alternative form of charitable action which Gandhi recommended even more strongly. Wealthy people, or public bodies such as municipalities, could open dairies for the public benefit, and shops where wholesome items of food would be sold at reasonable prices. The poor would thus gain access to cheap (but not free) nutritious food, especially unadulterated milk and milk products. Ideally, this could be done in every town and village. Such enterprises could, Gandhi believed, be run as financially self-supporting institutions. 'There is nothing to prevent them from becoming so except public disinclination to give the requisite skill and capital to such philanthropic concerns.'[110] Instead, the benevolence of the wealthy was exhausted in the effort to feed an ever-increasing army of beggars who were a burden on society.

Gandhi allowed one exception to his condemnation of *sadavarta*. It was commended for people who were lame, crippled or disabled by disease, for such people were not able to work. Even in these cases, however, relieving hunger was not the only objective; preserving their dignity and self-respect was no less important. 'Even the disabled should not be fed with thousands of people watching them. There should be a proper place, private and quiet, for feeding them.'[111] Also, those who could not work because of physical disability, and were not being looked after in private institutions, should be regarded as the responsibility of the state which should finance suitable institutions for this purpose.

The reasons which prompted Gandhi to denounce *sadavartas*, also led him to denounce giving alms to beggars. He would not, he stated, send away a beggar without offering him work and food, but if that person refused to work in return for food, he would let him go away hungry. The vast majority of street beggars, according to Gandhi, are professional idlers, 'when they are not much worse' and those who have money to spare do an ill-service to those beggars and to the country by giving them money, food or clothing. Since it is difficult for an individual to distribute charity judiciously, it was best to avoid indiscriminate charity altogether and only offer food for work done.[112] The long-run social consequences of begging, Gandhi believed, were so harmful that he recommended making both begging and giving alms to beggars punishable offences.[113]

Gandhi's view of charity was entirely characteristic of his realistic stand on social issues, and shows his consequentialist view of ethics at work. In this it differs sharply from the Buddhist view which regards the act of giving alms as conferring merit on the donor irrespective of consequences. It differs no less from the early Christian view which accepted the obligation of alms as a direct expression of true charity whereby the donor shared vicariously in poverty; and also from the later Christian view in which charity for the relief of poverty was seen both as a social obligation and a religious duty.

Gandhi's view of charity is also in keeping with his ethical pluralism. There are a number of different moral principles which could conflict: the principle of helping others justifies charity to beggars; the principle of self-reliance requires beggars to work. Gandhi's solution is a compromise between the two, an exercise in practical reasoning from ethical principles.

As was usual with Gandhi, his remarks on charity were meant to apply primarily to a specifically Indian context. They have, however, a more general aspect. Governments of Western countries are under increasing economic pressure to reform their existing schemes of welfare payments. Proposals have recently come up, for example, to link the eligibility of the unemployed to receive a dole to their willingness to work if jobs are provided. Such proposals have been attributed to a narrow 'economic' outlook and criticised on moral grounds. Gandhi would probably have approved of them but for moral rather than economic reasons.

Likewise, he had little sympathy for foreign aid as a means of promoting economic development in poor countries. The reasons which made charity harmful to individual recipients applied to nations, too, for it led to dependence, an erosion of incentives to work and save, and a loss of self-respect. And receiving charity becomes a habit that is difficult to shed. 'Heaven help the man, the woman or the nation that learns to live on charity.'[114] For these reasons, he consistently opposed foreign aid, food aid in particular.

Supposing a few millionaires from America came and offered to send us all our food stuffs and implored us not to work but to permit them to give vent to their philanthropy, I should refuse point blank to accept their kind offer.[115]

WORK, LEISURE AND THE DOCTRINE OF BREAD-LABOUR

In standard economic theory work (or 'labour') is a source of disutility, while consumption and leisure are sources of utility. The individual chooses between work and leisure by balancing the gains and losses in utility that an extra hour of work would bring and thus arrives at an equilibrium on the basis of his preferences, given the wage rate.

Gandhi, as we have seen, approached the problem of choice, and its bearing on welfare, in a different way. He took as his starting point what individual preferences should be rather than what they might happen to be at a given time; hence his heavy reliance on the concept of ethical preference. Gandhi found compelling ethical reasons for believing that work should in general be preferred to leisure, and work based on physical labour to work involving purely intellectual effort. The rationale for his view lies in the doctrine of bread-labour, which I shall now discuss.

The doctrine of bread-labour asserts the moral imperative that one must earn one's bread by the sweat of one's brow: 'he has no right to eat who does not bend his body and work'.[116] Bodily labour is a duty imposed by nature on mankind.[117] And one who eats but does not do any manual work in effect steals food.[118]

Gandhi borrowed the doctrine from Tolstoy whom, he noted, had himself taken it over from another Russian writer, but Gandhi also professed to find the roots of the doctrine in the *Bhagavadgita* which says that one who eats his bread without offering the necessary daily sacrifice was a thief. This sacrifice (*Yajna*), as interpreted by Gandhi, was bodily labour for the sake of humankind. The same lesson, he states, was taught in the Koran, the Bible and the Parsi scriptures and represents the moral consensus of humankind. Having satisfied himself that the doctrine of bread-labour was in correspondence with basic moral instincts of humankind Gandhi proceeded to interpret it in a way that would make it more relevant for addressing his own particular concerns, which were social and economic rather than religious.

Accordingly he laid down certain conditions which had to be satisfied in order that physical labour could properly be described as bread-labour. First, the term bread-labour in Gandhi's sense was inapplicable to work motivated by economic compulsion. Grinding toil for the sake of eking out a miserable livelihood, which is the lot of millions of poor peasants and factory workers throughout the world should not, he thought, be dignified by the name of bread-labour.[119] Such labour could not confer the benefits that he claimed for 'true' bread-labour. Addressing a labourers' meeting in Madras on 22 March 1925, Gandhi observed: 'But I know that the joy I can derive from labour is not your lot. Labour to most of you is painful toil without pleasure.'[120] That was not the kind of bread-labour Gandhi had in mind, for far from bringing to labourers the sense of achievement that *Yajna* should bring, it degraded them. 'Similarly compulsory obedience to the law of bread-labour breeds poverty, disease and discontent. It is a state of slavery. Willing obedience to it must bring content and health.'[121]

Second, it must be performed in a spirit of service to others rather than solely to please oneself. 'If a young man who has trained his body with rigorous exercise spends eight hours every day in doing such exercise, he is not doing bread-labour.'[122] Even though such exercise itself, states Gandhi, may be a good thing, it does not qualify as bread-labour because the element of service to others is lacking. For the same reason, while daily jogging, however healthy it may be, would not amount to bread-labour in Gandhi's sense participating in a meals-on-wheels project to help the sick or elderly, would.

Third, there must be scope for exercise of the mind. This depends not so much on the nature of the task itself as on its context and milieu and on the spirit in which it is performed.

> Where body labour is performed for mere wages, it is possible that the labourer becomes dull and listless. No one tells him how and why things are done: he himself has no curiosity and takes no interest in his work.[123]

Such labour cannot foster a blending of mental and bodily exercise, which Gandhi claims as flowing from true bread-labour. Even if one accepts the performance of manual labour as an ethical norm, the question remains, *how much* manual labour is it one's duty to perform? Both a strong and a weak version of this requirement may be found in Gandhi's writings on this topic. The former suggests that one must earn one's entire living through the performance of physical labour – presumably while contributing at the same time to the service of society, and this is the form in which Tolstoy preached the doctrine of bread-labour. The weaker version, on the other hand, simply requires one to perform *some* socially useful physical labour.

Some of Gandhi's early pronouncements on bread-labour do appear to suggest that everyone should do everything oneself, so that little scope is left for the division of labour which normally underlies social life. Gandhi, however, denied that this was what he meant.

> Man's dependence is no less than his independence. So long as he remains in society, and remain he must, he has to curtail his independence to fit into that of theirs, that is, society. Therefore, it can only be said that each person, as far as possible, must do his work himself... one must therefore exercise discretion in deciding whether a task is to be done by oneself or with the help of others.[124]

As an illustration of exercising such discretion, Gandhi states that if he wanted a drink of water he would fill his mug himself, but he would not try to dig a well. Not to fill the mug oneself indicated pride, to begin digging a well, stupidity. The weaker version of the requirement means that it is not morally incumbent on a person to earn the entire requirements for living by bread-labour but only that everyone should regularly perform *some* such labour.

Gandhi used the doctrine of bread-labour interpreted in this way, to serve a number of causes that were near his heart. One was that of breaking down caste barriers. Traditionally it was the function of the Sudras to serve those belonging to higher castes, and especially Brahmanas, by performing manual labour for them. The doctrine of bread-labour stated that *all* had to serve society by performing manual work: there was no distinction between, say, Sudras and Brahmanas in this regard. Gandhi found class barriers just as pernicious as those arising from caste. Here too the doctrine of bread-labour had relevance: respect for manual labour implied respect for manual labourers: 'A country where labourers are not respected but despised falls into decay.'[125]

Contempt for labour, and labourers, started during school days. Some parents objected to their children being taught manual labour at school because they would not have to labour for a livelihood, but Gandhi would not agree to exemptions.[126]

Another cause to which Gandhi was committed was greater equality in intra-family labour allocation. The doctrine of bread-labour came in handy, as Gandhi's advice to students on how they could best help put the doctrine into practice, shows: 'help in preparing your breakfast and milk, whatever you take, without waiting for your mother, or anyone else to prepare it and serve you; give a helping hand in sweeping and scrubbing; . . . help your mother with the cooking and in cleaning the dishes'.[127]

More generally, Gandhi wanted people to be resourceful and self-reliant. Again the doctrine of bread-labour helped.

> Able-bodied adults must do all their personal work themselves, and must not be served by others, except for proper reasons. But they must at the same time remember that the service of children, as well as of the disabled, the old and the sick, is a duty incumbent on every person who has the required strength.[128]

Again, Gandhi was committed to Basic Education, which relied on crafts as the 'medium' of primary education. The doctrine of bread-labour was an important component of his philosophy of education: that literary learning and craft learning must go together. The former represented formal intellectual knowledge, the latter socially useful manual labour. 'Efforts to separate them and break the link that binds them together results in the misuse of knowledge.'[129]

Perhaps the most important use that Gandhi made of his doctrine of bread-labour was to decry what he called the glorification of leisure. A standard argument in the debate on the costs of economic growth has been that GNP fails to take the value of leisure into account and accordingly that growth in national income may actually lead to a deterioration in the quality of life. Gandhi's position on the role of leisure is somewhat more complex. He accepts that a certain amount of leisure is necessary for each person, but notes that the amount that is necessary may not be the same for each person. In a properly functioning society everyone would be in a position to enjoy amounts of leisure, and of consumption, that were sufficient for their needs. The village *swaraj* of his conception is a place where 'everybody is a toiler with ample leisure'. That leisure is an essential component of the quality of life does not, however, imply that the greater the amount of leisure available the higher the quality of life will be. The principle of the limitation of wants applies just as much to leisure as to the consumption of goods and services. 'Leisure is good and necessary up to a point only.'[130] Beyond that point, leisure is not only unnecessary it can actually be harmful, for too much leisure tends to erode the human faculties.

The harmful effects of excessive leisure were not, for Gandhi, merely a theoretical speculation but something he claims to have observed. The point is connected with Gandhi's preoccupation with the moral and material effects of agricultural under-employment which, as he saw it, led to millions of rural people suffering simultaneously from too little consumption and too much leisure. This comes out clearly, for example, from the following exchange between Gandhi and an interviewer.

QUESTION: You do not seem to have regard to the question of leisure. Too much work leaves little leisure to the poorer classes for any intellectual thinking and recreation, and you are now seeking to make them work more.

ANSWER: Is that really so? I am trying to deal with people who do not know what to do with their enforced leisure. It is their enforced idleness that has made them like so many lifeless stones. There is so much inertia that some of them do not want to be disturbed.[131]

It could be argued that Gandhi's view of the value of leisure is distorted by a failure to distinguish between voluntary and involuntary leisure, but Gandhi denied that for the purpose of his argument this was a basic distinction. That modern technology could lead at the same time to greater output, higher incomes, reduced working hours and increased leisure was not a prospect that Gandhi welcomed. On the contrary he dreaded 'the prospect of our being able to produce all that we want including our foodstuff out of a conjurer's hat'.[132]

While the working day should not be too long, neither should it be too short. 'I know that socialists would introduce industrialisation to the extent of reducing hours to one or two a day but I do not want it.'[133] He preferred a working time of eight hours a day, which he believed left sufficient time for leisure as well as intellectual pursuits. The widely held assumption that a progressive reduction in working time, and increase in leisure, would enrich the quality of life was mistaken. People would not know what to do with their leisure, and would suffer from inertia and lethargy (just as those with enforced leisure in the Indian countryside already did).[134]

Gandhi's theorising on social issues invariably had a specific target. In the case of his doctrine of bread-labour the target was the contempt in which manual labour was held in Indian society. It was also intended to help build up a work ethic for a rural society; and it also tied in nicely with Gandhi's views on the place of craft learning in education. On the whole, however, bread-labour does not play an important role in Gandhi's social and economic thought and there are few references to it in his later writing.

The doctrine of bread-labour has sometimes been interpreted as a denigration of the intellect; and I shall conclude my discussion of the doctrine by considering whether such an interpretation is just. Gandhi tried to counter the impression that his doctrine was anti-intellectual by two arguments. First, he denied that he held bodily labour to be superior to mental labour: they were just different.

> I do not discount the value of intellectual labour, but no amount of it is any compensation for bodily labour which every one of us is born to give for the common good of all. It may be, often is, infinitely superior to bodily labour, but it never is or can be a substitute for it, even as intellectual food, though far superior to the grains we eat can never be a substitute for them.[135]

Gandhi's second argument, that manual labour intelligently performed is itself the best means of stimulating the intellect, will be discussed in the chapter on education. I find the first argument unconvincing: from the fact that to survive one needs food, not mere thought, we can hardly conclude that physical labour can never be substituted by intellectual effort. It is precisely substitution of this kind that has often stimulated both economic and scientific progress. The point really is that Gandhi disliked such substitution, for reasons that are examined in Chapter 4. In sum, while to suggest that Gandhi *denigrated* work of the intellect is perhaps an exaggeration, the charge that he denied such work its rightful place must stand.

Gandhi believed in balanced and harmonious growth of body, mind and spirit as the goal of human development. I share that belief. Nevertheless, I see his doctrine of bread-labour as tilting to one side, for it declares an ethical preference for bread-labour over pure intellectual labour for which no real case has been made out. In my judgement the bias comes from his instinctive distrust of specialised excellence, what he called 'intellectual voluptuousness', unrestrained by an over-riding commitment to the service of humankind. But a commitment to such service need not necessarily require the performance of physical labour.

I shall conclude with two brief remarks on Gandhi's overall approach to utility, preference and welfare, an approach which I characterised in terms of the concept of ethical preferences.

First, we must remember that when Gandhi started writing on these topics, economic theory was still dominated by classical, that is,

hedonist utilitarianism, with which Gandhi's moralist consequentialism had little in common. It is hardly surprising therefore that he
should have tried to de-link the goal of human welfare both from a
'felicific calculus' based on the balance of pleasures and pains, and from
the greatest happiness principle. Since that time the focus of economic
theory has changed. It is concerned with neither pleasure nor happiness
as such but rather with the individual's tastes, desires and preferences.
And both among economists and philosophers, there are now many
who would agree with Gandhi that the preferences, the satisfaction of
which could reasonably be regarded as contributing to human welfare,
should themselves satisfy certain prior conditions. For example, they
should be based on adequate information, they should not be 'mal-
conditioned' (e.g. drug-induced), they should not express simply the
whims of the moment but be based on reflection, they should include
considerations for others and not merely oneself, and so on.[136]

According to a recent study on the ethics of health care:

> having a conception of one's good is more than merely having a
> set of desires, intellectual or conditioned. People have a capacity
> for reflective self-evaluation, for considering what kinds of
> desires and character they want to have. There are, of course,
> limits to which people can change their desires. They can change
> their particular tastes in food, but not whether they have any
> desire to eat at all. In broad respects, our natures are fixed and
> given to us by our biological nature, but within these broad
> limits we adopt particular values and create a unique self.[137]

This is entirely in line with Gandhi's understanding of the bearing of
preferences on welfare.

My second comment is about difficulties that arise in applying the
principle of ethical preferences to particular issues. I pointed out
earlier one basic difficulty – namely that in a market economy it is
people's actual preferences, together with their incomes, that determine market demand for various goods and services. If actual
preferences happen to be the same as ethical preferences, there is no
problem, but they need not be. If they are not, the question arises: how
could effective preferences of individuals be made to reflect their
ethical preferences? Traditionally, 'ideal-regarding' reformers have
sought an answer either in direct coercion or in legislation. While
ruling out the former, Gandhi did rely on legislation to restrict or
regulate consumption as well as some other aspects of human
behaviour. His plea for the prohibition of alcoholic drink and drugs,

and of international trade in armaments, is a well-known example. However, he relied much more on moral suasion, as in the case of *khadi*. But as we have seen, despite Gandhi's unique moral authority, his life-long effort to create a wide-spread ethical preference for hand-spun cloth, and for *swadeshi* in general, failed. This has been attributed by some to the failure of India's urban middle classes to discard 'consumerism' in favour of an ethically responsible code of consumption behaviour. Others, including the present writer, would accept that there is much to be said for an ethical approach to consumption but deny that the use of inferior and costly products simply because they are locally or nationally made is particularly ethical.

I find some other preferences recommended by Gandhi more acceptable on moral grounds, especially his rejection of such 'charitable' acts as giving alms to beggars, indiscriminate foreign aid and providing the unemployment dole as a means of permanent income.

3

RIGHTS

The level of a society's well-being could be judged in terms of the rights that its members are guaranteed rather than the preferences that are satisfied or the needs fulfilled. Economists, it is true, have not been greatly concerned with rights as a measure, or even as a component, of the standard of living. It is differences in social welfare arising from how far individuals' preferences are satisfied on which, as a rule, they have focused their attention and they have also recently become increasingly concerned with the question of whether the basic needs of all individuals are being met. Rights, on the other hand, have been emphasised mostly by those writing on law, ethics or political science.

In his influential book, *Taking Rights Seriously*,[1] Ronald Dworkin noted that the language of rights had come to dominate political debate in the United States. Does the government respect the moral and political rights of citizens? Or does the government's foreign policy, or its race policies, violate these rights? Do a minority whose rights have been denied have the right to disobey the law? Or does the silent majority itself have rights, including the right to see that those who break the law are punished? These questions, he observed, had become prominent and he suggested a reason for this. 'The concept of rights, and particularly the concept of rights against the Government has its most natural use when a political society is divided, and appeals to co-operation or a common goal are pointless.'[2]

The questions raised by Dworkin are just as relevant now as in the 1970s and not for the United States alone. And whereas formerly they used to be discussed only from a legal or political point of view, they have started coming up in economic discourse as well. Indeed in some recent writings on welfare economics the connection between rights and welfare is regarded as of crucial importance. This is especially true of the so-called 'welfare rights', the rights to a living wage, decent

44

working conditions, health care, education and so on, which, as it happens, do not figure in Dworkin's list.

Gandhi's cause, as we have seen, was the individual. For him it was the individual rather than the group, class, caste, tribe, nation or state to which the individual might belong that was in the last analysis the relevant 'unit of account' in economic, political or moral reckoning. And his concept of civil disobedience rests on the individual's rights against the state. Yet he did not usually speak the language of rights. A scholar who is generally sympathetic to Gandhi's notion of the individual as an autonomous moral agent recently observed that 'Gandhi lacked a theory of rights: when he spoke about rights, they were derived from duties.'[3] I shall argue in this chapter that while the second part of this statement is certainly true, the first is not; and that it would be a mistake to infer from Gandhi's assertion of the primacy of duties that he did not take rights seriously. This chapter consists of four sections. The first presents Gandhi's basic approach to rights and duties. Some specific rights are discussed in the second section and a resolution on fundamental rights, of which Gandhi is generally regarded as the author, is discussed in the third. The final section tries to place Gandhi's concept of rights in a broader perspective.

RIGHTS AND DUTIES

Dworkin classifies political theories as belonging to one of three broad groups: goal-based, right-based and duty-based. A goal-based theory takes some goal, for example that of maximising social welfare, or perhaps a weighted set of goals, as fundamental. A right-based theory regards some right such as the right to liberty, or a set of rights, as fundamental. For duty-based theories it is the performance of a duty, or duties, that is the fundamental concern. Other goals, rights and duties could also be valued by an exponent of the theory in question but they would have to be treated as either subordinate or derivative. Dworkin cites utilitarianism as an example of a goal-based theory; Kant's categorical imperatives as constituting a duty-based theory and Tom Paine's theory of revolution as a right-based theory. In terms of this classification Gandhi's approach to political theory could be interpreted either as goal-based or as duty-based, for both elements can be found in his thought, but it is certainly not right-based.

Gandhi's discussion of rights contains two main ideas, that rights and duties are correlated and that it is duties that have priority, rights being in a certain sense derived from them. He repeats these views, sometimes using almost the same words, throughout his writings. 'The true source of rights', he wrote in an article published in 1925, 'is duty... If we all discharge our duties rights will not be far to seek.'[4] In 1939 he was making the same point in even more categorical fashion: 'Rights accrue automatically to him who duly performs his duties. In fact the right to perform one's duties is the only right that is worth living for and dying for. It covers all legitimate rights.'[5] The following year, commenting on the draft of a Charter on the Rights of Man prepared by H. G. Wells, Gandhi wrote: 'I feel sure that I can draw up a better charter of rights than you have drawn up, however, what good will it be? Who will become its guardian?'[6] Wells, suggests Gandhi, has started at the wrong end. 'Begin with a charter of duties of man and I promise the rights will follow as spring follows winter.'[7] In the same spirit, in 1947, he wrote to Julian Huxley, then Director-General of Unesco, expressing scepticism about a proposal for a Declaration of Human Rights;

> The very right to live accrues to us only when we do the duty of citizenship of the world. From this one fundamental statement perhaps it is easy enough to define the duties of man and woman and correlate every right to some corresponding duty to be first performed. Every other so-called right can be shown to be usurpation hardly worth fighting for.[8]

Gandhi had the same message for the restive masses of India on the eve of independence: 'The people should not merely run after rights. He who runs after rights does not secure them ... His right is illusory. When you do your duty the rights will drop into your lap.'[9]

SOME SPECIFIC CASES

The correlation of rights and duties may itself be interpreted in a variety of ways and so can the statement that duties have priority over rights. I shall try to discover what Gandhi meant by these assertions by first looking at his exposition of particular cases. The first such case that I shall consider bears on the right to equality.

> Every man has an equal right to the necessaries of life even as birds and beasts have. And since every right carries with it a corresponding duty and the corresponding remedy for resisting any attack upon it, it is merely a matter of finding out the corresponding duties and remedies to vindicate the elementary

fundamental equality. The corresponding duty is to labour with my limbs and the corresponding remedy is to non-cooperate with him who deprives me of the fruits of my labour.[10]

It is important to be clear about the content of the right that Gandhi is talking about in this passage. It is neither equality of earnings nor that of opportunity that he has in mind but simply that of an equal right to a minimum subsistence. To this right, which Gandhi asserts as holding for each individual, there corresponds some duty or duties on the part of some other individuals or institutions. This must be so because rights and duties are correlated. That is not, however, the duty which Gandhi describes here as either 'the corresponding duty', or 'the corresponding remedy'. Both these refer to duties devolving on the right-holders themselves. The former refers to the duty of bread-labour. Gandhi believed that if a person refused to undertake such labour when an opportunity to do so was offered and the person concerned was not barred by physical disability from carrying it out, the right in question no longer applied. This then was one of the ways in which a right could be contingent on the performance of a duty. Moreover, merely agreeing to work was not enough for the right to hold, one must try to work one's best.

> It is simple enough to understand that your right is to receive the hire for your labour and it is equally simple to know that your duty is to work to the best of your ability for the wages you receive.[11]

The other duty of the right-holder which Gandhi specifies in this passage is meant to apply in a quite different context. Suppose that one is in fact performing one's duty by working to the best of one's ability but the employer concerned nevertheless exploits the worker and denies him or her a living wage or proper working conditions. An employer who does so is of course guilty of not performing his (or her) own duty but that itself imposes a further duty on the right-holder, that of non-violent non-cooperation with the employer. For Gandhi it is this that justified the right to strike, which as he saw it meant that labour should try to impose its will upon the employer. But in exercising this right it was necessary for labour to know how far it could actually do so in any particular situation. Addressing a workers' meeting in Madras, Gandhi asked;

> If we find that we are not adequately paid, or adequately housed, how are we to claim and receive enough wages and good

accommodation? Who is to determine the standard of wages and the standard of comfort required by the labourers?[12]

He also provided an answer: 'The best way, no doubt, is that you labourers understand your own rights, understand the method of enforcing those rights, and enforce them.'[13] Going on strike was one such method. However, the strike should be conducted by non-violent methods and should be used only if the circumstances are appropriate, in the sense that the conditions of the argument hold. On the other hand, in these circumstances to strike is not only a right but also an absolute duty. Using the same reasoning Gandhi justified the workers' rights to share in the administration and control of industry, and to satisfactory working conditions, including suitable housing for workers without impairing their freedom in any way, decent facilities for rest and recreation at the workplace, sufficient water, satisfactory sanitary facilities, maternity leave for women workers and crêches for their infants. Some implications of his arguments for the structure of industrial relations are examined in Chapter 6.

Another example, which is more general in nature, and which has been discussed extensively in the political science literature, has to do with the respective rights and duties of the people and their ruler *vis-à-vis* each other. Gandhi starts by describing the way in which rulers usually perceive their own rights.

> He who is a ruler for a moment gets it into his head that he has been created by God solely to rule over people, that he has the right to hang some, to imprison others and to fine some others. He wants that all the duties should be discharged by the people. He says that he has derived his right to rule from God.[14]

The assumption of a Divine Right to Rule is however, quite unfounded, whether the rule imposed is foreign or indigenous. A ruler has a right to rule only if he carries out his duties satisfactorily, his basic duty being to serve the interests of the people and protect their rights.

> But if the Princes refuse to recognise the rights of the people, if they say that they will blow their subjects to bits with cannon, then they will not be doing their duty. What then should the people do? In that eventuality it becomes the duty of the people to fight against the ruler and remove him from the throne.[15]

This does not mean, Gandhi hastens to add, that they should set fire to the palace and destroy everything. The same principle applied to landlords *vis-à-vis* their ryots. The duty of the landlords was to serve the interests of ryots and to protect their rights. If the landlords failed to do so, not only did the ryots cease owing them any duty in return, but the duty also devolved on them of resisting the landlord's rule. Again, this does not give a right to indulge in murder, rapine and plunder, which are crimes against humanity.

Yet another right that received attention from Gandhi is the right to protection against forced labour by landlords. In India the use of forced labour usually has a caste as well as a class dimension. Gandhi points out, 'The system of forced labour exacted by petty land-owners from Harijans and other classes called backward is almost universal in India.'[16] The law provides rights against being subjected to forced labour but in practice the rights are often violated. Gandhi suggests a number of remedies. First, the existing legal provisions should be strengthened so as to decrease the scope for evasion. Second, the labourers affected must become more organised and more conscious of their rights. This, he thought was already happening. 'They are slowly but surely being awakened to a sense of their rights. They are numerous enough to enforce them.'[17] The land-owners, who are for the most part caste Hindus, must wake up to their duty of treating Harijans as brothers, and with the respect 'that belongs to man'.

Commenting on Gandhi's view of rights as flowing from duties Bondurant makes the point that in traditional Hindu polity the king was obliged to fulfil his kingly duties towards his people, proper fulfilment of such duties being the sole justification for expecting his subjects to obey him. Gandhi, 'who would make every man a king', regarded duties as prior to rights. But the effect of his reasoning was not precisely conservative in nature.[18] Gandhi's exposition of the rights of the Prince is certainly far from conservative, a point to which I shall return.

I now go on to consider another right discussed by Gandhi. This relates to the freedom of religion. A sect of Jain monks in India, known as the Digambar Jains, customarily went about naked. (The word *Digambar* literally means, 'those who have the sky as their garment'.) They raised the question whether under *swaraj* they would enjoy the right to nudity as part of their fundamental right to the free profession and practice of religion. In an article entitled 'Limits to Freedom',[19] Gandhi expressed the view that practising nudity was not a fundamental right. He put forward two main arguments in support of this view. One is essentially a consequentialist argument which appeals to the requirements of decency and public order. 'Freedom, both individual and religious, has always had and will always have many limits.'[20] Sadhus, especially when visiting cities, had an obligation to observe the minimum bounds of social decency. Complete nudity fell below the required minimum. The other argument has to do with doing one's duty. Gandhi was committed to the position that the right to perform one's duty was a fundamental right which was worth dying for. He maintained that 'nudity cannot be one's duty'.[21] It was only a custom which had to change. Gandhi does not confront the question, *what* makes something a duty, but treats duty as a 'primitive notion'.

There are also a number of other rights to which Gandhi refers. Of these the right to property, and the right to civil disobedience have some importance for the study of Gandhi's thought. I discuss the former in the chapter on trusteeship (Chapter 6) and the latter in the final section of the present chapter.

Gandhi's analysis of specific rights makes it abundantly clear that his belief in the primacy of duty does not imply a 'passive' view of rights. He observes: 'Exercise of a right requires a quality that gives the power to impose one's will upon the resistor through sanctions devised by the claimant or the law whose aid he invokes in the exercise of his right.'[22]

The requirement of legal sanction is part of the standard definition of a right. That the claimant can, if need be, resort to a sanction of the claimant's own devising, based on the principle of *satyagraha*, is a typically Gandhian contribution. In the case of a basic human right, the violation of which could be regarded as a crime, it might even be appropriate for persons other than the claimant to offer *satyagraha* in support of the claim. Gandhi used this argument on several occasions, notably when trying to implement the human rights of untouchables.

> Let me tell you that it is not enough for you to hold the belief passively that untouchability is a crime. He who is a passive spectator of a crime is really, and in law, an active participator in it.[23]

A RESOLUTION ON RIGHTS

Despite his declared scepticism about the usefulness of drawing up charters of rights there is a well-known instance where Gandhi himself took a prominent part in preparing such a charter, and a discussion of Gandhi's attitude to rights would be incomplete without taking it into account. The charter in question forms part of the Resolution on Fundamental Rights and Economic Change adopted by the Indian National Congress at its session in Karachi in 1931. The resolution is presumed to have been drafted by Gandhi,[24] who also moved and argued in favour of it at the open session of Congress. Subsequently he described it as the most important resolution passed at this session.

As the title of the resolution suggests it includes a list of fundamental rights and economic changes which the people of India, under Congress leadership, would seek to implement once *swaraj* was achieved. The following are said to be fundamental rights of the people:

(a) freedom of association and combination;
(b) freedom of speech and of the press;
(c) freedom of conscience and the free profession and practice of religion, subject to public order and morality;
(d) protection of the culture, language and scripts of the minorities;
(e) equal rights and obligations of all citizens, without any bar on account of sex;
(f) no disability to attach to any citizen by reason of his or her religion, caste, creed or sex in regard to public employment, office of power or honour and in the exercise of any trade or calling;
(g) equal rights to all citizens in regard to public roads, wells, schools and other places of public resort;
(h) right to keep and bear arms in accordance with regulations and reservations made in that behalf;
(i) no person shall be deprived of his or her liberty nor shall his or her property be entered, sequestered or confiscated save in accordance with the law.

Among other rights stated in the document are the following: religious neutrality on the part of the state; adult suffrage; free primary education; a living wage for industrial workers; limited hours of work; protection against the economic consequences of old age, sickness and unemployment; labour to be freed from serfdom or conditions bordering on serfdom; protection of women workers and adequate provision for leave during maternity; prohibition against employment of children of school-going age in factories; and rights of labour to form unions to protect their interests, with suitable machinery for settlement of disputes by arbitration.

On the face of it Gandhi's championship of the Fundamental Rights resolution appears to be at odds with his usual dislike of 'rights-talk'. Gandhi, it is true, went out of his way in his opening speech to emphasise that he was not presenting a Constitutional document. It was meant, he said, for ordinary people who were not legislators nor interested in intricate questions of constitution. The purpose of the resolution, according to Gandhi, was to give some indication 'to the poor inarticulate Indians' of the broad features of *swaraj*. Among these he gave special importance to religious toleration, to the quest for just and equitable relations between capital and labour, and between landlord and tenant (the clause about 'serfdom or conditions bordering on serfdom' was meant to apply especially to bonded labour in agriculture) and to the abolition of gender-bias in public employment. ('The moment this is done', he declared, perhaps with undue optimism, 'many of the disabilities to which women are subject will cease.')[25] Thus Gandhi saw the resolution as a vision of the future but this was not *all* it was.

Even though Gandhi took care not to present his resolution as providing a list of the claims to be made justiciable rights in free India, it was so interpreted by many. Such a reading appears, indeed, to be implied by the wording of the resolution and it underlies the political discussion that followed it. It is also implied by Gandhi's long-held belief that while rights, in order to be honoured and not merely talked about, require duties to be performed, both by the right-holder and by others, a right in itself is nevertheless a *legal* entity. As he stated on one occasion, 'there is no right but is legal. Divorced from legality moral right is a misnomer'.[26] It gains plausibility from Gandhi's persistent advocacy of legislation conferring legally enforceable rights on disadvantaged groups even before independence was achieved. Especially relevant for this purpose is his campaign for legal reform in order to secure the right of Harijans to enter Hindu temples. He argued that reform was needed simply to correct the bias in the existing law which not only allowed but even encouraged discrimination:

> What is wanted is that there should be no State recognition of untouchability. At the present moment there is this anomaly that the State not only recognizes untouchability, but helps believers in it to enforce their views against others, thus making what they believe to be a religious precept a matter of legal obligation. Seeking assistance of law therefore becomes obligatory for reformers in order to have the anomaly removed.[27]

He also maintained against some of his followers that the use of the legislatures in this way did not contradict the principle of non-cooperation with British rule,[28] though the scope of legislation in the cause of social reform would increase immensely with independence. Such legislation would, however, always have to be supported by properly conceived and carefully organised campaigns for educating the public on the issues involved.

In sum Gandhi's sponsorship of the Resolution on Fundamental Rights and Economic Changes was entirely consistent with his theory of rights. When he wrote to Wells or Huxley scoffing at their enthusiasm for a declaration of human rights he was not denying the relevance of rights in general nor of the special category of 'human rights'. Indeed he had a strong commitment to the notion that certain rights belonged to human beings simply by virtue of their being human; and I have argued elsewhere in this book that his concept of equality was based on this notion. In his campaign for the abolition of untouchability he explicitly and repeatedly appealed to the basic principle of giving 'equal rights to all human beings'. In expressing scepticism about the usefulness of a declaration of human rights Gandhi was making the point that rights, to be useful, must have effective legal protection, which opinions of experts or statements by Unesco could not give. He made the same point in justifying legislation to help towards securing rights for minorities: 'Civic rights will certainly be protected by law if they are to be worth anything.'[29] At the present state of development of human society such law could only be made, he believed, at the local or national, rather than an international level.

A SUMMING UP

Gandhi's discussion of the meaning of rights does not fit in easily with current preoccupations of political or economic theory. Nevertheless, it has a certain theoretical structure of its own. He draws on several distinct traditions of thought, and proper understanding of his views requires looking at them from a broad perspective. This I shall now try to do.

Perhaps the closest parallel to Gandhi's approach to rights is to be found in the language of the law. In insisting that rights, by definition as it were, are correlative with duties Gandhi was at one level simply stating a standard proposition in law, the discipline in which he had been trained. It is a commonplace of legal textbooks that where one person has a right another has a duty. Thus an individual's right to be given something, as for example to be repaid a loan, to be paid a living

wage or to be provided safety in the workplace involves a corresponding duty on the part of someone else to give it; and a person's right to
act, as for example to draw water from a public well, or enter a place of
worship or conduct legitimate business involves a duty on others not
to interfere.

The proposition that rights and duties are correlated does not, it is
true, carry the same meaning for all jurisprudents. Some see it simply
as a matter of logic and would regard the statements, 'A has a right
against B' and 'B has a duty towards A' as logically equivalent. Others
maintain that the duty is not so much a logical consequence of the
right as a legal protection for it. On this view the duty is a necessary
condition for making the right effective. This, for example, is the
opinion of White, who states: 'In many cases it would be pointless,
though not logically impossible, to give a right to A without laying a
correlative duty on B.'[30]

The difference between these two possible meanings of a correlation between rights and duties, or for that matter differences between
different kinds of rights, does not much matter for Gandhi's argument, for his concern was not so much with definitional precision as
with the way in which rights which he regarded as really important,
'rights worth living for and dying for', could be actually implemen-
ted. It is that concern which underlines the worry he expressed in his
letter to Wells that even the most impressive Declaration of Human
Rights would make little difference to the human condition unless
there was someone to act as 'guardian' of the rights declared. The
attribution of the duties corresponding to each right could at least
help in grasping more clearly what was involved and perhaps even
serve as a safeguard against a string of pious platitudes masquerading
as rights.

That Gandhi's doctrine of the correlation of rights with duties is in
line with legal thinking receives support from the well-known
judgment of a British court in the case of Broome v. DPP (1974,
AC 587) concerning the existence of a right to picket. The court held
that since Parliament could not have meant to impose a duty on
anyone to stop and listen to a picket it therefore had not given the
right to stop anyone and make him listen.[31] I am not concerned here
with the validity of this judgment but only wish to point out the
similarity of this mode of reasoning to Gandhi's.

Gandhi did not assert only that rights and duties were correlative
but also that rights were derived from duties which, therefore, was the
more important concept. I shall now take up this aspect of his view of

rights for consideration. It is tempting to see in Gandhi's view of duty as prior to right, a parallel to the view of rights in the idealist, and generally conservative, tradition in political philosophy. Thinkers in this tradition, too, tend to give priority to duties over rights. They believe that each individual member of society is assigned, whether explicitly or otherwise, certain tasks appropriate to his or her position in society, which it is the individual's duty to carry out. Rights are contingent on performance of the duties assigned. The logic of this school of thought was worked out most consistently by Bernard Bosanquet in *The Philosophical Theory of the State*, and I shall take his version of the argument as my point of departure.

Bosanquet defines rights as 'claims recognised by the State, i.e. by society acting as ultimate authority, to the maintenance of conditions favourable to the best life'.[32] His justification of rights forms part of a complex argument which presents four distinct concepts arranged in the following order of priority. First, the common good; second, social functions or 'positions' instrumental to the common good; third, duties instrumental to the performance of these functions and last, rights instrumental to the performance of duties. At the top of the hierarchy is the notion of the common good, which consists in self-realisation by each member within a community which promotes the good life. What each member of the community can contribute to this common good depends, however, on the position that the member occupies. 'The position, then, is the real fact – the vocation, place or function, which is simply one reading of the person's actual self and relations in the world in which he lives.'[33] Accordingly it is these positions that determine what the duties of particular individuals are. These duties, in turn, require rights for their satisfactory performance. All rights, thus, are powers instrumental to duties and so to making the best of human capacities within a system of positions embodied in the social order, and can only be recognised or exercised upon this ground.

> In this sense the duty is the purpose with a view to which the right is secured, and not merely a corresponding obligation equally derived from a common ground and the right and duty are not distinguished as something claimed by self and something owed to others, but the duty as an imperative purpose, and the right as a power secured because instrumental to it.[34]

Two important corollaries follow. First, there cannot be any unrecognised rights. Second, rights go with functions. 'It is to their differentiated functions which constitute their life and the end of the community, that the sub-groupings of rights, or conditions of good life, have to be adjusted each to each like suits of clothes.'[35]

There are clearly points in common between the theory of rights just described and the views expressed by Gandhi. Gandhi agrees with Bosanquet in assigning priority to duties over rights while both would reject the currently popular view that 'rights are trumps'. Several of Gandhi's statements which I have quoted above seem to echo Bosanquet's view that 'the duty is the purpose with a view to which the right is secured'. Likewise Gandhi agrees with Bosanquet that self-realisation by individuals can only be achieved within a community and hence that a justification of rights must appeal to the concepts both of individual autonomy and social well-being. Nevertheless, overall, Gandhi's notion of rights is very different from Bosanquet's.

A basic difference between them concerns the relevance of positions for a theory of rights. Gandhi, too, believed that there could be 'natural' differences in function corresponding to difference in occupation and gender, a point which I take up in Chapter 5. Nevertheless, for Gandhi both rights and duties attached to individuals. As Bondurant points out, 'Gandhian rights were not to be rigidly confined to rank and order.'[36] They were not meant, as with Bosanquet, to be tailor-made for social positions.

Gandhi's emphasis on individual autonomy has another important consequence for the theory of rights. In his account, unlike Bosanquet's, the individual's rights against the state have a central place. The right to civil disobedience, which Gandhi asserts, follows logically from this. According to Gandhi the state is justified only because, and to the extent that, it provides opportunities to individuals to realise their full potential. Obedience to the law is contingent on this condition being fulfilled. If it is not, the individual has the duty, and consequently the right, to disobey.

> I saw, during my pursuit of truth, that it was our duty to give willing obedience to laws. But I also saw, while doing this duty, that it was equally a duty to disobey a law if it fostered untruth. What form should such disobedience take? We should suffer the penalty for the breach of law involved in acting according to the truth. This is known as Civil Disobedience.[37]

Civil disobedience could be used in defence of basic human rights. 'To accept defeat in the matter of free speech and free association is to court disaster... In the general interest, therefore, we must defend these elementary rights with our lives.'[38] To offer civil disobedience in a just cause was the inherent right of a citizen, who could not give it up 'without ceasing to be a man'. There were of course problems in deciding if and when a cause was just.

'Who is qualified for such disobedience, and which law should be considered as fostering untruth, cannot be decided by laying down definite rules. Experience alone will help one to decide.'[39] It is for the individual to decide when civil disobedience becomes a duty and his ability to do so correctly improves as he gains experience with the technique of *satyagraha*. In the course of gaining this experience one could make mistakes. It was, therefore, quite legitimate to question the wisdom of applying civil disobedience in regard to a particular act or law or to advise delay and caution. But the right itself could not be allowed to be questioned, 'it is a birthright that cannot be surrendered without surrender of one's self-respect'.[40] This is far removed from Bosanquet's unquestioning acceptance of the sanctity of the established law and his consequent belief in the impossibility of unrecognised rights.

> Even if one succeeds in showing that some right is not being honoured, i.e. that some opportunities for one's self-realisation consistent with one's Position are not being provided ... all my showing gives no right till it has modified the law.[41]

To maintain a right against the state by force or disobedience is rebellion, which Bosanquet asserts cannot be a duty, at least in a state in which the law can, in principle, be altered by constitutional process. According to the Gandhian view, on the other hand, not only must society provide individuals with opportunities for growth, 'the final decision as to what constitutes that growth lies with the individual'.[42] This basic difference between Gandhi's view of rights and that associated with the traditional conservative view comes out sharply in the following exchange between Lord Hunter and Gandhi which took place when Gandhi was giving evidence before the Disorders Inquiry Committee, of which Hunter was president, at Ahmedabad, on 9 January 1920:[43]

HUNTER: My point is, having regard to the circumstances, a sort of sanctity attaches to the laws of the Government of the time being?

GANDHI: Not in my estimation.

HUNTER: That is not the best check on the masses?
GANDHI: Not blind adherence to laws, no check whatsoever.

In response to further questions, Gandhi made it quite clear that he did not intend his principle to be applied only to a colonial situation in which the government did not represent the will of the people. Indeed, he argued that it would be still more open to the masses to offer civil disobedience when India became free and had her own democratically elected ministers. In most democratic countries, stated Gandhi, there were ministers 'who have made themselves irremovable somehow or other', and he fully expected this to happen in India as well. 'In that event what is a poor respectable minority to do? Offer civil disobedience.'[44]

It is of some interest to note that Rawls' analysis of the right to civil disobedience closely matches Gandhi's. Rawls describes civil disobedience as 'a public, non-violent, yet political act contrary to law, usually done with the aim of bringing about a change in the law or policies of the government'.[45] Although Gandhi tended to emphasise the role of the individual and his conscience more than Rawls does, e.g. 'Civil disobedience relies for its success solely on the strength of the individual,'[46] and to interpret 'non-violence' much more stringently, his concept of what civil disobedience was about was much the same. Rawls goes on to state the conditions under which civil disobedience could be justified. These are, first, that laws to be disobeyed should be such as to inflict 'substantial and clear injustice'; second, that before taking resort to civil disobedience all available legal means of redress should have been fully utilised; and third, that one who exercises this right is willing to grant everyone else the right to use similar methods. Gandhi accepted the third condition fully, the second with some reservations (he would always inform the authorities concerned about any plans to embark on civil disobedience well in advance but would not necessarily try all available means of redress if he thought they were in violation of self-respect or would be fruitless), and did not accept the first. He did believe that civil disobedience should normally be offered only against laws which violated basic rights. His pledge of *satyagraha* during the campaign of civil disobedience against the Rowlatt Bills, for example, describes the bills as 'unjust, subversive of the principles of liberty and justice, and destructive of the elementary rights of an individual on which the safety of India as a whole and the State itself is based'. But civil disobedience could also be symbolic in nature and there was an element of this in the campaign against the salt tax laws. The decisive criterion for Gandhi was not the magnitude of the damage done but whether the law 'fostered untruth'. The right to civil disobedience as interpreted by Gandhi is therefore much more extensive than Rawls allows.

There are two specific aspects of Gandhi's concept of rights that I should like to comment on next. The first concerns his attitude to welfare rights, rights to a minimum level of such things as nutrition, shelter, education and health care which, taken together, could guarantee a 'decent minimum level' of material welfare for every individual. Such rights are also sometimes described as rights to positive freedom, or simply as 'positive rights', in order to distinguish them from civil and political rights required for 'negative freedom'. Whether welfare rights can properly be regarded as rights at all is a question which has received some attention from political theorists and philosophers. Such writers take a deontological view of rights, that is, they define rights as over-riding ('categorical') moral imperatives. From this perspective, they argue that because scarcity of resources may make it impossible for a poor country to guarantee a decent minimum standard to all its citizens, welfare rights may not exist at all.[47] Fried puts the point as follows:

> It is logically possible to respect any number of negative rights without necessarily landing in an impossible and contradictory situation ... Positive rights, by contrast, cannot as a logical matter be treated as categorical entities, because of the scarcity limitation.[48]

The point has little relevance for Gandhi who see rights not so much as categorical moral claims by the right-holder but rather as opportunities open to individuals for self-realisation. By exercising their rights individuals are enabled to develop their own potential to the full and by doing so contribute as best they can to the common good which it is their duty to do. For this purpose both a decent minimum standard and personal liberty are necessary. Gandhi, as noted earlier in this chapter, believed individual autonomy to be essential to 'personhood', hence his commitment to the individual's rights against the state. Likewise, he regarded ways of treating an individual that denied the individual the respect owed to all people, as morally impermissible, hence his life-long preoccupation with the rights of untouchables, and of women, and his belief that untouchability was an evil far worse than poverty. However, this only reflects his view that actions themselves are to count as part of the consequences, for means are also ends, and that certain actions could involve infinitely evil consequences. The belief that positive and negative rights are different *in kind* and that positive rights are not truly rights at all is inconsistent with the logic of Gandhi's position.

Gandhi's adherence to positive rights does not, as some have supposed, make him a socialist. On his view, for rights to become effective requires both appropriate assertion of the rights and willing performance of the corresponding duties by individuals in society. This applies to both positive and negative rights. While rights, by definition, must have legal sanction, the state is by no means their sole guarantor. Indeed, he feared that relying overly on the state for implementing a right might even be counter-productive. Thus, commenting on a programme of rights drawn up by M. R. Masani, a socialist, Gandhi asked: 'Does "the right of the child to care and maintenance by the State" absolve the parent from the duty of caring for the maintenance of his children?'[49]

This aspect of his thought seems to have been missed by Bondurant, when she writes,

> the Gandhian insistence upon selfless service to society, upon duty to the community as the more important correlative of right, and the final concept of a social well-being – these moral incentives provided by Gandhi, as by Green, could lead to a nationalization of industries, socialization of health and education and, in general, a form of liberal socialism.[50]

While Gandhi did agree, though somewhat reluctantly, that nationalisation of some industries might be necessary, he was strongly opposed to socialisation of health and education and, as I think I have shown elsewhere in this book, his views on social and economic organisation were far removed from socialism of either the liberal or the authoritarian variety.

My next comment bears on the concept of animal rights. In traditional political, and moral, theory only human beings can be regarded as right-holders. That animals, too, could have rights was argued by Gandhi long before the cause of animal rights was taken up by radical activists, and subsequently addressed by philosophers. In an article published in 1935, he wrote: 'If our sense of right and wrong had not become blunt, we would recognise that animals had rights, no less than men.'[51]

Attributing rights to animals does not pose any great theoretical difficulty for Gandhi's scheme, which makes rights correlative with duties. The rights of animals depend, therefore, on human beings recognising and carrying out certain duties towards domestic animals such as caring for their health and welfare, providing them with proper food and shelter, not burdening them with excessive work, treating them humanely, etc. as well as towards wildlife, such as refraining from wanton destruction, preserving their habitat and so on.

That human beings do have duties towards animals just as they have towards other human beings was something Gandhi took for granted. This is not surprising, given that the total separation between humankind and the animal kingdom that marks Christian theology was no part of the moral tradition in which Gandhi's own sensibilities had been nurtured. Indeed he once remarked that although he had been deeply influenced by the life and teachings of Jesus, one of the two main reasons which held him back from becoming a Christian was that Jesus did not appear to him to show the all-embracing compassion for all living beings that marked Buddha.[52] The other reason was the Christian belief that one could not reach salvation unless one accepted Jesus as the only-begotten Son of God.

Gandhi believed that his theory of trusteeship applied just as well to the relationships between human beings and animals as it did to those between different groups in human society: 'It is an arrogant assumption to say that human beings are lords and masters of the lower creation. On the contrary, being endowed with greater things in life, they are trustees of the lower animal kingdom.'[53]

Gandhi also tried to give some practical content to this concept through efforts to secure a better deal for animals. He drew public attention in particular to the ill-treatment of cows in India:

How we bleed her to take the last drop of milk from her, how we starve her to emaciation, how we ill-treat the calves, how we deprive them of their portion of milk, how cruelly we beat the oxen, how we castrate them, how we beat them, how we overlord them.[54]

For bringing about a change in the way animals were treated, Gandhi undertook campaigns to educate the public about their duties towards animals, to persuade municipalities and other bodies to adopt appropriate rules and regulations for animal care, and to enact legislation for the protection of animals at the state level. Some have seen these efforts by Gandhi simply as an expression of his veneration for the 'holy cow', and possibly this may have played a part, but Gandhi himself described his campaign for cow-protection as an aspect of the wider effort to honour animal rights. Cow-protection, he suggests, 'takes the human being beyond his species'.[55]

> The cow is merely a type for all that lives. Cow protection means protection of the weak, the helpless, the dumb and the deaf. Man becomes then not the lord and master of all creation but he is its servant.[56]

The cow, he suggests, was an appropriate choice to serve as a symbol of the animal kingdom because she was a companion and a giver of plenty, yielding milk and making agriculture possible.

Gandhi's concept of animal rights required human beings to perform the duty of taking care of animals but this duty did not necessarily over-ride all other considerations. He was willing, for example, to do injury to monkeys who damaged crops at his ashram at Sabarmati, approved of the putting down of rabid dogs and believed that for dealing with the nuisance of stray dogs civilised human beings should seek out a solution on a consideration of both ethics and expediency.[57] On the other hand he opposed experiments on animals for the purpose of scientific research in any circumstances.

For a deontological theory of rights it is much more difficult to provide a rationale of animal rights. Nozick, for instance, who regards rights as side-constraints on action which it is morally impermissible to violate on any account, concedes that such stringent limitation may not be considered appropriate for 'non-human animals'. In trying nevertheless to find a place for animal rights he has to take resort to some very contrived devices, such as treating animals as 'morally intermediate between persons and stones', and appealing to a composite principle of 'utilitarianism for animals, Kantianism for people'.[58] More logically, some others have reached the conclusion that on the deontological view of rights, it would be improper to speak of animal rights at all.[59] Similar difficulties appear, though to a lesser extent, in the treatment of the rights of children, or the mentally ill. These and other limitations of the analysis of rights as categorical moral imperatives have led some to look for alternative models. One such is the so-called 'goal-rights' model in which both rights and other objectives such as social welfare may be included as ultimate goals and rights are not treated as necessarily over-riding these other goals.[60] Another suggestion that has been made is that we should return to a duty-based approach to rights theory. Arnold suggests that it may well be that a theory couched in terms of duty is the sort of theory that needs reflecting in a moral philosophy;[61] and expresses the belief that 'the future may well regenerate the language of duty in order to promote interests in areas where the rights thesis is prevented from promoting them'.[62] If that happens, Gandhi's views on rights, and his attempts to apply them in order to secure a better deal for disadvantaged groups, may perhaps come to receive greater attention.

I shall conclude by recounting the main topics discussed in this chapter. I started with the two main propositions that make up the Gandhian view of rights: first, that rights are correlative with duties and second, that conceptually duties have priority over rights. I then tried to bring out the meaning of these propositions by looking at Gandhi's exposition of some specific rights. Next, I discussed Gandhi's view of rights from a broader perspective and argued that his assertion that rights are correlated with duties is best understood in a legal framework. I also compared Gandhi's understanding of the primacy of duty with that expressed by Bosanquet and emphasised in that context the role of civil disobedience. Finally I examined the implications of Gandhi's view for welfare rights and for animal rights. So far, I have been concerned with Gandhi's views on individual welfare. In the next chapter I shall consider his views on the technology of production.

4

INDUSTRIALISATION, TECHNOLOGY AND THE SCALE OF PRODUCTION

Among Gandhi's economic views it is perhaps those he expressed against the use of machines that have attracted the greatest public attention. His hostile attitude to power-driven machinery and large-scale production, and hence to industrialisation on modern lines as the path to economic development, gained him much notoriety both in India and abroad. His views on these topics are discussed in this chapter, which consists of four sections. The first contrasts Gandhi's view of industrialisation with the mainstream tradition of Indian economic thought and states some of the criticisms that have been made against his approach. Gandhi's arguments against industrialisation are set out in the second section. A number of qualifications to these arguments which Gandhi himself came to accept are stated in the third section, and the fourth section attempts a critical assessment of Gandhi's views on industrialisation in the light of recent developments in technology. The chapter concludes with a recapitulation of its principal arguments.

GANDHI VS RANADE

The central concern of Indian economic nationalism had always been to find a remedy for mass poverty. And at least since Ranade (1842–1901) the agreed remedy was industrialisation. Ranade had argued long, and – to most economic and political thinkers in India – convincingly, that the single most important cause of poverty in India was the overdependence of the economy on agriculture. While, in common with all pre-modern societies, India had always been predominantly agricultural, the position had worsened considerably under British rule. Competition from products of modern manufacturing industry, mostly British, had led to a decline of output and employment in indigenous craft industries. This, in Ranade's view, was a world-wide trend resulting from technological changes associated with the Industrial Revolution in Europe. However, the concerted efforts of the Government of India to serve the interests of British producers, rather than those of the people of India, had prevented the transition from occurring in a more orderly and gradual fashion and had made the process of de-industrialisation in India far quicker and more devastating than need have been the case. Ranade observed:

> Every class of artisans, the spinners, weavers and dyers, the oilsmen, the papermakers, the silk and sugar and metal workers etc. who are unable to bear against western competition resort to their land, leave the towns and go into the country and are lost in the mass of helpless people who are unable to bear up against scarcity and famine.[1]

But the indirect and long-run effects of the process could be even more damaging. 'The progress of ruralisation in modern India means its rustication, i.e. a loss of power, and intelligence and self-dependence, and is distinctly a retrograde step.'[2] There were, he thought, a few developments such as the growth of seaports and military and railway stations which had an opposite effect but they were too weak to counterbalance the economic forces tending towards ruralisation. Industrial development alone could halt, and eventually reverse, the process. Economic development in Indian conditions, therefore, required priority being given to industry and commerce over agriculture.

Ranade also developed a number of more general arguments purporting to show that industrialisation was the appropriate means of bringing about economic development not only in the special circumstances prevailing in India but in all countries. First, he appealed to a version of what has now come to be known in the literature of development economics as the argument for balanced growth. Taking a cue from the German school of historical economics, and in particular from Friedrich List, Ranade defined economic development as a full and all-round development of the productive powers of society. This required a proper balance among different sectors of production, ensuring that an adequate demand for the output of each sector could be sustained. Where, as in India, the structure of the economy was lopsided, a substantial increase in industrial output and employment was therefore a necessary condition for long-run economic growth to occur.

A related, though logically distinct, argument was based on the concept of certain well-defined 'stages of growth' through which an economy is expected to pass in the process of development. Ranade described the Indian economy of his time as being stuck in the stage of 'agriculture plus handicraft'. The stage to which it should advance was that of 'agriculture plus manufacture plus commerce'. In keeping with this vision Ranade and his successors tended to think of industrial growth in an open economy context.

Third, manufacturing industry, argued Ranade, allowed greater scope than other types of production for what he called 'art manipulation', in other words, the application of science and technology to the production process. This in his view explained why a society's output per head of the population was usually found to be proportional to the share of the labour force that was engaged in manufacturing. For the same reason manufacturing activity allowed far greater scope for learning by doing than traditional agricultural pursuits, which fostered 'rustication'.

While most Indian economists agreed with Ranade that the long-run solution to mass poverty was industrialisation they held differing views on what was stopping that solution from being achieved. For some it was the economic drain resulting from the exploitative financial mechanisms by which British rule in India was maintained. Others, like Ranade, placed greater emphasis on such factors as the lack of trained labour, a low rate of saving, and deficient facilities for mobilising available savings for investment in industry. Yet others put the blame on government for failing to give help or encouragement to Indian industry. All were, however, in favour of industrial development on the Western model and many suggested methods by which the process could be speeded up. Gandhi departed from the mainstream by rejecting the goal of industrialisation itself. On the contrary, he argued that economic development based on the use of modern machinery and large-scale production in urban centres should be avoided as far as possible. These would only create unemployment, increase economic inequality and concentrate power in the hands of an urban elite, while perpetuating the poverty and degradation of the village masses. Instead he proposed a massive effort to revive the traditional village and handicraft industries of India which had been destroyed under foreign rule. Only this, he maintained, could succeed in bringing about productive utilisation of human labour, and in restoring the human dignity of village people, who formed the overwhelming majority of the population of India. The alternative path to economic development that Gandhi proposed, based on the Constructive Programme and *swadeshi*, is described elsewhere in this book (see Chapter 2).

Gandhi's hostility to industrialisation and to the use of machinery not only set him apart from previous Indian thinkers such as Ranade or Gokhale but also from many of his colleagues in the Indian National Congress, including Jawaharlal Nehru, who later became India's first Prime Minister. Nehru took good care to dissociate both himself and the Congress from Gandhi's views on this topic, insisting both that the Congress was committed to the industrialisation of India once independence was achieved and that this was the only way in which mass poverty could be abolished.[3] Contemporaries in India, and economists in particular, tended to look on Gandhi's views on technology as a not quite harmless fad and often took him to task for, as Gandhi himself put it, 'talking things of bygone ages'.[4] Such talk also caused ridicule abroad. During an interview with Gandhi Charlie Chaplin remarked that while he was in sympathy with India's aspirations and struggle for freedom he was somewhat confused by Gandhi's abhorrence of machinery.[5] Aldous Huxley suggested:

> that by pleading for a return to nature and opposing the application of science and technology to agricultural and industrial production, people like Gandhi were in effect trying to take the world back to famines, death and barbarism. Tolstoy and Gandhi are professed humanitarians but they advocate a slaughter, compared with which the massacres of Timur and Jinghiz Khan seem almost imperceptibly trivial.[6]

Marxist critics, too, denounced Gandhi's desire to 'run from the Machine Age to the Stone Age'[7] which they saw not only as being rooted in his reactionary ideology but also as a reflection of the cultural backwardness and superstition characteristic of Indian society as a whole.[8] Marx himself had anticipated such criticisms of the Gandhian view when in an election appeal to 'the workers and the petty-bourgeois' in January 1849, he warned them against a programme for reviving the guilds. He told them that it was better to suffer in the contemporary bourgeois society, whose industry creates the means for the foundations of a new society that would liberate them, than to revert to a bygone society, which on the pretext of saving them would throw the entire nation back into medieval barbarism. How far such an indictment of Gandhi's views on industrialisation is justified is a question to which I shall return towards the end of this chapter, but first I look at the arguments which Gandhi himself put forward in support of his case.

THE CASE AGAINST INDUSTRIALISATION

Gandhi's opposition to the project of industrialising India on modern lines was based on moral as well as economic reasons. As was customary with Gandhi he did not distinguish sharply between the moral and the economic argument, but for the sake of clarity I shall try to do so here. I begin by looking briefly at the views on machinery expressed by Gandhi in *Hind Swaraj*. Earlier I described Gandhi's style of writing in that book as rhetorical and exaggerated and stated my belief that the views expressed there on various topics should not be taken to be representative of his mature thought. While this applies no less to the opinions on machinery which form Chapter 19 of *Hind Swaraj*, they are frequently quoted by critics and have a certain historical interest which I feel justifies my taking them as a starting point.

'Machinery', Gandhi states bleakly, 'has begun to desolate Europe. Ruination is now knocking at the English gates. Machinery is the chief symbol of modern civilisation; it represents a great sin.'[9] The mill workers of Bombay, he goes on, have become slaves and the condition of women workers is particularly shocking. If the machinery craze grows India will become an unhappy land. It would even be preferable, he thinks

> to send money to Manchester and to use flimsy Manchester cloth than to multiply mills in India. By using Manchester cloth we only waste our money; but by reproducing Manchester in India we shall keep our money at the price of our blood, because our very moral being will be sapped, and I call in support of my statement the very mill-hands as witnesses.[10]

Gandhi does not really tell us why machines, or mills using them, are such a great moral evil but appears to suggest that it is the low wages and poor working conditions of workers that he finds unacceptable. He does not, however, ponder on the question *why* the workers had migrated from their villages to seek jobs in the cotton mills of a big city despite working conditions there being so poor, a point which applies equally to the critics of the Industrial Revolution in England whom Gandhi seems to be echoing. Even in his later writings he never came to grips with the issue of rural–urban migration, even stating on one occasion that he 'did not think that the poor of India would leave their homes and migrate to the towns for work in the mill'.[11] Continuing with *Hind Swaraj,* he finds machinery guilty by association:

> Machinery is like a snake-hole which may contain from one to a hundred snakes .Where there is machinery there are large cities; and where there are large cities, there are tram cars and railways; and there only does one see electric lights.[12]

English villages, he adds approvingly, do not boast of any of these things. While Gandhi was sure machines were evil he was not so sure how the evil could be removed. The following passage brings this out.

READER: 'Are the mills, then, to be closed down?'
EDITOR: 'That is difficult. It is no easy task to do away with a thing that is established. We cannot condemn mill-owners; we can but pity them. It would be too much to expect them to give up their mills, but we may implore them not to increase them. If they would be good they would gradually contract their business.[13]

However, Gandhi goes on, whether or not the mill-owners do so people could always stop buying machine-made goods, an idea he later developed into the basic strategy of the movement for *swadeshi.* The discussion ends with an exhortation:

> Do not, therefore, forget the main thing. It is necessary to realise that machinery is bad. We shall then be able gradually to do away with it. Nature has not provided any way whereby we may reach a desired goal all of a sudden. If, instead of welcoming machinery as a boon, we should look upon it as an evil, it would ultimately go.[14]

Gandhi's condemnation of machinery, and modern civilisation, in *Hind Swaraj* rests on a kind of moral fundamentalism rather than on reasoned argument and it is on this element that critics have concentrated their attack. In his later writings, however, Gandhi developed a serious and sustained argument against relying predominantly on mechanised techniques and large-scale production for bringing about economic development. To this argument we now turn.

Essentially the argument is that the choice of techniques should be guided by the factor-proportions prevailing in the economy concerned. India by all accounts was deficient both in capital and in technical expertise. In order to develop large-scale machine-based industry India would require to import from abroad both machines and experts to run such machines.[15] This would take a very long time. On the other hand India had a relative abundance of human labour power. This, as Gandhi saw it, was due to a large population together with a high man–land ratio. And although the total land area of the country was also very large, because agriculture had been practised in India almost continuously from very ancient times, a high proportion of the cultivable land was already under cultivation, and the scope for increasing the area under cultivation was therefore fairly limited. At the same time, Gandhi pointed out, there was considerable under-utilisation of available labour. Because of the seasonal nature of agriculture, which was predominantly rain-fed, cultivators who tilled their own land – and a large majority of the population of India belonged to this category – had no work for at least four months in a normal year. If rainfall was scanty or irregular and the crops failed, the extent of under-employment would be much greater. Gandhi spelled out the logic of his argument in a letter to an American friend in 1934:

> What applies to America and England does not necessarily apply to India. India has in her teeming millions so many superfluous days that she does not need to free the energy of her sons for superior or more remunerative work through highly developed machinery. In her 350 million children she has so many living ready-made machines and if she can utilise their labour, half of which is running to waste, the double starvation of the body and the mind will cease. That is the problem that faced me when I returned to India in 1915 and has haunted me ever since.[16]

Gandhi's stand against mechanisation can be interpreted in large measure as a response to this specific problem. He makes the same point even more strongly in another letter, also written in 1934:

> In India, at any rate for generations to come, we shall not be able to make much use of mechanical power for solving the problem of ever-growing poverty of the masses. We are too many and we have so many idle hours at our disposal that it would be suicidal to make use of mechanical power to allow human power to run to waste.[17]

70

Interpreted in terms of the factor-proportions argument, Gandhi's stand against the adoption of mechanised techniques for industrial development in India need no longer be seen as advocacy of a 'return to nature'. Gandhi himself makes this quite explicit. In the course of justifying his opposition to the grinding of corn by a mechanical process in the mills he states:

> I have no partiality for return to the primitive method of grinding and husking for the sake of them. I suggest the return because there is no other way of giving employment to the millions of villagers who are living in idleness.[18]

His plea was not so much for using capital less as for using labour more. The same concern underlies his opposition to methods of production which involve utilising natural resources more intensively than labour. Any plan which exploited the raw materials of a country to the full while neglecting utilisation of man-power was lopsided and could not lead to equality.[19]

In most of his writings on industrialisation Gandhi had India's specific circumstances in mind, but he also tried to develop a stronger, and more general, case against 'modern' economic growth through the use of power-driven machinery and large-scale production. This too is based primarily on the threat of unemployment but it is derived not from the factor-proportions argument as such but rather from certain general characteristics that Gandhi attributes to machinery. He describes three such characteristics. The first is that a machine displaces human, or animal, labour instead of merely supplementing it or increasing its efficiency. The second is that there is no discernible limit to the growth and expansion of machines. It is quite otherwise with human labour which cannot go beyond a certain physical limit. A third characteristic follows from these two, namely that machines appear to have a will or genius of their own, which is always antagonistic to human labour. This leads not only to labour being displaced but to its being displaced at an ever accelerating rate. And this, suggests Gandhi, occurs not necessarily because such an outcome is considered by users of machines to be socially or economically desirable but as a consequence of the nature of technological progress itself. Gandhi's 'strong' case against industrialisation rests on this characterisation of machinery. 'I am against machines just because they deprive men of their employment and render them jobless. I oppose them not because they are machines but because they create unemployment.'[20]

The question of whether machinery necessarily causes unemployment had been discussed extensively in classical political economy with which Gandhi had a superficial acquaintance but for him the answer seemed self-evident. 'If one machine does the work of a hundred men, then where are we to employ those hundred men?'[21] One could argue, of course, that they would find employment elsewhere. Gandhi was aware of this argument and tried to answer it in his own way, 'You may say that workers thrown out of work by the introduction of improved machinery will find occupation in other jobs'.[22] This was unlikely especially in a developed economy with well-organised labour markets, such as that of Britain.

> But in an organised country where there are only fixed and limited avenues of employment, where the worker has become highly skilled in the use of one particular kind of machinery, you know from your own experience that this is hardly possible.[23]

Gandhi is using a two-fold argument here. First, that the aggregate demand for labour is given; and second, that as a result of specialisation in the production process workers have highly specific skills and cannot easily be re-employed elsewhere in the economy even if an opportunity for employment arises. The first argument seems to beg the question. If the use of machinery facilitates large-scale production, which in turn leads to an acceleration in the rate of economic growth, the aggregate demand for labour could be expected to increase. This, indeed, has generally been the historical experience of industrialising countries. The second argument, based on specialisation of labour is more plausible but does not allow for the possibility of retraining.

To sum up, Gandhi believed that machinery was by its very nature labour-displacing and that its tendency to throw workers out of their jobs was a general tendency operating everywhere. Its consequences, however, were particularly grave for a country such as India which had meagre capital resources but a large population, and which was already suffering from a serious problem of under-utilisation of the available labour-time, because of under-employment. The proliferation of highly mechanised, capital-intensive industries in such a country could, he feared, bring about large-scale unemployment with horrendous social effects.

Gandhi's second main argument against the pursuit of industrialisation through large-scale production was that it led to the concentration of production and distribution in the hands of a few and thereby promoted the concentration of economic power.

Organisation of machinery for the purpose of concentrating wealth and power in the hands of a few and for the exploitation of the many I would hold to be altogether wrong. Much of the organisation of machinery of the present age is of that type.[24]

If that kind of organisation were to spread in India it would lead to further encroachment of the cities on villages, making the villages even more dependent on the cities than they already were. Gandhi's vision of *swaraj* could not, he thought, be realised through such a process. If industrial production was concentrated in a few urban centres the economic as well as the political power of the urban elite would be strengthened at the expense of the village masses. Mass production in the usual sense of the term, that is production by the fewest possible number through the aid of complicated machinery, could not, suggests Gandhi, serve the interests of the masses themselves.[25] In his view a preferable alternative would be production by the masses through self-employment in village industries. 'If you multiply individual production a million times would it not give you mass production on a tremendous scale?'[26] This he describes as 'mass production in people's own homes'. Income distribution, he believed, could be equalised only when production was localised, in other words when the distribution and production of goods were simultaneous. Issues relating to this proposed alternative path to economic development are discussed further elsewhere in this book.

Both in India and abroad Gandhi's warning that large-scale production would increase the concentration of economic power and hence fail to remove inequality and exploitation struck a more responsive chord than his warning that machinery would lead to unemployment. This was largely because the former warning was taken to be directed against the capitalist system of production rather than the use of machinery as such. This was indeed *one* element of his thinking. In October 1924, in a conversation with a student who had come to interview him, Gandhi stated that what he objected to was the craze for machinery, not machinery as such.

> The craze is for what they call labour-saving machinery. Men go on 'saving labour' till thousands are without work and thrown on the open streets to die of starvation...Today machinery merely helps a few to ride on the backs of millions. The impetus behind it all is not the philanthropy to save labour but greed.[27]

He went on to say that scientific truths and discoveries should cease to be mere instruments of greed. 'Then labourers will not be over-worked and machinery instead of becoming a hindrance will be a help.'[28] He took up the same theme in a talk many years later:

> We should be as careful in using machines as a doctor is in prescribing poisonous medicines. Machine-power can make a valuable contribution towards economic progress, but a few capitalists have employed machine-power regardless of the interests of the common man and that is why our condition has deteriorated today.[29]

Such statements do appear to suggest that it is the capitalist rather than his machine that is to blame. However, he also explicitly and repeatedly states that his opposition was not directed *only* at the concentration of power that occurred in a system with private ownership of the means of production. 'I do not share the socialist belief that centralisation of the necessaries of life will conduce to the common welfare when the centralised industries are planned and owned by the State.'[30]

Gandhi also acknowledged that he held a different view on this point from some of his colleagues. 'Pandit Nehru wants industrialisation because he thinks that if it is socialised, it would be free from the evils of capitalism. My own view is that evils are inherent in industrialism, and no amount of socialisation can eradicate them.'[31] Issues related to this argument are discussed in Chapter 6, on trusteeship.

Gandhi also resorted to a number of subsidiary arguments to buttress his case against industrialisation as a means of economic development. One of these is that to achieve sustained growth of industrial output a country must enjoy some form of preferential access to foreign markets. 'If all countries adopted the system of mass production there would not be a big enough market for their products.'[32] Mass production would then come to a stop. Success required privileged access to foreign markets. 'Industrialism depends entirely on your capacity to exploit, on foreign markets being open to you, and on the absence of competitors.'[33] Gandhi, in common with many other writers of the time, looks on the quest for markets as an impetus to economic imperialism and he notes that the period of the Industrial Revolution in Europe was marked both by wars of conquest to acquire territories in the Asian and African continents and by wars between the European powers themselves. Britain, he points out, had been particularly successful in acquiring colonies all over the world, which served as captive markets for British manufactured products. The Indian subcontinent was especially valuable to Britain as a market for cotton textiles made in the Lancashire mills. 'England with her large-scale production has to look for a market elsewhere. We call it exploitation.'[34] Such exploitation, according to Gandhi, was carried out by a variety of means, both direct and indirect. Among the latter he includes attempts to encourage the adoption by 'natives' of a Western life-style which would cut them off from their own culture and stimulate a taste for foreign goods. Efforts by missionaries to convert Indians to Christianity is cited by him as a typical example of this hidden agenda. In India, he observes, Christianity had more to do with life-style and material consumption than with the Sermon on the Mount. The advent of a missionary in a Hindu household simply meant changes in 'dress, manners, language, food and drink'.[35] To become a Christian was commonly identified with having 'a brandy bottle in one hand and beef in the other'.[36] Gandhi sums up as follows:

> Let me say a word about your missionaries. You send them here for nothing, but that is also part of imperialist exploitation. For they would like to make us like you, better buyers of your goods and unable to do without your cars and luxuries.[37]

But England's capacity to exploit other countries in this way was rapidly diminishing. She now faced increasing competition from other countries, such as America, Japan and Germany and even a handful of cotton mills in India posed a threat to Lancashire. Soon, the industrialised nations of the West might cease to find in Africa a dumping ground for their wares. The problem, however, was not peculiar to the West but was inherent in industrialisation. 'The economic imperialism of a single tiny island kingdom (England) is today keeping the world in chains. If an entire nation of 300 millions took to similar economic exploitation it would strip the world bare like locusts.'[38] If India took to machinery and started producing cloth many times in excess of its domestic consumption, it would become dependent on foreign markets for its output and in due course turn into an exploiting nation like England. But by virtue of its size and population it would be much more dangerous than England was. India, when it begins to exploit other nations, which it must do if it becomes industrialised, will be 'a curse for other nations, a menace to the world'.[39] On the other hand, given that there were already powerful industrialised nations who were out to protect their own markets by all possible means, including the use of arms, the chances of India being particularly successful in exporting her manufactured products were hardly bright. In the end, Gandhi believed, the drive for exports would lead to a competitive struggle between nations to build up their military strength, and an industrialised India would have to stand against the military power of Britain, Japan, America, Russia and Italy.

SOME QUALIFICATIONS

Gandhi's rejection of machinery was not quite as absolute as some have supposed but, especially in his later writings, was hemmed in with certain qualifications and after-thoughts which I shall now consider. An important qualification arose from his explicit recognition that technological possibilities of production varied considerably from one type of product to another, and that the extent to which human or animal power could be used instead of machinery varied accordingly. In terms of the language of modern economics Gandhi regarded the elasticity of factor-substitution (a measure of the extent to which factors of production, such as capital and labour, could be substituted for each other in production of goods) as product-specific. For certain types of products the use of power-driven machinery was indispensable: without such machinery they could not be produced at all. He states, 'We want to cultivate hand processes to perfection but where it is found to be absolutely necessary let us not hesitate to introduce machinery.'[40] He provides a number of specific examples where he believes this to be the case. In a letter to a distinguished engineer in 1934 he wrote, 'I know that the heavy industries cannot be organised without power-driven machinery. I can have no quarrel with such use of machinery.'[41] Likewise he had no objection to the use of highly mechanised techniques of production in the steel industry, which 'does not lend itself to hand labour' or for making surgical instruments.[42] He acknowledged that some of the most delicate life-saving appliances could not have been made without the use of machinery, and did not want the production of such things to be abandoned because of that.[43] Asked by a correspondent whether his opposition of the use of machinery extended to the introduction of flush toilets in India for the purpose of improving the standard of sanitation Gandhi replied,

> Where there is ample supply of water and modern sanitation can
> be introduced without any hardship on the poor, I have no

objection to it, in fact it should be welcomed as a means of improving the health of the city concerned. At the moment it can only be introduced in towns.[44]

In the same spirit when asked by some socialists why he opposed the growth of industries in India through the use of machinery Gandhi demurred, pointing out that he did not oppose all such industries. 'You can use machines to manufacture cars, engines, aeroplanes and things of that kind.'[45] He also exempted public utilities which simply could not be undertaken without using machine-power.

In cases of this kind, where mechanical technology was required by the logic of production itself, Gandhi saw the problem of the choice of techniques as being subsumed under that of the choice of products. About some of these products Gandhi was far from enthusiastic. For example he wanted India to shun the production of cars, aeroplanes and armaments altogether. However, he had no such objection to the production of things that contributed to public health and sanitation nor to the provision of public utilities. Among the latter the case of electric power is particularly important and Gandhi's position on the use of such power in production shifted considerably over time. In *Hind Swaraj* he had condemned the use of electricity even for lighting. Some of his later writings appear to suggest that he had had second thoughts about this. In 1935 an American correspondent brought to his attention a scheme developed by Henry Ford for decentralising industry through the use of electric power which could be transmitted from a central generating board to the villages. The correspondent held up for Gandhi's approval a vision of 'small, neat, smokeless villages dotted with factories, run by village communities'. This involved the use of power-driven machinery but avoided the concentration of production in large urban centres. Gandhi did not condemn the scheme outright but withheld his approval on the ground that while it would indeed decentralise the production of goods, electric power itself would still be supplied by a single producing centre. Dependence on it for essentials, such as light, water and electricity placed too much power in the hands of a single, private agency.[46] Some years later when asked by a socialist who was strongly in favour of industrialisation: 'You would have nothing to do with electricity?' Gandhi replied, 'Who says so? If we could have electricity in every village home, I should not mind villagers plying their implements and tools with the help of electricity.'[47]

However, Gandhi insisted that for this to occur the power-houses had to be owned either by the village community itself or by the state. Clearly, despite his dislike of state control in general, he was as usual prepared to make what he called 'intelligent exceptions', and in this case he regarded depending on the state for an essential input as a lesser evil than depending on a private monopoly.

In some of his later writings Gandhi also qualified his opposition to modern industrial development by acknowledging that it had a place provided it did not result in stifling village industry.

> I do visualise electricity, ship-building, iron works, machine-making and the like existing side by side with village handi-crafts. But the order of dependence will be reversed. Hitherto industrialisation has been so planned as to destroy the villages and village crafts. In the state of the future it will subserve the villagers and their crafts.[48]

If that condition was satisfied Gandhi was willing to approve of the use of machines, even of importing them if need be: 'As long as we cannot make the machines required for utilising the hide of dead cattle, worth nine crores, available in our country, I would be ready to import them from any part of the world.'[49]

This was not, he claimed, inconsistent with his views on machinery nor with the vow of *swadeshi*. There is a large and important branch of production, that of necessaries of life such as food and clothing, where Gandhi's objection to the use of mechanised techniques ran much deeper. 'For food and clothing', he declared, 'I would be dead against industrialisation.'[50] Yet even here his position was more pragmatic than this declaration suggests. During the 1930s Gandhi was requested by American journalists on several occasions to clarify his stand on the role of mechanisation in agriculture. On one such occasion, asked if he agreed that the application of machinery to agriculture would make a great difference to India as it had done to the United States and to Canada, Gandhi said,

> Probably. But that is a question I do not consider myself fit to answer. We in India have not been able to use much complicated machinery in agriculture with profit so far. We do not exclude machinery. We are making cautious experiments. But we have not found power-driven agricultural machinery to be necessary.[51]

At that time, however, the question of mechanising Indian agriculture was merely an academic exercise with little practical relevance. By 1947, just about the time when India gained independence, Gandhi came to believe that this was no longer the case. In a discussion with Rajendra Prasad, shortly afterwards to become the first President of India, Gandhi asked, 'Have you given thought to the possible consequences of using tractors, and pumping machines to water the fields, and trucks instead of carts for transport of goods? How many farmers will become unemployed, how many bullocks become idle?'[52] After independence Gandhi continued to express strong opposition to the adoption of any policies by the central or state governments that might encourage the replacement of ploughs by tractors for cultivating the land. He was no less firm in opposing the use of machinery for grinding corn or manufacturing cloth. He told an interviewer that if he were Prime Minister of India he would stop all machine-driven flour mills and restrict the number of oil-processing factories. He would not, he said, destroy the existing textile mills but would not help them in any way and would not permit new ones to be set up. He described as ideal villages those which are self-reliant in food, which have not a single flour-mill and in which the residents grow all the cotton they need and manufacture their own cloth right up to the stage of stitching garments in their own homes. If he was in charge, he would reward such villages by giving them prizes and exempting them from all taxes.[53]

At some points in his writing Gandhi tried to develop a general principle for discriminating between proper and improper use of machinery. 'If we are able to judge when to use a machine and when to avoid it and if while using it we do so with understanding, quite a few of our difficulties will be solved.'[54] Apart from the *charkha*, which, somewhat quixotically, he insisted on describing as a sort of machine, his favourite example of a machine that one should *not* try to avoid was Singer's sewing machine. Not only did Gandhi regard sewing machines as beneficial, he also approved of the establishment in India of factories 'which would have to contain power-driven machinery of the ordinary type' for making them. However, he thought that these should be nationalised or state-controlled. Because Gandhi was prepared to make exceptions, despite his stand against the use of machinery, he was asked by an interviewer who saw a logical difficulty in this position if he made an exception of the Singer Sewing Machine and his spindle, where would the exceptions end? Gandhi replied, 'Just where they cease to help the individual and encroach upon his individuality.'[55]

In the same spirit, he defined as a helpful machine 'any machine which does not deprive masses of men of the opportunity to labour but which helps the individual and adds to his efficiency and which a man can handle at will without being 'its slave.'[56] The distinction that Gandhi draws here between helpful and unhelpful machines will be discussed in the next section of this chapter but I should like to point out that Gandhi himself failed to apply it in a systematic way. Towards the end of his life he observed, 'Every machine that helps every individual has a place but I must confess that I have never sat down to think out what that machine can be.'[57] The failure to think this out suggests, at least to this writer, that he did not take the distinction very seriously but assumed that most machines were unhelpful. The same impression is given by his answer, many years earlier, to a village worker who had wondered, 'But why not accept the machine with all its good points, eliminating the bad ones?' Gandhi simply repeated his standard economic argument, 'I cannot afford to keep our human machines idle.'[58] Usually, it is true, he welcomed improvements in what he called 'cottage' or 'hand' machines and was involved himself in an effort to develop improved versions of the *charkha*. On one occasion he recommended the use of improved ploughs, arguing that even though such innovation could harm the village carpenter by reducing the demand for his labour this deprivation could be out-weighed by increases in the earning capacity of the farmer. On the other hand he opposed a scheme for developing rubber-tyres to be fitted on bullock-carts, arguing, somewhat implausibly, that this would not make things easier for the villagers but on the contrary would increase their requirements, make them dependent on others and provide yet another means of exploitation.[59]

CONCLUSION

By way of a summing up I shall offer some comments on Gandhi's views regarding industrialisation and technology. My first comment is about Gandhi's application of the factor-proportions argument. In arguing that a labour-abundant society should try, as far as possible, to adopt labour-intensive techniques, Gandhi was ahead of the econo-mists of his time. The argument now forms part of the received doctrine of development economics. A recent and widely used text-book on the subject by A. P. Thirlwall states, *inter alia*, that the efficient use of resources in a relatively labour-abundant economy would normally require the use of labour-intensive techniques of production and generally the encouragement of activities that utilise the abundant factors of production; that if the labour-supply and the rate of investment are given, the more capital-intensive the technique the greater the unemployment; that techniques imported by a developing country from abroad often suffer from the labour-saving bias characteristic of technical progress in the country of origin (where it is labour that tends to be the more scarce factor) and that they may therefore represent an inappropriate technology from the importing country's point of view; and that such considerations have led to a movement in the developing countries to create an intermediate technology using more labour per unit of capital and less foreign inputs.[60] All these propositions are consistent with Gandhi's approach to the problem even though the context in which the problem is raised is not precisely the same.

Gandhi's 'strong case' against industrialisation is much more vulnerable. The case rests, as we have seen, on his characterisation of machines. For the purpose of his argument their most important characteristic is a tendency to replace human labour at an ever accelerating rate. This, he believed, would lead to certain irreversible changes in the way production was organised, involving a rising trend in the scale, and capital-intensity, of production, and in the degree of its concentration between different firms and regions. Gandhi saw these as the predominant features of industrialisation and concluded that if it spread, especially in a country with a largely agricultural population, unemployment and inequality would increase and economic power become concentrated in the hands of an urban elite while the peasant masses would remain poor and powerless. Such a reading of the long-run trend of modern technology lies at the heart of Gandhi's hostility to industrialisation. He did not reject the necessity of economic growth itself. On the contrary he had a life-long commitment to the eradication of poverty and recognised that increase in income and employment was necessary to achieve this end. He did not, however, see industrialisation on modern lines as a means of achieving it. 'That the crores in India should be guaranteed a certain income is only right and to achieve this ideal large-scale machinery is not only not necessary but wholly destructive.'[61]

Gandhi's reading of the trend of technology has something in common with that of Karl Marx. Marx, too, believed that industrial capitalism had an inherent tendency to become increasingly capital-intensive (the law of increasing organic composition of capital), and that this led in the long run both to the substitution of competition by monopoly and to increasing misery for the masses of working people. However, Marx believed this process to be historically self-correcting for it would lead to society becoming divided into two warring classes, the capitalists and the working class, and ultimately to the overthrow of capitalism and the rise of a different kind of society in which the means of production would be held in common. Gandhi's vision was very different. He wanted to avoid the evils of the industrial system by avoiding industrialisation itself.

This gloomy view of the consequences of industrialisation is hardly justified by historical experience. Industrialisation, wherever it has occurred, has been accompanied in its early phase by the displacement of labour, urban squalor and social unrest. Over a longer period, however, standards of living in all industrialising countries whether measured by per capita income, or by social indicators such as the expectancy of life at birth, have increased substantially. This has been just as true of the less developed countries during their post-independence period, as it was of Western countries in the past.[62] It is the secular rise in productivity, brought about in the main by technological innovation, which has made this possible, though organised efforts by labouring people in defence of their wages and working conditions, and in some cases action by the state, have also played an important part. The increasing misery of the masses of working people under industrial capitalism that was forecast both by Marx and by Gandhi failed to happen. The rate of unemployment, while it has shown considerable fluctuation over the business cycle has not shown an upward long-run trend, while the proportion of the population that is economically active has steadily increased with industrialisation. Fears have recently been expressed that the spread of automated techniques of production may lead to a substantial part of the work-force of industrialised countries becoming unemployed within the next few decades. But the same advances in information processing technology that have made automation possible are also opening up new work opportunities and at the same time in some ways changing the concept of work itself. They may help towards dispersing work activities over space; blurring time-honoured distinctions between production and consumption and between workplace and home; making work-patterns more flexible; and creating entirely new types of work. Some of these outcomes Gandhi himself would probably have approved but it is modern technology, not village handicrafts, that has made them possible.

I shall now consider briefly another of Gandhi's criticisms of industrialisation: that it makes a country dependent on foreign markets, which in turn leads it to embark on economic imperialism.

This idea did not originate with Gandhi. It had been held by some Indian economic nationalists, who deplored the influence of Lancashire on the economic policies of the Government of India. It also formed part of the standard Marxist analysis of imperialism. Unlike them, however, Gandhi used the argument not so much against imperialism as against industrialisation itself.

That the argument has substance, as applied to Indo–British economic relations during most of the nineteenth century and the early part of the twentieth, has been demonstrated by historical research. By 1830, while cotton textiles still accounted for over half the value of total British exports, Britain had started losing its early markets in Europe and the United States, which were developing their own manufacturing sectors. India helped to fill the gap. Between 1820 and 1855 while Britain's total cotton goods exports grew at a rate of less than 2 per cent per year, her cotton goods exports to India grew at about 6 per cent per year. 'None of this', observe Cain and Hopkins, 'could have taken place without British control, which was steadily extended in scope throughout the period.'[63] That trade-patterns were not determined simply by comparative advantage, as economic theory suggests, but by the needs of empire is shown by Gallager and Robinson who point out that 'in this supposedly *laissez-faire* period India ... was subjected to intensive development as an economic colony along the best mercantilist line'.[64] During the second half of the nineteenth century the links between the metropolitan economy and India were further strengthened. As a purchaser of British export goods, in 1870 India had stood third and in 1890–92 second: on the eve of the First World War India stood first, with 60 per cent of her imports coming from Britain. During 1870–1914 India served as the 'third leg' in a triangular pattern of settlements between Britain and the rest of the world, financing over two-thirds of Britain's balance of payments deficit with Europe and the United States of America. Britain's political domination of India enabled her to manipulate Indian tariffs and monetary system to the advantage of British industry and British investors.

This historical link between industrialisation and empire influenced Gandhi's thinking but it does not prove his case. That would require him to show that industrialisation can *only* be sustained by foreign rather than domestic demand; and that foreign markets can *only* be acquired by force of arms rather than by supplying cheaper or better goods and services. Neither of these propositions appears to be true. Even in the case of those industrialising countries of Europe which gained most by imperialism, growth in domestic demand probably played a more important part in sustaining economic growth than did foreign demand. And in more recent times the newly industrialising countries of South-East Asia have achieved conspicuous economic success without imperialist expansion overseas.

Gandhi's critique of industrialisation is only 'good in parts'. Some have interpreted his views essentially as a plea for the use of labour-intensive, rather than capital-intensive, techniques in industrial and agricultural production. This is a legitimate interpretation of one aspect of his thought and it represents a valuable insight which continues to have relevance for development economics. However, Gandhi was also making a much more radical claim: he was arguing in favour of handicraft or cottage industry as against modern manufacturing industry based on the factory. Here I should like to go back to Ranade. In arguing for industrialisation as the only long-run solution to mass poverty, Ranade had pointed to the dangers of 'rustication' and the advantages of a well-balanced economic structure that would not be so utterly dependent on agriculture. Gandhi's remedy for rustication was his Constructive Programme, and while he, too, sought to reduce the degree to which people had to depend on agricultural pursuits for a livelihood, he wanted to do so by developing village industries. Both these proposals of Gandhi's have merit and I have discussed them elsewhere in this book but they will not bear the burden which he wished to place on them.

Gandhi, as we have seen, started by condemning both the use of machinery as such and the civilisation which it represented. He moved away from that position as time went on but even his later writings show little enthusiasm for the positive contribution that machinery could make. There are two points bearing on this that I should like to make. First, Gandhi did not always distinguish clearly between issues relating to the scale of production and those related to the use of power-driven machinery. In principle power-driven machinery could be used just as well by small-scale as by large-scale units of production. Gandhi was surely right in thinking that increase in the scale of either political or economic organisation does not necessarily bring about greater efficiency, and that it often leads to excessive centralisation and a loss of involvement in decision-making. On the other hand his objection to power-driven machinery appears to be based on instinctive dislike rather than reasoning.

Second, Gandhi failed to grasp the enormous potential of modern technology for improving the quality of life of ordinary people. He once expressed the wish to 'make the machine our slave', adding: '"Our slave" means the slave not of the rich but of the poor.'[65] Yet by insisting that machinery had no place in the production of the necessities of life, he in effect excluded it from playing such a role. This, to my mind, represents the basic weakness of Gandhi's view of technology. It also justifies the critics who attacked his view as being unrealistic and backward-looking, but those critics ignore certain elements of strength that are also part of his approach.

In many less developed countries self-employed producers such as agriculturists and artisans form a large part of the workforce. Economic analysis, whether of the neo-classical or the Marxist variety, has paid relatively little attention to the social and economic constraints operating on their behaviour or the factors which influence their decision-making. Gandhi's preoccupation with village industries was in part a response to the economic problems of people belonging to this social category. Nanda puts the point well:

> The disintegration of the small peasant and the artisan economy, and the growth of large-scale enterprises based on modern technology, form a common ground between the advocates of the capitalist and the communist models of development. But Gandhi sensed the difficulties and dangers of alienating millions of small producers, who formed the bulk of the population, from the means of production.[66]

Perhaps Gandhi's most valuable contribution to an understanding of the role of machinery lies in his warning that humankind could be in danger of becoming a prisoner of its own artifacts. One cannot, he is saying, gain proper understanding of the limits of technology if one sees technology only in terms of its own logic, 'the will of its own' as Gandhi put it. Technology has to be assessed from a wider perspective, and for Gandhi the only valid perspective is a humanist one.

> Machinery is a grand yet awful invention. It is possible to visualise a stage at which the machines invented by man may finally engulf civilisation. If man controls the machines then they would not; but should man lose his control over the machines and allow them to control him, then they could certainly engulf civilisation and everything.[67]

For making judgements of this kind the relevant unit of aggregation for Gandhi was necessarily the individual. The question of whether humankind was in control of the machines had therefore to be resolved at the level of the individual. And the distinction that Gandhi tried to draw between a helpful and an unhelpful machine was indeed posed at this level. Although, as I pointed out earlier, Gandhi did not actually make much use of it, conceptually it is a useful distinction and corresponds broadly to that which some have drawn between a tool and a machine. In a perceptive essay on how computer technology could contribute to the human spirit Twerkle states the distinction as follows: 'Tools are extensions of their users; machines impose their own rhythm, their rules, on the people who work with them, to the point where it is no longer clear who or what is being used.'[68]

A similar point is made by Simon who points out that the word 'machine' carries with it connotations of rigidity, simplicity, repetitive behaviour and so on and suggests that since computers, by and large, do not share these attributes we should stop calling them machines.[69] The view has also been expressed that the long-run impact of computers on individuals, and society, will depend on whether future trends in computer technology are based more on developing their tool-like or their machine-like characteristics. Ultimately, as Gandhi saw so clearly, the nature of technology is a matter of human choice. What he did not see as clearly is the fact that making the right choice requires striking a balance between the welfare costs of technological progress and those of trying to revert to pre-modern technology. In a tribute to Gandhi on the occasion of his seventieth birthday Aldous Huxley wrote:

> Too much mechanical efficiency is the enemy of liberty because it leads to regimentation and the loss of liberty. Too little efficiency is also the enemy of liberty because it results in chronic poverty and anarchy. Between the two extremes there is a happy mean, a point at which we can enjoy the most important advantages of modern technology at a social and psychological price which is not excessive.[70]

In his writings on technology Gandhi did not succeed in reaching that happy mean, even though he tried in his own way to move towards it.

I shall conclude this chapter with a recapitulation of its principal arguments. I started by pointing out that Gandhi rejected industrialisation as a solution for mass poverty and that in doing so he dissented from the mainstream of Indian economic thought. I then discussed the two main arguments that Gandhi used against industrialisation. The first is that large-scale machine-based production on which industrialisation is based tends to create unemployment. Gandhi argued both that machinery was by nature labour-displacing anywhere and at all times; and that the widespread use of mechanised techniques of production would have disastrous social and economic consequences for countries such as India which had meagre capital resources but a large labour force and which were already suffering from rural under-employment. His second main argument was that the pursuit of industrialisation on modern lines would further increase the concen-tration of economic power, in favour of an urban elite and to the detriment of the village masses. On both counts Gandhi concluded that methods of production should be guided by the aim of utilising labour to the maximum possible extent. His solution was to rely predominantly on the development of village handicrafts, rather than on industrialisation, as the preferred path to economic development. In his later writings, especially, Gandhi modified his opposition to industrialisation and the use of machinery by a number of qualifica-tions which I considered next. Finally I examined the long-run relevance of Gandhi's views on technology.

5

INEQUALITY

Gandhi spent his entire public life fighting inequalities of various kinds: racial discrimination in South Africa, political domination of India by British imperialism, social oppression resulting from the caste system, economic exploitation of the rural masses of India by an urban elite, and the subjection of women in patriarchal society. Not surprisingly, how best to redress inequality was a central theme in his published work. Yet he was concerned not so much with the *economics* of inequality, with its focus on disparities in income, consumption and wealth, as with inequalities of other kinds such as gender and caste inequality, to which economists have traditionally paid relatively little attention. Despite his aversion to hierarchy and discrimination, Gandhi was not, strictly speaking, an egalitarian in the sense that the word is now used in the literature.

I shall describe Gandhi's views on inequality in four sections of this chapter. I begin with his concept of equality, then give an account of his views on economic inequality proper. I consider his views on inequalities generated by the caste system, untouchability in particular, in the third section, and those on gender inequality in the following section. I conclude with a few remarks on Gandhi's ideas on inequality as a whole.

EQUALITY AS RESPECT

Gandhi's concept of what equality is about rests on the notions of human dignity and the respect which is owed to each person as an autonomous moral agent. Since each person is equally such an agent, the respect is equally owed to all. This notion of equality as respect is often described as Kantian but its roots go back to Buddha.[1]

As Gandhi sees it, inequality, defined as the existence of differences, is pervasive in nature. No two leaves of a tree are exactly alike. And the same is true of human beings, who are a part of the natural world. At any moment, he points out, people will be seen to vary in respect of height, physique, metabolism, intellect, ability and earnings. We need to think of and strive towards equality precisely *because* there is great inequality in the physical world. That men are not equal is only a half-truth. The other half is that they are.

> For though they are not all of the same age, the same height, the same skin, and the same intellect, these inequalities are temporary and superficial, the soul that is hidden beneath this earthly crust is one and the same for all men and women belonging to all climes.[2]

An immediate consequence of equality as respect for all persons *as* persons is that it rules out notions of superiority and inferiority. The word 'inequality', observed Gandhi, 'has a bad odor about it and it has led to arrogance and inhumanities, both in the East and West'.[3] For him what is bad about it is its close link with the notion of superiority, 'the high and low belief',[4] as he calls it. It is this belief, he states, that sustains untouchability and caste distinctions in India, class war and racial feuds in Western society, and insolent exploitation of the nations of Asia and Africa by those of Europe. Gandhi rejects this belief as incorrect. We can indeed observe differences between individual human beings and perhaps between groups of human beings as well. But this does not make some individuals or groups superior to others. In his opinion there is no such thing as inherited or acquired superiority. Moreover, Gandhi finds the very notion of superiority loathsome and morally offensive. 'Assumption of superiority by any person over any other is a sin against God and man.'[5]

I shall next consider Bernard Williams' critique of the notion of equality as respect which is at the heart of Gandhi's writings on inequality. His main criticism is that the notion lacks an empirical underpinning. 'It is not... in their skill, intelligence, strength or virtue that men are equal, but merely in their being men. It is their common humanity that constitutes their equality.'[6] This, Williams suggests, is too general a notion and 'there is not much to it', it cannot provide any 'solid foundation' for the idea of equality.

As against Williams I should like to argue first that in such matters solidity is not necessarily a virtue. That Gandhi's concept of equality is suggestive rather than 'solid' and can be interpreted in a variety of ways, should I believe count in its favour rather than against it.

Second, the argument from common humanity is neither empty nor trivial, for the domain to which the principle applies is not obvious. Those opposed to equality as a principle at some point invariably suggest that all persons are *not* to be reckoned as part of the community for which considerations of common humanity hold good. Accordingly, in all societies some group or other has always been excluded from the reckoning in some respect. Such exclusions have applied, depending on the time and place, to voting, standing as candidates for electoral office, holding property, being able to choose one's occupation or one's place of residence and to many other things. Among those excluded have been slaves, untouchables, those belonging to a different race or tribe, the poor, immigrants and women. Such exclusions, and the resulting deprivation have been sought to be justified by both theological and 'scientific' arguments which contend that the exclusion is due to some lack or defect in those excluded and hence that the inequalities or oppression that may be associated with such exclusion are deserved.

The distinction between deserved and undeserved inequality has appeared in some writings in the economic literature on inequality, for example, in Rawls[7] and more recently in Temkin who holds strong egalitarian views, but writes:

> I think egalitarians are not committed to the view that deserved inequalities – if there are any – are as bad as undeserved ones. In fact, I think deserved inequalities are not bad at all. Rather what is objectionable is some being worse off than others *through no fault of their own.*[8]

Since neither Temkin, nor to my knowledge any one else, has suggested a principle whereby deserved and undeserved inequalities could be distinguished, such a distinction can only serve as a means of justifying existing inequalities. Gandhi's concern with equality as flowing from the respect owed to human beings as such irrespective of whether they 'deserve' to be worse off than others or not, provides a useful corrective.

Gandhi's concept of equality also fits in nicely with the distinction drawn by Dworkin between treating people equally and treating them as equals.[9] The former concern leads to the advocacy of an equal distribution of resources (for example income and wealth), opportunities (such as access to public health care), and burdens (such as taxes) and this, and its implications for society's welfare, has been essentially what the economics of inequality is about.

Gandhi, as we shall see, also sometimes touched on this aspect of equality but his primary concern was always with treating people as equals, that is with the same concern and respect. This might itself sometimes require greater equality in the distribution of resources. Nevertheless, it was treating people as equals that remained the basic goal and this might not always imply equal distribution of resources. Dworkin adds that a commitment to treating people as equals rules out ways of treating an individual that are inconsistent with recognising the individual as a full member of the human community. Racial, caste and gender inequalities belong to this category and Gandhi's concept of equality was entirely appropriate for analysing them.

ECONOMIC INEQUALITY

For an analysis of economic inequality Gandhi's approach is not, perhaps, quite so suitable and his discussion of it is somewhat superficial. He has, however, an important point to make, namely that it is the consumption level of the poorest that should be our primary concern. 'Economic equality', stated Gandhi, 'must never be supposed to mean possession of an equal amount of worldly goods by everyone.'[10] He did not regard complete equality in either income or property as an acceptable social goal. On the other hand mass poverty and a very wide gulf between rich and poor were both entirely unacceptable. His ideas on what constitutes poverty have been discussed earlier. How wide the gulf between rich and poor would have to be before it became morally unacceptable is a question that Gandhi never attempted to answer precisely but he provides some clues. One occurs in a letter he wrote to Lord Irwin in 1930. 'Take your own salary... You are getting Rs 700 per day against India's average income of nearly annas 2 per day... Thus you are getting much over five thousand times India's average income.'[11]

Gandhi points out that the British Prime Minister at that time was estimated to be earning only 90 times Britain's average income. There appears to be an implicit suggestion that while a maximum income of the order of five thousand times the national average is unacceptable a ninety times differential just might be. Elsewhere Gandhi argues that the acceptable degree of inequality in a society should be seen in terms of differences in consumption, life-style and the standard of living rather than just income. The British conquerors and rulers had set up a standard of living which took no account whatsoever of the conditions in which the conquered lived. Gandhi was very much concerned that

91

rulers in independent India should not follow that example. After Congress ministries were formed in several provinces during the 1930s Gandhi repeatedly warned against the danger that they might do just that; and urged that in a country where many millions lived in semi-starvation its elected representatives should not live in a style and manner out of all correspondence with their electors. Correspondence, rather than strict equality, should be the governing principle. 'By all means let monied people have tasteful ornamentation, whether in dress or in other surroundings,'[12] but even their consumption of luxury goods should take some account of the level of consumption prevailing among the masses of the poor, for in a well-ordered society, even if it is unequal, a due sense of proportion is always observed. Gandhi held that the process of economic growth should not be allowed to abandon that sense by letting the gap in consumption between rich and poor increase without limit. This, he thought, could easily happen if the benefits of growth went mostly to people in the higher income groups, whose consumption levels increased spectacularly, while the *minimum* level of consumption in the society concerned was little affected.

> Let not those who would raise this minimum and multiply India's wants in order to wake her up to action, think that they would achieve the end by first multiplying their own wants at the expense of the poor, and without in the same proportion enabling and inducing the latter to raise their standard of living.[13]

His writings on the eve of, and just after, India's independence express the same concern. He insists that while he did not want to taboo everything above and beyond the bare necessities, the consumption of luxuries, 'must come after the essential needs of the poor are satisfied. First things must come first'.[14] Gandhi's approach is thus similar in spirit to Rawls' maximin principle of justice, according to which a society's political, social and economic institutions may be said to be just if they maximise the level of welfare of the representative member of the worst-off group.

I come now to questions of policy. In a less developed country with mass poverty and highly unequal initial distribution of endowments economic growth based on market forces does not automatically ensure that first things will come first. Indeed, during the early stages of modern economic growth inequality is believed to have increased *because* the growth process often worked in the way that Gandhi describes. Analysis of this historical experience led Kuznets to his hypothesis that inequality of incomes would increase with industrialisation and economic growth, declining only at a much later stage.[15] Gandhi deplored such an outcome and sought to avoid it by avoiding industrialisation itself. However, other than fiscal measures such as progressive income tax and high death duties, he could not suggest any effective means of preventing it in the existing economic milieu. Nor was economic inequality in India simply a *future* problem. The gap that separated zamindars from peasants was certainly unacceptable to Gandhi. The terrible inequality between them, he stated on many occasions, had to be removed. But while he called for an end to permanent settlement he was not in favour of the total abolition of the zamindari system itself, nor did he regard the parcelling out of the zamindars' land among the peasants as a viable solution. In agriculture as in industry he rejected the socialist solution: planned economic growth based on state control rather than market forces and the removal of inequality by radical redistribution of property. The logic of his position will be further examined in the next chapter, on trusteeship.

INEQUALITY, UNTOUCHABILITY AND THE CASTE SYSTEM

The social basis of traditional Hindu society lay in a four-fold hierarchical division by *varna* or caste group, corresponding to occupational category and determined by birth. There are four basic *varnas* in descending order of status: Brahmanas, who pursue knowledge and perform the priestly functions; Kshatriyas, who are warriors; Vaisyas, who carry out farming and commerce; and last, Sudras, who serve persons of the other castes, especially the Brahmanas, through manual labour. In addition there were certain groups following occupations regarded as particularly lowly or defiling who were classified as 'untouchables'. Because they were outside the four-fold *varna* classification, people belonging to these groups were also called *avarna* (non-caste) or *panchama* (the fifth) and were subjected to severe social, economic and legal discrimination.

Gandhi became convinced quite early in his life that the most important source of inequality in India was untouchability, and it was against this that he fought hardest and longest. For this reason I shall deal with his views on this in some detail. For the purpose of an analysis of inequality three aspects of Gandhi's views on untouchability are particularly relevant; first, the role of untouchability in generating economic inequality; second, the contradiction between the practice of untouchability and the notion of equality in the sense of equal respect for all beings; and third, the claim made by defenders of untouchability that the inequalities associated with it were in some sense 'deserved'.

I begin by considering Gandhi's views on the contribution of untouchability to social and economic inequality. Most untouchable households were landless. This was, according to Gandhi, both a result and a cause of their endemic poverty, but it was also due to legal restrictions on their owning land which had existed from ancient times and continued under British rule. People regarded as untouchable were forced by custom to live in separate areas, some distance away from where *savarnas* (caste Hindus) lived. Comparing their position to that of Jews in Europe who had to live in ghettos, Gandhi observed that 'though we have no ghettos there is nothing to choose between them and untouchability'.[16] Untouchables were restricted, by definition as it were, to the lowest paid and most menial occupations and even there they faced discrimination in both labour and product markets. 'As labourers they do not get employment as easily as the others, and as artisans they do not find customers for their wares.'[17] As a rule they were denied access to village tanks, wells and other sources of public water supply; to hotels or restaurants in cities; to publicly maintained schools; and to temples or other places of worship. In some parts of India they were barred from entering certain streets or localities, which led Gandhi to exclaim, 'How dare an untouchable ever think of entering streets inhabited by Brahmins!'[18]

Untouchables have long formed the hard core of the rural poor in India, and Gandhi believed, correctly, that the eradication of untouchability would have the effect both of improving the economic position of the worst-off group and of reducing the extent of economic inequality in society as a whole. (Since most untouchable households belonged to the lowest income group, any improvements that occurred in their income would, other things being equal, inevitably improve Rawlsian (maximin) inequality and reduce the inequality of the income distribution as measured for example by the Gini coefficient.) The movement for the abolition of untouchability was not, as Gandhi saw it, a political movement to protect the interests of untouchables:

Nor is it intended purely for the economic amelioration of the

Harijans nor yet for their social regeneration. But this does not mean that we do not aim at the Harijans' social, economic or political advancement. We want all these improvements. If we are honest about our work, progress in these directions is bound to follow from our efforts.[19]

Similarly, the Constructive Programme was geared to the special needs of untouchables. By developing such crafts and industries as tanning in which Harijans had traditionally been engaged it tried to improve their employment and earning opportunities and to remove discrimination against them in respect of employment and wages.

Gandhi was generally in favour of measures to reduce inequality even if they led to a loss in economic efficiency, but in this case the equality and efficiency objectives went together. The abolition of untouchability would not only reduce untouchability but also help in increasing efficiency. 'It is no small waste deliberately to stunt the mental and moral growth and to make the least economic use of one-sixth of the population of India.'[20] If an economist, using proper statistical techniques, were to estimate the economic loss due to untouchability, Gandhi reckoned that the figure would be staggering.[21]

Clearly, Gandhi was aware of the importance of untouchability in generating inequalities of income, consumption and assets, but for him this was not the heart of the matter. Asked if he agreed that the whole Harijan problem was in the last analysis an economic problem, Gandhi said he did not.

> You may solve the economic problem, but unhappily the Harijan problem, which is essentially that of the eradication of a disease in Hinduism, will not be solved thereby. Dr Ambedkar who is economically better off than most of us is still regarded as an untouchable.[22]

While most untouchables were poor, there were also a few groups among them who were better off than many caste Hindus. This had not brought about any improvement in their social status.[23] The issue of poverty and that of untouchability were distinct in principle and should not be confused. To Gandhi the removal of untouchability had moral priority over the removal of poverty.

> My religion will not be destroyed if I do not solve the problem of poverty of a poor peasant. But if I allow untouchability to persist

even in the case of a wealthy Harijan, my religion will cease to exist.[24]

A more important component of Gandhi's notion of equality is the idea, which I referred to earlier, that we owe equal respect to all men and women on the ground of their common humanity, or by virtue of their all being children of God. In his long campaign against untouchability Gandhi used both the secular and the theological versions of the argument for equality as respect. The former underlies his frequent reminder to caste-Hindus of their duty to regard Harijans as their blood-brothers, entitled to the respect that belongs to man,[25] while the latter comes out in his renaming the untouchables as Harijans (children of God) and choosing the title Harijan for the daily in which the bulk of his writings was published.

Gandhi was also much concerned with the distinction between 'deserved' and 'undeserved' inequality referred to in an earlier section. It is 'undeserved' inequalities which call for redress. There was, however, a strong body of Hindu orthodox opinion which maintained that the inequalities from which the untouchables suffered were deserved, for being born as an untouchable was not just an accident but the result of sins committed in a previous birth. By the doctrine of *karma*, one was responsible for one's actions, including actions in a previous birth, and the untouchables had, therefore, no one but themselves to blame for their condition. Gandhi totally denied this imputation and asserted that untouchability was an evil custom imposed by society and that it could, and should, be removed by social action. 'Let us never say their misery is due to their *karma*, but let us say we have made up our minds to discharge at least a portion of our debts to them.'[26]

Gandhi's understanding as to which aspects of inequality were morally the most important determined the nature and direction of his movement against untouchability. It was the belief that untouchability was 'earned' and had religious sanction that he wanted to wipe out from the hearts and minds of Indians. To this end he conducted an intense and prolonged campaign of public education through writings and speeches. He started by arguing that untouchability had nothing to do with religion but was only an evil custom which should be given up. 'What there is of it is all due to the persistence of custom.'[27] Customs died hard, especially if they were ancient and that untouchability was an ancient custom nobody could deny. 'But if it is an evil, it cannot be defended on the ground of its antiquity.'[28]

Customs, traditions and institutions, however ancient or widespread they might be, still required to be justified by the principles of reason and morality.

> I do not advocate surrender of God-given reasoning faculty in the face of ancient tradition. Any tradition, however ancient, if inconsistent with morality, is fit to be banished from the land. Untouchability may be considered to be an ancient tradition, the institution of child widowhood and child marriage may be considered to be ancient tradition, and even so, many an horrible belief and superstitious practice. I would sweep them out of existence if I had the power.[29]

Gandhi had little doubt that he had the power and he intended to use it to the full in the cause of removing evil customs and undermining the beliefs which sustained them. He found reassurance in recalling that some other evil customs had been swept out in the past, in India and elsewhere. 'Was there not cannibalism in some parts, and the custom of suttee in India? They had to disappear.'[30] Some other evil customs such as child marriage, the dedication of *Devdasis* to virtual prostitution in the name of religion, as well as untouchability itself, which Gandhi regarded as the worst evil of all, were still there but would not survive long.[31] Customs practised by Hindus were not, however, necessarily part of Hinduism; and the same applied to other religions. The real danger in India as elsewhere was that 'horrible beliefs and superstitious practices' which were actually in decline could be sought to be revived in the name of religious or cultural fundamentalism, for 'many who are professing to revive ancient culture do not hesitate to revive old superstitions and prejudices'.[32]

To defenders of untouchability, who described themselves as *sanatanists* (followers of the permanent, or eternal, tradition) untouchability was not, as Gandhi would have it, simply an old and outworn custom: it was an essential part of their religion. They argued that the practice had a 'theoretical' basis in the doctrine of *karma* and that it had been approved by Hindu scriptures precisely on that ground. This was anathema to Gandhi who professed to believe in the doctrine of *karma*, but not, of course, in this particular application of it. The argument of his opponents threatened his entire strategy which was to persuade the caste Hindu masses that the indignities and inequalities from which the untouchables suffered were in no way their own responsibility. Accordingly, Gandhi maintained his offensive against untouchability, describing it as a 'Satanic' activity, and on one occasion as 'Dyerism' (after General Dyer who had ordered the massacre at Jalianwalabagh), and denouncing the 'savarna lynchers' for their persecution of the innocent Harijans. He also continued to urge that untouchability was no part of Hinduism and the myth that it was, had been created by a priestly elite who were not interested in religion but simply in preserving their own privileges. By giving untouchability a religious tone they were doing immense harm to religion itself. 'It is a painful fact, but it is a historical truth that priests who should have been the custodians of religion have been instrumental in destroying the religion of which they have been custodians.'[33] The *sanatanists* were wrong: 'the curse of untouchability had no sanction of the Shastras, it should be eradicated from society'.[34]

Some of the *sanatanists*, who were more familiar with the texts, and the language in which they were written, than Gandhi was, now started quoting chapter and verse, especially from *Manusmriti*, which expounded the theory and practice of untouchability. This made little impression on Gandhi who, as Parekh puts it, 'shifted the debate on to a different plane where he felt more comfortable'.[35] He did this in two distinct ways. One was to move away from analysis of textual evidence to the 'spirit' or 'essence' of Hinduism, which he identified with the principles of truth and nonviolence. 'The essence of Hinduism is contained in its enunciation of one and only God as Truth and its bold acceptance of *ahimsa* as the law of the human family.'[36]

Passages in the smritis, or even in the Veda, which appear to contradict these two principles – and any statement in approval of untouchability belonged to this category – must be rejected as interpolations.[37] The meaning of texts, observed Gandhi, was a matter of interpretation, which changed over time. Learning, whether linguistic or theological, did not necessarily make someone a good interpreter. 'That belief in untouchability can co-exist with learning in the same person adds no status to untouchability but makes one despair of mere learning being any aid to character or sanity.'[38] It might be difficult for Gandhi to establish his point by quoting authorities from the *Bhagavadgita* or *Manusmriti*, but he claimed to have understood the spirit of Hinduism.[39]

Gandhi's second line of defence was a return to his standard argument which placed morality and reasoning not only above prevailing custom but also above anything Hindu, or any other, scriptures might say. 'Nothing in the Shastras which is manifestly contrary to universal truths and morals can stand. Nothing in the Shastras which is capable of being reasoned can stand if it is in conflict with reason.'[40] Since untouchability was manifestly contrary to both reason and morality any Shastras which appeared to condone it became null and void. Accordingly, Gandhi refused to accept the authority of a Shastra which supports untouchability, i.e. which condemns a certain class of people by reason of their birth as untouchable.[41] Such a Shastra, he maintained, 'far from purging us of sin, adds to our load of sin'.[42] Religion itself, in his view, was inseparable from morality, which in the last analysis, was a matter of conscience.

> Even if all the Hindus of India were to be ranged against me in declaring that untouchability as we know it today has the sanction of the Shastras or the Smritis, I will then declare that these Shastras and these Smritis are false.[43]

In the same spirit, he continued to assert both his belief that untouchability was no part of Hinduism and his resolve that if he ever became convinced that it was, he would renounce Hinduism. This looks suspiciously like having one's cake and eating it too, but when opponents tried to point this out, Gandhi remained unapologetic. 'Untouchability is a hydra-headed monster. It is therefore necessary each time the monster lifts its head to deal with it.'[44] And deal with it he did.

Although Gandhi always relied on reasoned argument as the principal means of social reform he did not rely on argument alone. From the beginning of his campaign against untouchability, he was aware that 'the filth that has accumulated over a long period cannot be washed away all at once merely through argument'.[45] Some defenders of untouchability just could not be reached by reasoning: those of the priestly class who had important vested interests to protect, and certain individuals with a degree of irrationality bordering on the pathological. A habit of taking a purificatory bath every time one had accidentally brushed against an untouchable could, he suggested, be 'a question for a psychoanalyst to dissect and consider'.[46] In order to remove untouchability a programme of action was required. His programme included such things as organising the untouchables, especially in the villages, so that they were better able to protect their human rights; offering *satyagraha* in order to secure their rights of entry to hotels and restaurants and places of worship ('But not a single Hindu restaurant should be allowed to function which does not permit the entry of Harijans'),[47] and making the abolition of untouchability an election issue. Some of these techniques were later adopted by the Civil Rights movement in the United States during the 1960s.

Under Gandhi's leadership the Indian National Congress started working actively for the removal of untouchability, and discarding the practice in one's own behaviour was made a condition for membership. Mass action was undertaken to remove some of the discriminatory measures to which the untouchables had traditionally been subject, and many of these were banned by legislation enacted by Congress ministries during 1937–39. After independence, the Constitution of India declared untouchability in any form to be a legal offence and although the practice has not entirely ceased to exist belief in its legitimacy has.

'No reform', wrote Gandhi, 'has ever been brought about except through intrepid individuals breaking down inhuman customs or usages.'[48] This is not, perhaps, a bad description of his own role in the eradication of untouchability.

So far I have been concerned with Gandhi's attitude to the inequalities associated with untouchability. While untouchability was an integral part of the caste system, one could also look at that system as a hierarchical division by status, abstracting from questions relating to the condition of those at its lowest step, and sometimes Gandhi did look at it in that way. I shall now look briefly at Gandhi's attitude to caste division. The essence of his view is contained in his statement that caste 'insofar as it connotes distinctions in status is an evil'.[49]

Analytically, caste ranking may be regarded as an instance of non-redistributable assets. As Scanlon has shown, in the case of social inequalities such as distinctions of rank or social caste, the logic of a commitment to equality may require the elimination of such 'assets'.[50] Likewise, Rawls observes that aristocratic and caste societies are unjust because they make contingencies of birth and social circumstance the basis for organising society into 'more or less enclosed and privileged social classes'.[51] While Rawls' concern is with justice rather than equality, such societies can, on the same ground, be described as unequal as well. Gandhi's view of caste agrees broadly with both these views.

Gandhi did not, however, attack the caste system as such with quite the same fervour which he brought to his fight against the theory and practice of untouchability. For this reason he has been accused of being an apologist for caste distinctions.[52] In my judgement the accusation is incorrect but Gandhi himself bears some responsibility for making it appear plausible.

First, his early view of caste was not only conservative but even reactionary. At this stage he described the caste system as a perfectly natural institution, defended prevailing taboos against marrying, or even dining with, a person of a different caste, and criticised the anti-caste movement in India, even while acknowledging some evils that had 'crept into' the operation of caste.[53] Over the years, however, there occurred, in Nanda's words, ' a progressive hardening' in his attitude to caste.[54] As a result of direct experience of caste in India and his own reflections on the roots of ethics, he came to condemn the caste system, called on the people of India to give it up and made it obligatory for inmates of his own ashrams to give up caste taboos. His early writings approving of caste no more reveal an ingrained reluctance to throw off the caste system than his early writings in praise of the empire show ingrained reluctance to throw off the British Raj.

Much more confusing was Gandhi's half-hearted attempt to draw a sharp distinction between caste and *varna*. The four-fold division by *varna* which was characteristic of ancient Hindu society could, he suggested, be thought of simply as a taxonomy of occupational categories, that is, as a functional division of labour without any connotation of a hierarchical order. That, he claimed, was the essence of the *varna* system in ancient India which must not be confused with the caste system existing now.

Gandhi was really making two separate points but did not distinguish them with sufficient care. One is that a separation of functions is not the same as a hierarchy. It was the latter that he found morally offensive, not a group-wise division of labour even it this was maintained on a hereditary basis. Indeed, he approved of *varna* as a kind of 'spiritual economics' which encouraged people to follow their ancestral occupations (unless there were compelling reasons to the contrary) and helped in preserving traditional skills, restraining excessive competition and maintaining social cohesion. For much the same reasons he approved of the guild system in medieval Europe. However, Gandhi was also making a historical claim: that the *varna* system as it existed in ancient India was based on the separation of functions rather than on hierarchy. Few were convinced of the validity of this claim, not even, perhaps, Gandhi himself. He wrote:

> in the Satyayuga, or golden age, whenever it was, the society I dare say was better ordered than today. Ours is an ancient land where civilisations have come and gone, and it is difficult to say what exactly we were like in a particular age.[55]

If so, the claim that there ever existed a *varna* system from which hierarchy was absent remains at best a piece of wishful thinking. The historical evidence suggests on the contrary that from its earliest beginnings the system was based on both principles, hierarchy and separation working together. Nevertheless, Gandhi's attitude to the caste system must be seen in the context of his moral theory as a whole. Gandhi had little use for Brahmanical rites and rituals: 'sacred ash, sandlewood paste and vermilion powder', minute study of holy texts, or 'astrology and what-not'.[56] He insisted on the sanctity of 'bread-labour' and would require every person to perform some amount of manual work, including in particular the cleaning of latrines, an occupation which tradition had reserved for the untouchables. He argued that one should try to combine in oneself the spirit of all four *varnas*.

> Let us accept the *dharma* of service. Let us accept Shudradharma. This does not mean that we should discard learning. . . . We should acquire as much valour, that is fearlessness, as we can. We must develop commerce and industries to the greatest possible extent.[57]

The occupational categories were thus so redefined that neither the traditional *varna* classification nor the hierarchy it embodied made sense any longer. Parekh sums up succinctly:

> Since he undermined their traditional occupations there was no place for a distinct *Brahmana* class in his society. Because he opposed violence, *Kshatriyas* had no role. If all citizens performed Sudras' work, they too ceased to exist as a separate class.[58]

In the kind of society Gandhi was trying to build there was little room left for either *varna* or caste.

The fact that Gandhi chose to concentrate his attack on untouchability rather than caste does not necessarily show a weakness in his attitude towards caste. On the contrary he seems to have thought that this was the right strategy for fighting both the institutions. The struggle against the enormous absolute and relative deprivation generated by untouchability was, he believed, the best way to redress the inequalities of caste as a system. Nehru recalls repeatedly asking Gandhi why he did not hit at the caste system directly. 'I am undermining it completely', Gandhi would reply, 'by my tackling untouchability.'[59] He did not, it is true, see caste as being quite as evil as untouchability: while the latter was an 'unpardonable sin and great

102

blot on Hinduism', the former was 'an obstacle to our progress and an arrogant assumption of superiority by one group over another'.[60] But the two were not unrelated, for untouchability represented caste at its worst and both had to go. 'It is really high time that we get rid of the taint of untouchability and the taint of caste.'[61] In the same spirit he described the anti-untouchability movement as 'an attack on the evil underlying the caste system'.[62] If the movement succeeded in achieving its goal, the caste system could not survive long. 'Untouchability is the last word on caste, and as soon as untouchability goes, caste goes... Take untouchability out and the fabric of caste is destroyed.'[63] His belief was not illogical even though it may now look over-optimistic.

In concluding this discussion I should like to make a general comment bearing on Gandhi's moral epistemology. Gandhi's writings on economic and social issues invariably bear the stamp of his moral sensibility. But his use of moral language is not 'all of a piece'. He often switches abruptly and without any warning to his readers from a religious idiom to a secular humanist one, from talking about *Ramrajya* to talking about rights and human dignity. His analysis of the inequalities generated by untouchability and caste is not free from this tendency. It should not, however, be taken as indicative of sloppiness of mind or inability to pursue rational discourse. A recent philosophical study by Mohanty offers a more persuasive interpretation, which turns on the difference between criticising a moral tradition from within and from outside that tradition.[64] To be an effective critic of a tradition or society to which one belongs, it is not required that one must begin by throwing away that tradition in its entirety and trying to become a 'transcendental ego'. One may instead try to play a dual role: as one living within the tradition and up to a point committed to it, but at the same time as a critic examining it from outside. Such a role, suggests Mohanty, was Gandhi's. In an article written just two years before his death Gandhi distinguished sharply between two aspects of Hinduism.

> There is, on the one hand, the historical Hinduism with its untouchability, superstitious worship of stocks and stones, animal sacrifice and so on. On the other we have the Hinduism of the *Gita*, the *Upanishads*, and Patanjali's *Yoga Sutra*.[65]

He judged much of the former, caste and untouchability in particular, to be inconsistent with the rational, humanistic and individual-centred core of Hindu ethics which he found in the texts he mentions and elsewhere. Accordingly, he reinterpreted the tradition so as to eliminate the jarring components. Mohanty comments:

> Committed to the Hindu tradition in general, he reinterpreted the talk of *varna* so as to make it acceptable to his moral sensibility and thereby contributed towards the transformation of the Hindu *Sittlichkeit* into a more coherent ethical substance.[66]

GENDER INEQUALITY

Writing to a woman correspondent who had suggested that the treatment of women in India was 'a disease as bad as untouchability', Gandhi said that he disagreed.[67] He did express on numerous occasions, however, his belief that not only in India but to a greater or lesser extent throughout the world, women held a social, political and economic status distinctly inferior to that of men, and that they were subjected to many forms of inequality, discrimination and injustice. He believed also that this was the result, ultimately, of the rules of conduct imposed by patriarchal, male-dominated societies. Such rules were maintained by a complex network of beliefs, norms, customs, laws and conventions in the framing of which women had historically played little part but which they, too, had come to accept, comply with and acquiesce in.

The history of the world could not, however, on Gandhi's view confer moral validity. Men and women are one, their problems are the same. 'The soul in both is the same. The two live the same life, have the same feelings.'[68] Gandhi rests his case for equality for women on their fundamental equality as human beings, hence as autonomous moral agents entitled to equal respect. It was in essence the same principle which he had invoked in his campaign against untouchability. The principle had not only to be asserted but fought for.

Gandhi's understanding of the nature of gender inequality shaped his plan of attack. His first and most direct strategy was to help towards making women themselves active and self-conscious agents of change by drawing them into the political process. Gandhi believed that it was neither the physical nor the economic weakness of women as compared to men that kept them down but a sense of helplessness culturally imposed on them by male-dominated society and their own acceptance of inferiority.[69]

Hence, as Gandhi put it, 'the first thing is to free her from mental slavery'.[70] Participation in the political process was, he thought, a necessary first step. Early in his public career in India, Gandhi declared at a woman's meeting in Bombay: 'So long as women in India do not take equal part with men in the affairs of the world and in religious and political matters, we shall not see India's star rising.'[71]

Under Gandhi's leadership the national movement in India began to grow in strength, and from the beginning he tried to induce women in large numbers to participate in his campaigns of *satyagraha* beyond the narrow confines of the household. It would, he believed, broaden their mental horizons, encourage women to think for themselves and improve their self-esteem. Because such activity was highly visible, it could also help in winning acceptance from a wider public of equal status for women, and in the long run it would also help bring about legislative action for the abolition of discrimination against women, for, to a large extent, it was laws passed by men that had held women back:

> If law-making had been the business of women they would not have given themselves fewer rights than men enjoy. In countries where women have a hand in law-making they have had the necessary laws enacted for themselves.[72]

Gandhi's chosen forms of struggle were often especially designed to encourage greater participation by women and he describes his own contribution towards women gaining their rightful place in society as lying essentially in his adherence to truth and non-violence in every walk of life: 'The beauty of non-violent war is that women can play the same part as men. In a violent war the women have no such part in it as men.'[73] With this objective in mind Gandhi encouraged women not only to participate in mass movements but in some cases to take up the leadership. In his campaign for prohibition, for example, he specifically required that the principal work of picketing, of persuading people and pleading with them, and of taking deputations to the liquor-broth, should be done by women alone.[74] Kishawar comments:

> The programmes of action undertaken as part of non-violent *satyagraha* were such that women would not feel limited or unequal to men, as they inevitably do when sheer muscle power or capacity for inflicting violence, are to determine the outcome of a struggle. Thus women's traditional qualities, such as their lesser capacity for organised violence, were not downgraded but were held up as models of superior courage.[75]

Apart from taking an active part in the national movement, Gandhi also wanted women to enrol as voters and stand for electoral office. He strongly supported the representation of more women as candidates for elections or for official posts and suggested that it was the duty of men, 'to give such encouragement to women as will enable them to outshine men'.[76] At the same time he stressed that women who take part in politics should not simply act at the behest of their parents or husbands, who might happen to be politically active, but develop the habit of thinking and acting independently. That habit, he foresaw, would be sorely needed when women finally won their battle for legal and political equality: 'Women must have votes and equal legal status. But the problem does not end there. It only commences at the point where women begin to affect the political deliberations of the nation.'[77]

Gandhi's second line of attack on gender inequality was targeted at social customs which both expressed and contributed towards the inferior status of women: child marriages, the seclusion of women, the dowry system, polygamy and so on. Gandhi condemned such practices vehemently: 'I passionately desire the utmost freedom for our women. I detest child marriages. I shudder to see a child widow and shiver with rage when a husband just widowed with brutal indifference contracts another marriage.'[78]

Child marriage, Gandhi argued, was not only immoral, it also weakened the claim to *swaraj*.[79] It was the practice of child marriage that led to there being so many child widows in Hindu society and Gandhi held that such child widows should be remarried: 'In the case of child widows there can be no question of opinion. They should be remarried by the parents.'[80] Clearly, Gandhi's condemnation of child marriage did not extend to the authority exerted by parents over their children with regard to marriage.

His attack against the seclusion of women (*purdah*) was more consistent. In his article 'Tear Down the Purdah', he declared that this barbarous custom was doing immense harm to the country by impeding the personal growth of Indian women.[81] Because this custom had long forced women to remain 'caged and confined in their homes and little courtyards', their vision had become narrowed and they often had little interest in problems beyond their own immediate surroundings, for 'they knew nothing of them having been never allowed to breathe the fresh air of freedom'.[82] Tearing down the *purdah* was necessary for gaining freedom for the nation as a whole.

Similar arguments were used by Gandhi in his writings against the dowry system which, he pointed out, was closely related to caste.

'Marriage must cease to be a matter of arrangement made by parents for money.'[83] Instead it must be seen as a partnership between friends and equals. Wife and husband were, he held, co-sharers of equal rights and equal duties. 'Their obligation towards each other and towards the world must, therefore, be the same and reciprocal.'[84] In such a relationship there was no place for dowry. Addressing students at Karachi, he asked them to promise him that *deti-leti* would be wiped out. Unless that was done they could not be deemed to be ready for freedom.[85]

Among other customs affecting the social position of women was polygamy, which he argued was contrary to the ideal of marriage as an equal partnership. No matter what the custom in India might decree, the moral sense of the world held up monogamy as the highest ideal.[86] For the necessary reforms to occur the Hindu marriage law had to be changed, but the more important, and more difficult task was to bring about a change in widespread and long-held beliefs. Passages in the *Manusmriti* which approved of an inferior status for women were, Gandhi declared, to be rejected either as interpolations or simply as contrary to reason and morality. Here he followed the same strategy which he used in his campaign against untouchability.

Gandhi not only condemned specific customs which helped keep women in subjection, he also deplored the general climate of subservience of the wife to the husband which appeared to characterise Hindu marriage.

> Hindu culture has erred on the side of excessive subordination of the wife to the husband and has insisted on the complete merging of the wife in the husband. This has resulted in the husband sometimes usurping and exercising authority that reduces him to the level of the brute.[87]

Gandhi advised women that putting up with brutality was no part of wifely duties. In a particular case of this kind brought to Gandhi's attention, he offered the following advice: 'It is quite evident that the husband himself does not care for the wife. She may therefore without breaking the legal tie live apart from her husband's roof and feel as if she had never been married.'[88]

It is typical of Gandhi that he should concentrate on the woman's *feelings* rather than the economic constraints to which she may be subject. For this reason his 'solution' appears unrealistic. However, in fairness to Gandhi, we must note that he urged parents not to bring up daughters simply to be married off but to ensure that they learnt some useful and potentially marketable skills; that in this particular case he also advised the woman's parents, who were well off, to take her back and that he favoured the growth of voluntary institutions which would provide permanent shelter to ill-treated women, similar to women's refuges of today, noting with approval that the number of such institutions was growing.[89]

Gandhi's attack on gender inequality also included an economic element. Although he did not consider the lack of assets and earnings on the part of women to be of crucial importance in keeping them in an inferior social position he did regard it as a contributory factor which called for redress. Hence social arrangements that tended to keep women economically weak as compared to men, needed to be reformed. To this category belonged laws relating to income and property and the practice of gender discrimination in the labour market. Gandhi's concept of marriage as an equal partnership implied that the wife had an equal right to her husband's income and assets. 'It is my firm belief that a wife has full right to the husband's earnings. She has an inalienable right to his property.'[90] The inheritance laws, he urged, should also be changed so as to give equal shares to sons and daughters.[91] He points out the difficulties in bringing this about, noting that property is bound up with power.

> Man has always desired power, ownership of property gives this power. Man hankers also after posthumous fame based on power. This cannot be had if property is progressively cut up in pieces as it must be if all the posterity become equal co-sharers.[92]

Nevertheless, the required changes in law, he insists, must be carried out in a free India (and they were).

As regards working women, Gandhi spoke out strongly against the wide gap between men's and women's wage rates which he described as being arbitrary and unjustified. 'Men get almost double the women's wages for identical work.'[93] He supported the principle of equal pay for equal work and was in favour of enacting legislative measures to implement it. Likewise, he was committed to the principle that all offices, professions and employment must be open to women, for 'otherwise there can be no real equality',[94] and that gender discrimination in employment should be made a legal offence. He did not, however, regard quotas, or reservations of jobs, for women as an appropriate means of bringing about the desired outcome. This he believed offended against the principle of efficiency (of which he approved, unless there were strong ethical reasons to the contrary) and tended to make the beneficiaries passive recipients of 'charity'. 'I am not enamoured of equality or any other proportion in such matters. Merit should be the only test.'[95] On the other hand Gandhi approved of a weak form of reverse discrimination: if a male and a female candidate for the same job were judged to be of equal merit, the female should be chosen. Seeing, however, that it has been the custom to decry women, the contrary custom should be to prefer women, merit being equal to men, even if this should result in men being entirely displaced by women.[96]

The principle of merit itself should not, however, be overturned. 'It would be a dangerous thing to insist on membership on the ground merely of sex. Women and for that matter any group should disdain patronage. They should seek justice, never favours.'[97]

As in the case of untouchability Gandhi's attack on social customs which oppressed women was driven by his concern with the consequences of such customs, especially consequences for the oppressed; but sometimes, whether in discussing customs or setting norms for individual conduct, he also appealed to the principle of gender equality as such, irrespective of other consequences. I cite some instances below.

The principle of equality applied to sexual behaviour. If chastity was a good thing, and Gandhi certainly thought it was, it could not simply be good for females alone, as popular morality appeared to believe.

And why is there all this morbid anxiety about female purity? Have women any say in the matter of male purity? We hear nothing of women's anxiety about men's chastity. Why should men arrogate to themselves the right to regulate female purity?[98]

When someone sought to justify the practice of *suttee* on the ground that it is an expression of love and loyalty, it was again to the principle of equality that Gandhi appealed.

If the wife has to prove her loyalty and undivided devotion to her husband so has the husband to prove his allegiance and devotion to this wife. You cannot have one set of weights and measures for the one and a different one for the other. Yet we have never heard of a husband mounting the final pyre of his deceased wife.[99]

He used the same principle to condemn the prevailing taboo against the remarriage of widows. Pointing out that the taboo was in fact confined to the upper castes and that the vast majority of Hindu widows freely remarried, apparently without any untoward consequences occurring, Gandhi suggested that even if such consequences did occur, the determining principle must be gender equality.[100] 'Justice required that as long as widowers have the right to remarry, widows, too, should have it.'[101] In this matter as in others, argued Gandhi, certain restrictions might be necessary for the protection of society but they should be the same for both men and women.[102]

Similarly, when an opponent of the changes in inheritance laws that Gandhi favoured argued that economic independence for women might lead to the spread of immorality among them, Gandhi's response was a counter-question.

> Has not independence of man and his holding property led to the spread of immorality among men? If you answer 'yes', then let it be so also with women. And when women have rights of ownership and the rest, like men, it would be found that the enjoyment of such rights is not responsible for their vices or their virtues.[103]

Characteristically, Gandhi went on to add that whether for men or for women, a morality which depends on helplessness has not much to recommend it.[104]

There is an important area in which Gandhi did *not* wish gender equality to apply. This concerns women's role in the workplace. He did, it is true, support the principle of equal opportunity as well as that of equal pay for equal work. At the same time he held the traditional, conservative view that the spheres of work of men and women were distinct, the primary work of women being to look after the home and care for children. In his early writings he expressed the opinion that in an ideal society women should not have to earn their livelihood at all. If for economic reasons they had to work, working hours and practices should be adjusted in order to take duties at home into account. The vast majority of Indian women, who lived in the villages, could, he argued, achieve a measure of economic independence by participating in village and handicraft industries, while continuing to perform their duties at home. He was also concerned with the problems faced by women workers in the cotton mills and other organised industry. His campaign for prohibition was partly motivated by this concern, which is also reflected in his pioneering attempt, as an organiser of industrial labour, to make the provision of maternity care and opening of crèches conditions for the settlement of industrial disputes. Nevertheless, these he regarded only as a 'second-best' solution.

Ideally, women would not need to work, nor would infants have to be snatched from their mothers' hands. There was a 'natural' division of labour by gender. The father was meant to be the bread-winner while 'it is a woman's work to bring up her little ones and mould their character'.[105] It was a serious injustice to deprive a child of the tender care which only a mother can give.[106] Caring, for Gandhi, included teaching. Much of what young children really needed to learn he thought could only be learned at home, and mostly from the mother. The mothers themselves had to acquire the capability of carrying out this task and special educational programmes were needed to make village women familiar with modern infant and childcare practices, but nevertheless, there was no substitute, for otherwise children would remain without education 'despite their attending hundreds of schools'.[107]

On this issue, unlike many others, Gandhi's view remained substantially unchanged over the years. His writings during the 1930s, a time when thousands of women were responding to Gandhi's call for joining the national movement, clearly bring this out.

> I do not envisage the wife, as a rule, following an avocation independently of her husband. The care of the children and the upkeep of the household are quite enough to fully engage all her energy. In a well-ordered society the additional burden of maintaining the family ought not to fall on her.[108]

In an article entitle 'What is Women's Role?', published in *Harijan*, 24 February 1940, Gandhi repeats this view, arguing that while men and women were fundamentally one, in the forms there was a vital difference between the two, and hence that the vocations of the two must also be different. He spells out the difference: 'He is the bread-winner, she is the keeper and distributor of the bread.'[109] This expresses exactly the same view he had stated decades earlier and it is only slightly qualified in another article written in the same year (1940): 'Women in the new order will be part-time workers, their primary function being to look after the home.'[110]

Gandhi's attempt to maintain a gender stereotype in regard to spheres of work – which is inconsistent both with his commitment to gender equality as such and with his emphasis on the individual as the relevant 'unit of account' – led him into some strangely convoluted arguments, as in the following passage:

Equality of the sexes does not mean equality of occupations. There may be no legal bar against a woman hunting or wielding a lance. But she instinctively recoils from a function that belongs to man. Nature has created sexes as complements of each other. Their functions are defined as are their forms.[111]

The argument is confused. First, Gandhi clouds the issue by lumping together individual differences and gender differences. There may well be many women who would instinctively recoil from becoming professional hunters or lance-wielders but so would many men – including the present writer! Second, he mixes up an argument against women taking up work which makes heavy demands on physical strength as in agriculture, construction, the defence forces (or lance-wielding), with the argument against their taking up independent full-time careers outside the home. This particular confusion appears elsewhere in Gandhi's writing as well, for example in his article on 'What is Women's Role?'[112] in which he argues that a natural division of labour between the genders is responsible for the facts that there are no women carpenters or blacksmiths and that while both men and women work in the field, the heaviest work is done by males.

The argument that a woman's work is primarily in the home and the argument that there is a 'natural' division of labour are two quite different things. Perhaps it is also worth noting that in Gandhi's own ashram at Sabarmati women were placed on a footing of absolute equality with men in all activities and were not subject to any constraint which was not imposed on the men as well. No ashram task was assigned to women to the exclusion of men, cooking being done by both men and women. The only distinction maintained was that women were exempted from heavy work which could be beyond their strength. The consideration that male and female forms were different played no part in determining the functions which individual men or women were asked to perform.

Kishawar has described Gandhi as 'one of those few leaders whose practice was at times far ahead of his theory and his stated ideas'.[113] This is perhaps one such instance.

There is a basic ambiguity in Gandhi's writings on women's role in the workplace. The proposition that for a woman the home *is* the workplace forms the cornerstone of the traditional view of women's role in society. Gandhi accepts the proposition yet in much of his writing attacks that same traditional view which, he suggests, is itself the product of patriarchal society. 'Woman has been suppressed under

112

custom and law for which man was responsible and in the shaping of which she had no hand.'[114] As a result men had come to consider themselves to be lords and masters of women instead of considering them as their friends and co-workers. This was especially so in India. 'Today, the sole occupation of a woman amongst us was supposed to bear children, to look after her husband and otherwise to drudge for the household. This was a shame.'[115] There was nothing 'natural' about this and no reason to believe that women 'were created to cook and clean utensils'.[116]

In a passage which I quoted earlier, Gandhi opposes a wife following an independent avocation on the ground that 'the care of the children and the upkeep of the household are quite enough to fully engage all her energy'.[117] But this may itself be due to the traditional, and inequitable, intra-family allocation of labour time, which requires a woman to 'drudge for the household'. Gandhi himself argues for greater sharing of household chores and suggests that food requirements should be kept simple, so as to save time.

> Food should be cooked only once and that too should be very simple, so that the kitchen may not occupy all one's time . . . A woman is not born only to cook meals. Since cooking must be done, both [husband and wife] should take a hand in it.[118]

Gandhi regarded the care of children as more important and as a more specifically female activity than household management. However, even this was not something females, *qua females*, could carry out adequately for it involved education and training, not instinct alone. Gandhi deplored the fact that in India children were born anyhow and most women were ignorant of the science of bringing up children. The solution was an intensive and properly designed educational campaign which would teach village women the basics of hygiene, sanitation and nutrition science and make them familiar with modern infant and childcare practices, and help in reducing the infant mortality rate. But if having to bring up children is not something women know by instinct but a science which has to be learned, why should men not be able to learn it too? Then men too, in time, could come to share in this function as well as in cooking and cleaning. Gandhi writes: 'The division of the spheres of work being recognised, the general qualities and culture required are practically the same for both the sexes.'[119] If so, the division itself appears to be socially, rather than 'naturally', determined.

Unlike some, Gandhi could not consistently argue that women

should seek fulfilment *just* in being wives and mothers. His commitment to the individual as being the relevant unit for moral reckoning ruled out such a view. While a woman had certain special duties, she had also a duty to herself, to realise her own potential as an individual. This duty had an economic aspect: 'Indian economic independence', he wrote, 'means to me, the economic uplift of every individual, male and female, by his or her own conscious effort.'[120] In the same spirit, he declares that 'in a plan of life based on non-violence, woman has as much right to shape her own destiny as man has to shape his'.[121]

There is a logical inconsistency between holding such a position and requiring women to regard their duties at home to be primary, because nature had so decreed. Gandhi, despite all his good intentions, did not succeed in resolving this contradiction, which badly damages the credibility of his concept of gender equality.

How then should we assess Gandhi's ideas on gender equality as a whole? I believe it has three important positive features. First, in his concept of equality between man and woman within the marriage relationship, Gandhi was much ahead of his time. This is especially true of his views on the appropriate intra-family allocation of labour time. There is now ample evidence to show that even when women work full-time outside the home they have to bear an inordinate share of the housework, a fact which is described in feminist literature as 'doble jornada', the 'double day'. Gandhi sought to avert this by getting people at large to accept the crucial importance of gender equality in housework. He even wrote a textbook, a primer for school children, in which a mother is teaching her son the importance of such equality. Here are some relevant extracts:

MOTHER: Why should a boy not do housework?

SON: Because the boy has to earn money when he grows up, therefore he has to study well.

MOTHER: You are wrong my son. Women also make an earning for the family. And there is a lot to learn in housework, house cleaning, cooking, laundry. Men and women both need to be educated equally in housework because the home belongs to both.[122]

Second, Gandhi had the valuable insight that, in a large part of the world, women's liberation to be really meaningful must occur among the village poor. That women should have the same share of inherited property as men was, Gandhi thought, only just but this would not have any effect on the millions who had no property to inherit.[123]

Middle-class women were co-sharers of the powers and privileges of their husbands and would not easily give them up to benefit women less fortunately placed.[124]

Educated, urban, middle-class women, he believed, do have a special role to play but they 'will have to descend from their Western heights and come down to India's plains'.[125] While men were undoubtedly to blame, for their 'ill use of women' and had to do 'adequate penance' it was the women who had shed superstition and become conscious of the wrongs done to them who had to start the constructive work of reform.[126] The struggle for women's liberation had to be linked to the question of changing the nature of village life as a whole.

> This question of the liberation of women, liberation of India, removal of untouchability, amelioration of the economic condition of the masses and the like resolve themselves into penetration into the villages, reconstruction or rather reformation of the village life.[127]

Gandhi did not follow through what this implied, but even the recognition itself cannot be found in the thought of nineteenth-century social reformers in Europe and India who had called for the emancipation of women and whose tradition Gandhi followed. It is missing no less from the works of some modern feminists who, safely perched on Western heights, pronounce a doctrine of 'sisterhood' that takes little account of class, culture or rural realities. Third, despite his opposition to women working full-time, he did bring out the importance of women doing *some* work outside the home. Asked how to remove the economic dependence of women, he said: 'The easiest way is for every woman to take up some form of work.'[128]

Last, despite his inconsistencies, Gandhi had an open mind. He regarded his own views on woman's role in society as only provisional and was willing to accept that women themselves must decide what their role is to be. 'Only the toad under the harrow knows where it pinches him. Therefore ultimately woman will have to determine with authority what she needs.'[129]

Because laws had been made by men, women's experience was not represented in them. But the tyranny of patriarchy had run its course: 'When woman, freed from man's snares, rises to the full height and rebels against man's legislation and institutions designed by him, her rebellion, no doubt non-violent, will be none the less effective.'[130] In the end Gandhi's message was feminist in at least one respect: 'Women alone can emancipate themselves, not men.'[131]

I shall conclude with two brief remarks. The first concerns whether Gandhi can be said to be an egalitarian at all. Egalitarianism, in recent discourse, is usually defined as a belief in distributive equality. Gandhi did not share that belief. He did, it is true, have a commitment to improving the lot of those on the lowest rung of the ladder but that could be an expression of 'extended humanitarianism' rather than a belief in equality. Again, Gandhi was strongly opposed to economic disparities being wide, or becoming wider in the process of economic growth. But provided such disparities were kept within reasonable limits, he did not find them a matter of great moral concern nor did he particularly want them to be abolished altogether. A recent study by Beteille, which starts by defining equality in the sense of distributive equality, the equality of outcomes, goes on to recognise the possibility that 'the pursuit of equality limits the attainment of other ends, such as those of efficiency, liberty and even the self-realisation of the individual'.[132] Gandhi shared this opinion and he would not agree to give up these other ends for the sake of equality.

My second remark concerns Gandhi's neglect of the class dimension of both economic and social inequality. Gandhi may well have been right in refusing to see the class structure as the sole or even the decisive factor bearing on inequality but I believe he was quite wrong in not paying it any serious attention at all. I shall return to this point in the next chapter which discusses his concept of trusteeship. It is of some interest, however, to note that Gandhi's non-class approach to inequality won a tribute from a senior leader of the Communist Party of India, writing in 1969, who observes that the Marxist approach to social change did not call for any serious specific attention being paid to problems such as caste, untouchability and so on:

> And our practice reflected the understanding that if we organised and led the workers and peasants to fight militantly for their class demands . . . the divisions based on religion, caste, untouchability, language etc. would somehow be eliminated in the course of time.[133]

Perhaps, he suggests, Gandhi understood the complications and complexities of the task 'far better than we did'. Gandhi has been criticised for neglecting the economic basis of inequality and exploitation. Thus, Kishawar concludes that for women as well as for Harijans, Gandhi failed to put an economic content into his concept of

116

emancipation. 'Gandhi failed to realise that among other things, oppression is not an abstract moral condition, but a social and historical experience related to production relations.'[134]

This statement is inaccurate. As my discussion in this chapter should have shown, Gandhi placed moral issues squarely in the context of social and historical experience, but he not merely 'failed to realise' but strongly opposed the view that social and historical experience is determined by, or even necessarily related to, production relations. The point raises issues that I have touched on elsewhere in this book. The view that the origin of inequality lies in private property is a view held by both Rousseau and Marx and it is still influential. But as Dahrendorf points out: 'if social inequality were really based on private property, the abolition of private property would have to result in the elimination of inequality'.[135]

The experience of communist countries does not bear this out. Gandhi, despite the limitations of his world view, understood the nature of village realities and saw why *swaraj* 'requires emancipation from India's own traditional inequalities as well as those imposed from outside'.[136] In fighting against both, he also helped to clarify some of the issues involved.

6

THE THEORY OF
TRUSTEESHIP

THE THEORY EXPLAINED

Gandhi's theory of trusteeship was developed as an alternative to doctrines of socialism and communism (the two words are used more or less interchangeably in Gandhi's writings) which started becoming popular in India, following the Russian revolution of 1917. These doctrines, wrote Gandhi, had brought to the forefront the question of what 'our' attitude towards the wealthy should be.[1] Gandhi took socialist doctrine to mean essentially that the property of the rich princes, millionaires, big industrialists and landlords should be confiscated and they should forcibly be made to earn their livelihood as workers. Gandhi disagreed.

He held instead that all that one could legitimately expect of the wealthy was to hold their riches in trust and use them for the service of society as a whole rather than solely for their own private profit. This involved both the management of existing economic resources and responsibility for their growth and development in the public interest. For doing this they were entitled to a commission which would, on one hand, provide them with a reasonable standard of living and on the other, have some correspondence with the nature and extent of the services they rendered.

This chapter discusses Gandhi's ideas on trusteeship and is organised in five sections. The present section states the theory and explains Gandhi's reasons for believing that it provided a preferable alternative to communism. The following section provides a brief exposition of the principles of the Law of Trusts from which, I believe, Gandhi's concept of trusteeship was derived. The third section states some of the implications of trusteeship for industrial relations and the fourth, those for landlordism. The final section attempts a summing up.

118

The idea of trusteeship played a central role in Gandhi's view of what constitutes an acceptable economic ordering of society. Not only did he attach considerable importance to it, he described it as having 'a permanent association with his name'.[2] 'My theory of trusteeship is no makeshift, certainly no camouflage. I am confident that it will survive all other theories.'[3]

It was, however, with trusteeship as a *theory*, an idea, a social and moral norm, that he was concerned. He paid relatively little attention to practical difficulties involved in making it work, and was given to brushing aside with some impatience, questions bearing on whether it could ever be made to work at all. Thus, for example, he describes a society based on trusteeship as follows: 'The rich man will be left in possession of his wealth, of which he will use what he reasonably requires for his personal need and will act as a trustee for the remainder to be used for the society.'[4]

Gandhi adds; 'In this argument honesty on the part of the trustee is assumed.'[5] That the assumption was perhaps unrealistic did not bother him for this he thought was the nature of theoretical models. When critics pointed to the lack of any historical evidence for trusteeship operating on a society-wide basis and covering the entire range of private property, Gandhi remained unimpressed. 'That possessors of wealth have not acted up to the theory does not prove its falsity, it proves the weakness of the wealthy.'[6] Towards the end of his life, asked if he knew of any industrialist who had fully lived up to the ideal of trusteeship, Gandhi replied, 'No, though some are striving in that direction.'[7] This did not, however, appear to him to be an issue of much importance from the point of view of the theory of trusteeship itself. In the course of answering questions at a Gandhi Seva Sangh meeting, he states:

It may be asked how many trustees of this type one can really find. As a matter of fact, such a question should not arise at all. It is not directly related to our theory. There may be just one such trustee or there may be none at all. Why should we worry about it?[8]

Such a stance is quite consistent with Gandhi's view of the relationship between ideals and reality. An ideal *had* to be defined in its pure form, but this could never be realised, it could only be approximated, and that too only in the very long run.

You may say that trusteeship is a legal fiction ... Absolute

119

trusteeship is an abstraction like Euclid's definition of a point
and is equally unattainable. However, if we strive for it we shall
be able to go further in realising a state of equality on earth than
by any other method.[9]

Gandhi was not unaware of the immensity of the task and of the
pitfalls in the road to trusteeship but the only method that he believed
to be a serious alternative to trusteeship was communism, and that
method he could not accept. As he saw it, he was 'engaged in solving
the same problem that faces scientific socialists'.[10] He is far from sure
that trusteeship *will* work, asserting only that it could. 'It is highly
probable that my advice will not be accepted and my dream will not be
realised. But, who can guarantee that the socialists' dream will be
realised?'[11]

Gandhi put forward three main arguments in support of his belief
that trusteeship was a better, and in the long run a more sustainable,
means of dealing with the inequality and exploitation found in
societies based on private ownership of the means of production.
First, Gandhi justified trusteeship by the principle of non-violence.
The communist alternative of dispossessing the wealthy of the means
of production by confiscating their property violated that principle.
The Soviet communist system had some good aims, such as the
elimination of exploitation of the poor by the rich, but it was based on
the use of force which was unethical. Because of this Gandhi had
strong doubts about its final success.[12]

Second, as I pointed out earlier, Gandhi held that it is perfectly
possible to combine benevolence with self-interest. The acquisition of
wealth in a capitalist society did not necessarily carry a moral taint. 'It
is my conviction', he wrote, 'that it is possible to acquire riches
without consciously doing wrong.'[13] He refused to believe that the
capitalists 'were a necessarily bad lot or worse than members of any
other class'. Accordingly he would not say to the capitalists that unless
they renounced all the riches they had, he would have nothing to do
with them.[14]

Complete renunciation of one's possessions was, in any event,
suggested Gandhi, something which very few, whether poor or rich,
were capable of. All that one could legitimately expect of the wealthy
class was to hold their riches in trust and use them for the service of
society. To insist upon more would be to, 'kill the goose that laid the
golden eggs'.[15] For these reasons, Gandhi never asked his followers or
friends who had a business background to give it up. Typical of his

attitude in this matter is his advice to Kamalnarayan Bajaj, the eldest
son of Jamnalal Bajaj, a prominent industrialist who had been a
personal friend and a political ally, and also in Gandhi's judgement a
real trustee:

> If you are already engaged in business, continue to do so; earn
> wealth if you want but like Jamnalalji all your earnings should
> be fair earnings. Again bear in mind that for the good of the
> people, you too have to be a trustee of your wealth.[16]

Third, natural ability was unequally distributed. While we all have a
right to equal opportunities 'nevertheless we have not all the same
abilities'.[17] Entrepreneurial ability, in particular, was scarce and if
properly harnessed could be of much benefit to a poor, underdeveloped
country. 'We must not under-rate the business talent and know-how
which the owning classes have acquired through generations of
experience and specialisation. Free use of it would accrue to the people
under my plan.'[18]

The same concern comes out in Gandhi's response to some critics
against the management of Kasturba Gandhi National Memorial
Fund, to which capitalists had made most of the donations. The
criticism was that capitalists, who were in a majority on the Board of
Trustees of the fund, would come to dominate the organisation, but
Gandhi did not accept this, for he wanted 'not only their donations
but their talent, goodwill and services for the cause'.[19] That the
communist system failed to take into account the importance of
individual capabilities, entrepreneurial and managerial capabilities in
particular, was one of Gandhi's major points of criticism against that
system.

> Wealthy people should act as trustees of their wealth. But if they
> are robbed of their wealth through violent means, it would not
> be in the interest of the country. This is known as communism.
> Moreover by adopting violent means we would be depriving
> society of the services of capable individuals.[20]

In most of his writings on trusteeship Gandhi's main concern was with
the nature and implications of trusteeship rather than with how a
social system based on it could be brought about. There was one basic
principle to which Gandhi would allow no exception. A better society
could not be brought about by the use of violent means. Hence a
change from an existing social system based on exploitation and class
conflict to one based on trusteeship and cooperation, had to be

achieved by morally acceptable means, which included patient persuasion and non-violent, non-cooperation. But there was always the possibility that they might *not* agree to act as trustees.

> If, however, in spite of the utmost effort, the rich do not become guardians of the poor in the true sense of the term and the latter are more and more crushed and die of hunger, what is to be done?[21]

The answer was one that came naturally to Gandhi, 'non-violent non-cooperation'. The rich cannot accumulate wealth without the co-operation of the poor. In an article written on the eve of India's independence, he considers the possibility that even if capitalists agree, formally, to accept the role of trustees they may actually continue to act as exploiters. The assumption of honesty that a *theory* of trusteeship finds it necessary to make, might not apply in practice. 'They might insist that they should become trustees and yet they might choose to remain owners.' This time his answer was more categorical, 'We shall then have to oppose and fight them.'[22] This implied campaigns of non-violent non-cooperation with property owners by the masses of people. Only in the last resort, if all other means had failed, would he condone direct dispossession of property, by the state, for the purpose of placing it under the control of a trustee.

Gandhi's doctrine of trusteeship has usually been given a theological interpretation. From this point of view, the rationale of trusteeship is that everything on earth came from, and belonged to, God. If an individual had more than a 'proportionate' share of ability, talent or wealth, that person became a trustee of that part for the people as a whole. It followed that the rich should use their talents to increase their wealth, but for the sake of the nation. Trusteeship was thus a form of moral responsibility but it was different from either charity or benevolence. While Gandhi's doctrine of trusteeship indeed rests on a certain concept of moral responsibility, the religious element is only *one* of its components. Abrol is one of the few writers to have pointed out that the legal element was perhaps no less important: 'Not only Gandhi, the religious man, but Gandhi the lawyer, had a hand in the origin of this concept. Gandhi found this idea of trusteeship in books of jurisprudence, too.'[23]

TRUSTEESHIP AND THE LAW OF TRUSTS

Asked by a visiting journalist to define a trustee, Gandhi provided the following definition: 'A trustee is one who discharges the obligations of his trust faithfully and in the best interests of his wards'.[24] The definition has a clearly legal ring. Indeed it is related to the concept of trusteeship in the law of equity which Gandhi had studied at Lincoln's Inn, and on occasion practised as a barrister. I believe that Gandhi derived his concept of trusteeship from the law of trusts, and for this reason, I shall try in this section to provide an exposition of the basic principle of fiduciary obligation which underlies that law.

The literature of jurisprudence offers a number of definitions of a trust, which may differ from one another on some point of detail. I shall start with a classic definition due to Sir Arthur Underhill, who described a trust as:

> an obligation binding a person (who is called a trustee) to deal with property over which he has control (which is called trustee property) for the benefit of persons (called beneficiaries).

The definition has four basic elements. The first is that a trust is a kind of obligation. Second, this obligation has to do with some transaction in property. Third, the property concerned need not be owned by the trustee; the exercise of control will suffice. Finally, the benefits are meant to accrue not to the trustee but to the beneficiaries. Next I quote a more recent definition by Ford and Lee:

> A trust may be defined as an obligation enforceable in equity which rests on a person (the trustee) as owner of some specific property (the trust property) for the benefit of another person (the beneficiary) or for the advancement of certain purposes.[25]

According to this definition, the trustee has ownership of, rather than merely control over, the property in question, and the fulfilment of certain specific purposes is allowed as a legitimate purpose of a trust, as well as the achievement of benefits for certain purposes. The last definition of a trust that I shall cite comes from the Hague Convention on the Laws Applicable to Trusts and on their recognition:

> For the purposes of this Convention, the term 'trust' refers to the legal relationships created – *inter vivos* or on death – by a person, the settlor, when assets have been placed under the control of a trustee for the benefit of a beneficiary or for a specified purpose.[26]

This definition, too, allows a specified purpose, other than the benefit of a beneficiary, but requires control, rather than full ownership, of the assets concerned by the trustee.

Despite some variations among the different definitions, the general thrust of the legal meaning of a trust is clear enough. The essential feature is that some individual, or individuals (who are the trustee or trustees) of certain property (or assets) assume a legal obligation to use their position (whether this is one of ownership or simply the exercise of control over the property in question) for the benefit of some other person or persons, or for the advancement of a specified and impersonal purpose.

Subject to the broad features described, trusts may take many different forms. A trust may be a small-scale entity, a trustee holding a small number of beneficiaries, or it may be on a very large scale where the trustee holds very large sums of assets in trust for the benefit of thousands of people. A trust may be held by a single person or by a board of trustees. It may be held by a private or a public body. Historically, the trust developed from what was called a 'use' in medieval England, and represented a transfer of property by its owner to third parties for the use of himself or some beneficiary. These third parties then become the legal owners of the property but they held it for the benefit of the transferor and/or any other nominated beneficiary. As could perhaps be expected from the circumstances of its origin, the trust was often used as a tax avoidance device. It has, however, been widely used for more worthy purposes too, such as facilitating investment, preventing family assets from being squandered, helping to protect the environment, and so on. This last purpose is currently regarded as being particularly significant especially in North America. In the USA, the so-called Public Trust Doctrine imposes on each state a fiduciary obligation to ensure that public lands, which constitute the coastline as well as tidal rivers and bays of the sea, are made continuously accessible to the public at large, while in Canada the Environmental Fund, which is operated as a trust, is regularly used to finance the reclamation of land.

In law the concept of trusteeship is itself derived from the more general concept of fiduciary ties. The duties of a trustee are a particular instance of fiduciary obligation. This was made very clear by the classic judgment in the law of Meinhard v. Salmon:

> Many forms of conduct permissible in a workday world for those acting at arms length are forbidden to those bound by fiduciary

ties. A trustee is held to something closer than the morals of the market place. Not honesty alone, but the punctilio of an honour the most sensitive, is then the standard of behaviour.[27]

The ethics of fiduciary law, as distinguished from say, the law of contract, is strongly moralistic, the fiduciary being bound to act in such a way as to 'further the interest of others (the beneficiaries) and not his or her own'. In contract, on the other hand, the parties act in their own interests and try to do the best for themselves through a process of bargaining; there are no legal sanctions against the pursuit of self-interest as such, only against failure to observe the terms of the contract. (According to some authorities they might also apply if the contract itself was not 'fairly' arrived at.)

The difference can be seen by considering the foremost duty of a trustee, that of 'loyalty', as legally prescribed. This requires the trustee to observe the terms of the trust and to act solely for the economic well-being of the trust and the personal welfare of all the beneficiaries. The first part of the requirement, that of adhering to an agreement, voluntarily made, applies to the law of contract as well, but there is no counterpart in contract to the second. As against this, it could be argued that the law of trusts does not exclude the trustee from being one of the beneficiaries. On the other hand, the concept of fiduciary obligation does exclude a trustee from attaching more weight to his or her own benefit than to that of others.

> The trustee must manage the trust property in any event for the benefit of *all* the beneficiaries and the trustee will be in breach of trust if he or she acts for the benefit of some and to the detriment of others.[28]

TRUSTEESHIP AND INDUSTRIAL RELATIONS

Gandhi's concept of trusteeship has wide-ranging implications for the structure of industrial relations. It implies in particular that industrial relations should be built on cooperation rather than conflict. This would require a change of outlook on the part of the mill-owner, who should stop looking on labour simply as a means of earning profit, but rather as partners in a common enterprise.

> What I expect of you therefore is that you should hold all your riches as a trust to be used solely in the interests of those who sweat for you and to whose industry and labour you owe all your

position and property. I want you to make your labourers co-partners of your wealth.[29]

Specifically, Gandhi thought that this implied an obligation on the part of the employers not only to pay a living wage but also to ensure a clean working environment and provide facilities for cheap nutritious food, sanitation and elementary education for workers' children.

Trusteeship, according to Gandhi, implied that workers had certain obligations too. In the prevailing climate of industrial relations, while the capitalists tried to get maximum work from the employees, paying them only as much as they had to, the workers hit upon all sorts of tricks to put in as little effort as they could get away with. This was, he conceded, a natural response. 'The labourers are dissatisfied with their lot. They have every reason for dissatisfaction.'[30] The result was, however, that even if wages increased under the threat of strikes or because of legislation by government, this often did not lead to an improvement in efficiency. If industrial relations came to be based on trusteeship all this would change, for there would not be 'a single mill-hand who does not regard the mill in which he works as his own, who complains of sweating and over-work, and who therefore nurses in his breast nothing but ill-will towards his employers'.[31] Instead there would be a sense of willing participation in a common enterprise.

> From the moment your men come to realise that the mills are theirs, no less than yours, they will begin to feel towards you as blood-brothers, there would be no question of their acting against the common interest and the need for having a heavy supervisory establishment over them.[32]

Such a system, according to Gandhi, had economic as well as ethical merit, for if it came to prevail, strikes and breakouts would become much less frequent, productivity would increase and the costs of monitoring labour performance would be substantially reduced. Trusteeship could also lead in a natural way to profit-sharing and to workers' participation in management.

TRUSTEESHIP AND LANDLORDISM

Gandhi intended his theory of trusteeship to apply not only to industrial capitalists but also to landlords, although in their case he did not manage to develop the theory in as much detail as he had done for the labour–capital relationship. During the 1930s radical movements among the peasantry aiming at the total abolition of landlordism were gathering strength in some parts of India. Gandhi saw class war in the countryside as a threat to the unity of the national movement against imperialism. His doctrine of trusteeship provided an alternative.

A zamindar, Gandhi maintained, could be a nationalist too, but only if he tried to 'live like a non-zamindar'. This required that he had to regard his tenants as his co-proprietors. In other words, he will hold his zamindar in trust for his tenants, taking a moderate commission for the use of his labours and capital.[33] As a historical precedent, Gandhi held out the practice of the samurai in Japan as a model for Indian zamindars to follow. 'They must regard themselves, even as the Japanese nobles did, as trustees, holding their wealth for the good of their wards, the ryots.'[34]

Gandhi also tried to draw up a list of things that a 'model' zamindar was required to do in order that he might be described as a trustee. The list is formidable. Such a zamindar would study the economic condition of the ryots under his care; establish schools for the villages where his own children would be educated alongside the children of the ryots, provide the village wells and tanks, throw open his own gardens for the unrestricted use of the ryots, and convert into hospitals, schools and the like most of the unnecessary buildings which he keeps for his pleasure.[35]

Another list prescribes that a zamindar who seeks to be a trustee must provide his tenants with fixity of tenure, run well-managed schools for the ryots' children as well as night schools for adults, look after village sanitation and, in a variety of ways, make them feel that they, the zamindars, are their true friends, taking only a fixed commission for their services.[36]

In order to qualify as a trustee, a zamindar would also have to make a drastic change in his consumption behaviour and way of life in general. At present, Gandhi observed, there was a total lack of proportion between the 'unnecessary pomp and extravagance' that marked the life-style of landlords, and the 'squalid surroundings and the grinding pauperism' of the ryots in whose midst they live.[37] By this Gandhi did not mean that the zamindar's standard of living must become the *same* as the ryots'. Gandhi was not an 'absolute egalitarian', but he did not want the gap to be too glaring: 'I would not mind your using gold plates provided your tenants were comfortable enough to afford silver plates but where their life is a long-drawn-out agony, how

127

dare you have these luxuries?'[38] 'With the great awakening among the *kisans*, there must be growing dissatisfaction with their lot, and a growing assertion of their rights.'[39]

This, Gandhi whole-heartedly welcomed. It not only strengthened the national movement, it was also an essential condition for trusteeship to work. Trusteeship did not simply rest on the goodwill of the landlords. Organising the peasantry, spreading basic education among them, helping them realise their own strength, and become conscious, in particular, that the landlords could not continue to exploit them without tacit cooperation, whether forced or voluntary, on their own part – all these, according to Gandhi, were just as necessary to build up a social and political climate in which trusteeship could become a possibility, as they were for developing the class struggle, which Gandhi wished to avert.

> The kisan or the peasant whether as a landless labourer or a labouring proprietor, comes first ... But in the non-violent way, the labourer cannot forcibly eject the absentee landlord. He has so to work, as to make it impossible for the landlord to exploit him. Closest cooperation among the peasants is absolutely necessary. To this end special organising bodies or committees should be formed where there are none and those already in existence should be reformed wherever necessary. The kisans are for the most part illiterate. Both adults and young persons of school-going age should be educated. This applies to men and women.[40]

Gandhi was asked what his phrase, 'so as to make it impossible for the landlord to exploit him', precisely meant, whether for example it included, apart from campaigns of *satyagraha*, 'administrative reforms that the peasants may oblige the state to make through the exercise of their franchise, and minimise the powers of the landlords?'[41] Gandhi's response is typical of his general stance on techniques to be used for achieving social change:

> Civil Disobedience and non-cooperation are designed for use, when people, the tillers of the soil, have no political power. But immediately they have political power, naturally their character will be ameliorated through legislative channels ... If the legislature proves itself to be incapable of safeguarding the kisan's interests, they will of course, always have the sovereign remedy of civil disobedience and non-cooperation.[42]

In some passages Gandhi appears to recognise that to convert the landlord–tenant relationship into one of trusteeship was even more difficult than bringing about a similar transformation in the labour–capital relationship. In India, as in a number of other countries which had long been under colonial rule, landlords had been little more than revenue-collecting agencies serving the interests of the foreign ruler, and enjoyed power and privilege without contributing significantly to the production process (which was not the case with industrialists). Gandhi repeatedly pointed this out to the landlord class on the eve of India's independence.

> But some of the extraordinary privileges that pass muster under the British rule are themselves in the nature of an usurpation. The history of British rule is a history of usurpation. Those who helped the British government in this process got certain rights as a reward for their services.[43]

Gandhi's message to the landlords was that whether they become trustees or not, they would not enjoy such special privileges in free India. He returned to this theme the following year.

> For a long time during the British regime you have been exploiting the labourers and peasants. Therefore, I advise you in your own interest that if you do not see the writing on the wall, it will be difficult for you to adjust.[44]

He was only repeating a warning he had given before:

> In the final analysis land belongs to the man who has worked on it. The present system which divides people into capitalists or landlords on the one hand and the have-nots or serfs on the other should not be tolerated.[45]

CONCLUSION

I shall conclude with a few remarks on the wider significance of Gandhi's concept of trusteeship from a 'political economy' point of view. I begin by arguing against interpretations which regard trusteeship either as a halting step towards, or practically indistinguishable from, socialism.[46] Dantwala writes:

> In the last analysis, for all practical purposes, the concept of trusteeship is not very different from that of socialised owner-

ship. In neither case can the ownership be exploited for private benefit ... Both will be controlled in the interest of society.[47]

He goes on to suggest that the schedules of the rights and obligations of the trustee very much resemble those of the manager of a socialised farm or factory as regards both remuneration and freedom of action, which further supports the thesis that trusteeship is only a variant of socialised property. I believe this judgement to be mistaken. The second sentence of the passage quoted appears to suggest that socialised ownership cannot be exploited for private benefit. The history of nationalised industry both in the Soviet Union and in less developed 'planned economies' provides much evidence to the contrary. The last sentence implies that private enterprise by its nature *cannot* be controlled or regulated in the interest of society. Not only does this opinion contradict standard economic theory, it is one that Gandhi never held. As far as the rights and obligations of the trustee are concerned, these can be parallelled by examples from *any* enterprise organised in the form of a trust, whether in the public or the private sector. Furthermore, the view that trusteeship is 'really' a variant of state socialism is flatly contradicted by Gandhi himself.

Legal ownership in the transformed condition is vested in the trustee, not in the state. It was to avoid confiscation that the doctrine of trusteeship came into play, retaining for society the ability of the original owner in his own right.[48]

Similar statements occur repeatedly in Gandhi's writings on trusteeship. A more important issue is whether Gandhi's doctrine of trusteeship was designed to reduce, or on the contrary to maintain, existing inequalities in the distribution of economic and political power. A Marxist scholar describes Gandhi's theory of trusteeship as 'the haves looking after the have-nots as a result of a change of heart',[49] and calls it an insidious and effective weapon against the struggles of workers and peasants against their exploiters. As against this view Frankel has argued that in the Indian context Gandhi's theory of trusteeship has a radical effect, for it 'subtly encouraged a shift in the basis of legitimacy of the upper castes'.[50] The theory implies, she argues, that land-owning castes could no longer claim moral or economic justification for land-ownership from the fact of ownership itself.

Ascriptive status, standing alone, was no longer sufficient to bestow political authority. This was instead justified according to moral standards of political behaviour. Foremost among these was the duty of the propertied castes to use their resources to provide for the minimum well-being of the poor. The reciprocal of this duty was the *right* of the low-status landless castes to demand that the elite allocate resources in equitable fashion.[51]

On this interpretation, the trusteeship theory provides a curb on landlords' power, for it makes them subject to removal if they fail to honour their trust. Further, from a Gandhian perspective, the trustee-ship theory and the Constructive Programme went together. That programme, which sought to improve health, sanitation, transport and educational facilities for villagers, at the same time weakened the links of dependence and patronage that bound the peasantry to the dominant landed castes. Frankel concludes: 'The trusteeship doctrine, allied to the Constructive Program actually held revolutionary im-plications for the distribution of economic and political power.'[52]

It is worth noting that Gandhi himself, in his exposition of trusteeship, had drawn attention to the caste aspect of economic domination by the landlord class in rural India. 'The hideous caricature of *varnashrama* is responsible for the air of superiority that the so-called *kshatriya* assumes and the status of inherited inferiority the poor ryot submissively recognises as his deserved lot in life.'[53]

My own judgement on trusteeship is that while the Marxist critique is over-simple, Frankel's view is over-optimistic. The overall political impact of Gandhi's doctrine of trusteeship in land was to hold back rather than accelerate the process of radical land reform in India. This was not so much because he preached in favour of cooperation between landlords and tenants. 'I never said that there should be cooperation between the exploiter and exploited so long as exploita-tion and the will to exploit persist.'[54] His point rather was that the exploited themselves cooperated with their exploiters: 'All exploita-tion is based on the cooperation, willing or forced, of the exploited. However much we may detest admitting it the fact remains that there would be no exploitation if people refused to obey the exploiter.'[55]

Trusteeship, backed up by the sanction of *satyagraha*, seemed to Gandhi to offer the possibility of a way out. Historical experience suggests that as a means of bringing about an end to landlordism this is unrealistic. For the management of industrial enterprise, trustee-ship offers greater scope, and some elements of it are included in the so-called 'Japanese' style of management, with its tradition of life-long employment and emphasis on cooperation, rather than conflict, between labour and capital.

131

7

EDUCATION

INTRODUCTION

Most of the developing countries of today were in the past colonies of one or other of the European powers and at the time of independence they inherited a burden of mass illiteracy. This was in large measure the product of colonial policy which discouraged even the most elementary educational facilities. Gandhi's ideas on education developed in direct response to the colonial system of education that he experienced in India. As he wrote in 1909, 'I had been under the sway of Macaulay's ideas on Indian education . . . I have now been disillusioned. I wish that others should be.'[1] But Gandhi's response to that disillusionment was a creative one.

At the time of independence only about 15 per cent of the population of India was literate and less than a third of the children of school-going age were enrolled at school. Indian nationalists had predicted that such an outcome would be the inevitable consequence of educational policies adopted in India for over a century. While, they pointed out, the administrative structure within which these policies were carried out had improved considerably over time, their basic purpose remained unchanged. Education in India was designed neither to develop the mind nor to help achieve economic progress but simply to maintain the stability of the British Raj.

In his famous Minute on Education of the 2 February 1835, Lord Macaulay laid down the fundamental principle that was to govern educational policy in India:

> We must at present do our best to form a class who may be interpreters between us and the millions whom we govern – a class of persons Indian in blood and colour but English in tastes, in opinions, in morals and in intellect.[2]

132

In order that this class of persons could eventually come to adopt English manners and values, they had to be familiarised with English ideas and the English language. Giving them an 'English' education was all that government need be concerned with. The job of spreading primary education among the masses could safely be left to the English-educated 'interpreters'.

The principle stated by Macaulay was endorsed by Lord William Bentinck and his council, who decided accordingly that 'all the funds appropriated for the purpose of education would be best employed in English education alone'.[3] The same spirit underlies Sir Charles Wood's Educational Dispatch of 1854 which is credited with having laid the basis of a 'modern' system of education in India and which led among other things to the founding of the three 'presidency' universities in Calcutta, Bombay and Madras in 1857 and the restriction of government jobs to English-educated persons. Initially this approach enjoyed wide support. Singhal sums up succinctly:

> Missionaries sought to impart Christian knowledge through the medium of English, the British government needed clerks and cheap educated labour for administration and Indian social reformers advocated the cause of English education to modernise static Indian society.[4]

Towards the latter part of the nineteenth century English education itself helped spread nationalist ideas among the Indian middle classes. Yet a nationalist such as Ranade found nothing particularly objectionable in the system of education established by the British. In his opinion it was only the literary and mercantile classes, constituting some 10 per cent of the population, which needed to have a higher education, so that they could provide leadership to the community. For the rural masses a practical knowledge of the rudiments of reading and writing was all that was required and this could be provided cheaply and efficiently through the indigenous school system.[5] That system consisted of village *pathsalas* where caste Hindu children traditionally had a chance of acquiring the three Rs, untouchables as a rule being denied access, and the *maktabs* and *madrasas* which performed a similar function for Muslims, mainly for boys. Not many, however, shared Ranade's confidence in the competence of the indigenous schools. In most parts of the country, the Bombay region which Ranade probably had in mind being something of an exception, they had already started decaying by the time of the British conquest and had reached a state of near collapse under the Raj. Being now dependent entirely on voluntary fees or private charity, and slow to change with the times, they were low on morale and starved of resources. And as Lord Mayo had duly noted in the 1870s, the assumption by Macaulay and his successors that the Baboos would use their newly acquired English learning to educate the masses was hardly realistic.[6] This had certainly not happened in Britain itself, where the church, and to an increasing extent during the second half of the nineteenth century, the state, played a significant role in extending elementary education to working-class children. Whereas in 1833 only about a third of the children of school-going age in England were receiving any kind of regular instruction, by the end of the century this proportion had nearly doubled.[7]

In India, in contrast, there was hardly any progress. By the turn of the century it came to be generally recognised that village children were, in effect, not receiving any education at all, a fact recorded by the statistics on literacy, which for the population of British India was less than 5 per cent in 1901, and school-enrolment: the vast majority of children of school-going age did not attend school. The demand for mass education gathered strength and found its voice in Gokhale who was the first in India and one of the first anywhere to insist that mass education was a prerequisite for economic development. Gokhale fought all his life for the cause of education in India, writing, speaking, sometimes legislating in favour of female education, technical and higher education but above all, primary education.[8] Education alone, urged Gokhale, could enable the peasant to resist exploitation by the money-lender, to improve sanitation, to shake off superstition, to increase his earning capacity and to take an intelligent interest in public affairs. The basic task with which education should be concerned was the eradication of illiteracy. 'The quality of education is of importance that comes only after illiteracy has been banished.'[9] Without mass literacy India could not develop; for an ignorant and illiterate nation, stated Gokhale, could not make solid progress.

In 1911, as a non-official member of the Imperial Legislative Council, Gokhale introduced his Elementary Education Bill which sought to make elementary education compulsory in certain selected areas. It also provided that school fees were not to be charged to parents whose income was less than ten rupees a month. Gokhale himself regarded his proposal as only a first step towards making elementary education free and compulsory throughout India. However, it met fierce opposition from the provincial governments on both economic and political grounds. The Governor of Bombay, for instance, warned the Viceroy that the movement for mass literacy was the work of agitators who 'well realise that their power to stir up discontent would be immensely increased if every cultivator could read'.[10] In the event Gokhale's bill was rejected.

Gokhale died in 1915. A year after his death, Gandhi, who described himself as Gokhale's disciple, summed up his legacy as follows:

> The Congress must, of course, be kept alive, the true condition of the country should be placed before the people through speeches and writings, and efforts made to have education provided to every Indian.[11]

Gandhi pledged his commitment to each of these tasks. From around this time education for the masses became one of his most pressing concerns. 'If therefore you desire to work for the good of India, give primary education to its three hundred million people.'[12] Gandhi's ideas and example encouraged many of his followers to found, administer, and teach in schools in their local areas. Educating the people came to be regarded as part of *sarvodaya* and was a distinctive feature of the Indian national movement under Gandhi's leadership.

Gandhi's approach to education differed from Gokhale's in important respects. Gokhale wanted primary education to be free and compulsory and relied on public expenditure as the principal means of extending education to the masses. Gandhi started with more modest aims. In a speech on 20 October 1917 at the Second Gujrat Educational Conference, Ahmedabad, he speaks only of the desirability of making primary education generally available and suggests that it should be 'free but optional'.[13] It was only much later that he came to accept the general opinion that spreading education among the masses required attendance at school being made compulsory by law. That the state should be responsible for financing primary education out of its general revenues was another wide-spread belief that he never accepted. Instead, he wanted schools to be financially self-supporting. And unlike his mentor, Gandhi gave much more importance to the content and quality of primary education than to literacy as such.

This chapter considers Gandhi's ideas on education and consists of five sections. The present section has tried to provide a historical introduction. The second describes Gandhi's views on the aims of education; and the third his scheme for making education vocational. The fourth section gives his reasons for believing that schools should be financially self-supporting; and some of his thoughts on higher and university education are presented in the fifth. The last section offers a few concluding comments.

AIMS OF EDUCATION

Gandhi's understanding of what education is about is linked to his world outlook, which regards life as a quest for self-realisation. The etymological meaning of the word 'education' is 'drawing out'. The corresponding Gujrati word, *kelavani*, has just the same meaning. Pointing this out, Gandhi observes that education is a kind of 'unfoldment', an endeavour to develop our latent faculties.[14] Being educated means undertaking such an endeavour. But human beings have *many* latent faculties. Theories of education differ in the relative emphasis they place on them.

Gandhi accepts the usual classification of the human faculties into three broad groups: the mind, the body and the spirit. Among these, the spirit is regarded in Hindu philosophy as being not only the highest but also the only permanent element in human beings, a view which Gandhi shared. Accordingly, to hold the development of the spiritual aspect of man to be the predominant goal of education was, states Gandhi, logically a valid position; and that was indeed the rationale for the traditional system of education prescribed for members of the Brahmana caste in ancient India. It was not, however, Gandhi's own position nor did he want India, once she was free from British rule, to return to a Brahmanical system of education.

Education, observes Gandhi, could also be understood in another sense: as that leading to 'a full or maximum development of all the three: body, mind and spirit'.[15] On this interpretation it is *all-round* development of the human being that constitutes education, and this is what Gandhi wanted education to be: 'By education, I mean an all-round drawing out of the best in child and man – body, mind and spirit.'[16] Singling out the spiritual or, indeed, any one out of the three basic human faculties in a scheme of education could lead to a lack of balance. 'Man is neither mere intellect, nor the gross animal body, nor the heart or soul alone. A proper harmonious combination of all the three is required for the making of the whole man and constitutes the true economics of education.'[17]

By emphasising the need for education to be an all-round development of the human being Gandhi was, in effect, dissociating himself as much from the advocates of a return to a spiritually oriented

'Hindu' educational system as from the admirers of the 'English' system that was in place. This comes out clearly in the following passage, which Gandhi wrote on the eve of independence.

> The ancient aphorism 'Education is that which liberates' is as true today as it was before. Education here does not mean mere spiritual knowledge nor does liberation signify only liberation after death. Knowledge includes all training useful for the service of mankind and liberation means freedom from all manner of servitude even in the present life.[18]

By linking the aims of education to the ancient religious ideal of liberation which he interprets in a characteristically secular and humanist fashion Gandhi was reiterating a point he had been making for over three decades: his definition of education had practical implications for the choice of a curriculum and methods of teaching.

Spiritual development as Gandhi saw it required neither minute study of holy texts nor performance of elaborate religious rites and ceremonies but training in ethical behaviour based on the principles of truth and non-violence. The mind was not developed by filling it with a lot of information which one commits to memory but by learning to think for oneself and being able to solve problems by the exercise of one's thought. The aim of physical education was not bigger muscles but a trained and flexible body, one not only 'healthy, vigorous and sinewy' but more importantly, one able to carry out without fuss or fatigue any task it was required to perform, whether this consisted in trudging 30 miles, or climbing a mountain, or wielding a pick-axe, a shovel or a hammer.[19]

Education in Gandhi's sense was a demanding task. The social conditions prevailing in less developed countries such as India made it even more demanding. The village masses who formed the overwhelming majority of the population knew only physical labour.

> From their childhood they toil and labour in their fields from morning till night like their cattle in the midst of whom they live. Their existence is a weary endless round of mechanical drudgery unrelieved by a spark of intelligence or higher graces of life.[20]

Village people had little access to education of any kind. But neither did schools and colleges in the towns and cities give their students an education properly so called.

Gandhi saw education from childhood onwards as an active process of self-development rather than a means whereby a given store of knowledge could be passed on to passive recipients. By this criterion what passed for education in colonial India hardly deserved that name. It simply made children 'crammers and imitators, unfitted them for original work and thought and disabled them for filtrating their learning to the family or the masses'.[21] This, Gandhi believed, was due principally to the excessive importance given to English which not only served as the medium of instruction from high school onwards but also formed an important part of the primary school syllabus. Most of the children's time at school was taken up with memorising English words and phrases which they could neither understand nor relate to. The only result of this fruitless quest was that they sometimes forgot the proper use of their own language. Undue emphasis on a foreign tongue was not, however, the only barrier to education in India. The syllabus, the methods used for teaching and examination, and so on all emphasised memory rather than understanding and had the effect of robbing the learning process of interest and stimulus. History, for example, was taught as a chronicle of kings and their wars whereas it should really be taught as the history of man.[22] Moreover, what pupils were taught at school had no relationship with their home or their social and economic environment. Although over four-fifths of the population were engaged in agriculture, it had no place at all in the school syllabus. The educational system thus contributed towards bringing about total separation between home and school. The education that was given had no impact on the students' homes, 'although as a rule, the whole country should be influenced by the lives of students'.[23]

Gandhi's argument has an important corollary. If the educational process succeeds in doing its job of bringing about balanced development of individuals' mental, physical and spiritual faculties, the so-called social aims of education such as helping to make democracy work or contributing to gainful employment would also be easier to achieve. Gandhi was once asked whether he believed in the capacity of the average man to judge correctly provided he had enough knowledge of facts. He replied: 'Not knowledge of facts. What passes for facts is only impressions or estimates of things and estimates vary... What is really needed to make democracy function is not knowledge of facts but right education.'[24]

Gandhi's writings also show an appreciation of the human capital aspect of education. He advised educationists not to consider 'economic calculations in connection with education as sordid or out of place'.[25] In his opinion the education of children ought to be 'a kind of insurance against unemployment'[26] and school education should equip the school-leaver to earn an honest livelihood through the exercise of a profit-yielding vocation. This applied even more to higher education. When criticised for suggesting that the Gujrat Vidyapith should adopt a syllabus conducive to providing its graduates with a reasonable livelihood, Gandhi not only remained unrepentant but also described the success of Vidyapith graduates in securing jobs with good incomes as 'an excellent result'.[27] He added, however, that this was not the *principal* aim of education.

For many years Gandhi had been carrying out experiments in education, using a variety of curricula and learning techniques, in his ashrams. In 1937 he sponsored an educational conference at Wardha where he presented his ideas on education to an audience consisting of prominent educationists as well as the education ministers of provinces in which the Indian National Congress had been elected to govern. Gandhi's presidential address to the Conference began with an indictment of the prevailing system of education:

> The present system of education does not meet the requirements of the country in any shape or form. English having been made the medium of instruction in all the higher branches of learning, has created a permanent bar between the highly educated few and the uneducated many. It has prevented knowledge from percolating to the masses.[28]

The excessive importance given to English had placed upon the educated class a burden which had maimed them mentally for life and made them strangers in their own land. Primary education had been grossly neglected, but this was not just due to inadequate funding.

> Money spent on primary education is a waste of expenditure in as much what little is taught is soon forgotten and has little or no value in terms of the villages or cities. Such advantage as is gained by the existing system of education is not gained by the chief taxpayer, his children getting the least.[29]

The whole system had to be built afresh so that the children of the peasant, who was 'the chief taxpayer', could benefit from it. To this end the conference, under Gandhi's leadership, passed a number of resolutions of which the following are the most important:

139

1 that free and compulsory education be provided for seven years on a nation-wide scale;
2 that the medium of instruction be the mother tongue;
3 that the process of education throughout this period should centre around some form of manual and productive work, and that all the other abilities to be developed or training to be given should, as far as possible, be integrally related to the central handicraft, chosen with due regard to the environment of the child;
4 that this system should gradually be able to cover the remuneration of the teachers.

These are the aspects of education about which Gandhi was concerned the most. (University education was not discussed at the conference.) Some issues relating to resolution (3) are discussed in the next section and others, relating to the financing of school education, in the following one.

NAYEE TALIM

The programme of education for school children that Gandhi proposed came to be known as Nayee Talim (New Education) and is also described by some as Basic Education. It was based on three basic principles: it would be given entirely through the mother tongue, it would have a vocational rather than a literary orientation, and it would be financially self-supporting. It is the second principle, that of vocational education, that forms the topic of the present section.

Gandhi had long been committed to vocational education. 'In the education of this country', he had stated in 1928, 'the vocational aspect should constitute its dominant part.'[30] The rationale of the principle was spelled out by Gandhi in some detail. By vocational education he did not mean the teaching of handicrafts side by side with literary education. Rather he wanted that the whole of the school syllabus should be taught using some craft or crafts as a medium. The craft that he particularly recommended for this purpose was handloom spinning but other crafts could be used as well. The principal requirement that it had to satisfy was that the craft should be one widely practised by people in the area, so that the pupils were likely to have already acquired some familiarity with the tools and processes involved by the time they entered school. Not only would pupils be taught such crafts at school, these would be used as a springboard for learning mathematics, history, geography and science.

Many educationists believe that vocational training tends to impart a certain narrowness of vision which could frustrate the broader aims of education. Gandhi recognises this danger and observes that during the Middle Ages, both in European countries and in India, most students were taught only handicrafts, which did not give them an education. Proficiency in a craft did not necessarily develop intellect or originality in the artisan who might go on plying the *charkha* for generations without ever making any improvement therein. That, says Gandhi, had been the history of India: 'Artisans never paid any attention to the improvement of their tools and those who did mental work were not concerned with the crafts,'[31] and as a result both lost their creative instinct. The separation between manual and mental work was a direct result of the caste system, higher learning being supposed to be the province of Brahmanas, while those who did manual work such as spinners, weavers, carpenters or shoe-makers belonged to lower castes. This had impeded technical progress.

> And we have had no Cromptons and no Hargreaves, because of this vicious system of considering crafts as something inferior, divorced from the skilled. If they had been regarded as callings having an independent staus of their own equal to the status learning enjoyed, we should have had great inventors from among our craftsmen.[32]

Caste distinctions had to be fought directly but Nayee Talim could do its bit towards breaking down such barriers. In Gandhi's scheme crafts would be used to develop not only the manual dexterity of the pupils but also their intelligence. To maintain that intelligence could be developed only by literary training was, he argued, a superstition. In a country where more than 80 per cent of the population was agricultural and another 10 per cent industrial, a merely literary education could never succeed in doing that. On the other hand the spinning wheel could only be an effective educational tool if it was used in an appropriate, that is, a scientific rather than a merely mechanical, way. *How* something was taught was even more important than *what* was taught. 'The child should know the why and the wherefore of every process.'[33] By explaining the mechanism of the spinning wheel to the child, by showing the child the reason for each process, by relating it to the history of cotton, and cotton in turn to the history of civilisation, by teaching the child to count the number of rounds spun and to measure the strength and evenness of the yarn, one could hold the child's interest and train the hands, the eyes and the mind simultaneously.

In such a perspective proper planning of the curriculum was crucially important. Gandhi's own ideas on what constituted a proper curriculum for elementary education were spelled out in a number of articles on Nayee Talim and also reflected in his school at Wardha. Handicrafts, which included spinning, weaving, carpentry, horticulture and animal care were to provide the foundation. Music, drawing, arithmetic, citizenship, history, geography, science and languages were also to be taught, both directly and through the crafts, a learning-by-doing approach being used wherever possible. Schools would also give lessons in practical sanitation and hygiene, including efficient use of water and the repair and maintenance of village wells, knowledge which students would take back to their parents, taking on the role of silent revolutionaries. Cooperation between home and school would be encouraged by operating primary schools on a shift system, with two half-day shifts so that the children could also work in the field or help in household tasks. This, Gandhi believed, would go some way towards reducing the reluctance of parents to send their children, especially their daughters, to school.

Yet another innovation advocated by Gandhi was to postpone the time at which a child started on the alphabet. He believed that trying to do so at the very beginning of the learning process hampers the natural process of the intellectual growth of a child. 'The signs of the alphabet may be taught later when the pupil has learnt to distinguish wheat from chaff and when he has somewhat developed his or her tastes.'[34] A child at that stage would learn to read and write much faster and more effectively than at present, leading to overall economy in the use of resources. A saving in costs would also result from a reduction in the reading material required, such as primers and first readers.

The thrust of Gandhi's argument is that vocational training, if properly designed, is entirely consistent with the basic aim of education, the all-round development of the mental, physical and spiritual faculties. 'By regarding vocational training as something that is opposed to intellectual education, we are labouring under a great misapprehension and thereby retarding the progress of the people.'[35]

Bookish education, argued Gandhi, was by no means the same as intellectual education. On the contrary, it shut out the masses of the people from a chance of educating their intellect. Nayee Talim could give them this chance. 'If a cobbler could become a Shakespeare, why cannot other cobblers become, if not great poets, at any rate, experts in the field of chemistry, economics and such other subjects?'[36]

Education should also enable an individual to earn a livelihood. Vocational education could help in achieving this while the literary type of education prevalent in India only hindered it. In a speech on the occasion of the anniversary of the Gurukul Vidyapith on 20 March 1916, Gandhi had extolled the virtues of industrial education:

> He will lose nothing if he knows a proper use of tools, can saw a piece of board straight and build a wall that will not come down through a faulty handling of the plumber's line. A boy who is thus equipped will never feel helpless in battling with the world and never be in want of employment.[37]

By 1937, in which year he delivered the presidential address at the Educational Conference at Wardha, Gandhi thought he had worked out a way of achieving this. His plan was to turn the village school 'into an educative workshop in as economical and efficient a manner as possible'.[38] This, he claimed, would amount to 'a revolution in the education of village children'.[39]

WHY SCHOOLS SHOULD BE SELF-SUPPORTING

Giving the school student a vocational rather than a literary education had, according to Gandhi, a double purpose: the first, and purely educative, purpose was to 'develop the whole man or woman in him or her through the vocation learnt at school', the other, which was economic, sought 'to enable the pupil to pay for his tuition through the products of his labour'.[40] This ability to pay, he believed, would increase progressively. If in the first year each boy was able to earn two *piece* a day, he would be able to earn one *anna* a day the next year. 'In this way the power of production would go on increasing and they shall be able to earn their living in later life.'[41]

Providing primary education is widely accepted as being the responsibility of the state. Even economists with a commitment to *laissez-faire* tend to regard primary education as an exception to their rule and take it for granted that expenditure on it should be a charge on the public revenue. Gandhi disagreed. Early in his public life he wrote with deliberate paradox that since education to be universal must be free, 'our children must be made to pay in labour, partly or wholly, for all the education they receive'.[42] This did not mean that school students should be charged fees, to be paid by their parents. Making education universal required that 'our schools and colleges should become almost if not wholly self-supporting, not through donations or state aid or fees extracted from students but through remunerative work done by the students themselves'.[43]

In later writings he was a little more specific about which items of expenditure pupils should be required to pay for in this way. The rent of the school building, teachers' salaries and running expenses of the school should, he suggested, be met from remunerative work done by pupils during the first seven years of school. They should not, however, have to pay for food when at school. Food should be provided, or paid for, by parents except in the case of very poor families for whom the school should pay. Gandhi believed that his scheme for financing school education was perfectly viable, provided only that the content of the education itself was properly designed – if, that is, instead of teaching pupils only the three Rs, teaching was given in and through the handicrafts. From the very beginning pupils would learn how to make marketable products. The sale of the product of their manual work would provide the funds required.

Gandhi's proposal came under attack on both educational and economic grounds. The fear was expressed by educationists that the attempt to make education pay for itself would turn teachers into slave-drivers and encourage exploitation of child-labour. Some also argued that if, as Gandhi's proposal seemed to imply, the schools provided their pupils with free material for the practice of handicrafts as well as free marketing of the resulting products, professional artisans would be faced with unfair competition.

To the first criticism Gandhi's answer was that the professional ethics of the teachers themselves would prevent them from exploiting their pupils. As regards unfair competition, he claimed that this, if it arose at all, would be felt not by village artisans but rather by organised industry and in particular by the cloth mills, who were in a position to look after themselves. Also people might well decide to buy school products for reasons of sentiment even if the price they had to pay was a little higher, in which case the problem of marketing such products would not arise. As far as handloom cloth was concerned Gandhi suggested that the state should buy up surplus stocks if any from the schools at a favourable price.

Deeper reasons, too, divided Gandhi from his critics. Gandhi's view that education should be self-supporting was in part a consequence of his commitment to prohibition. The school budget in India was a charge on the provincial revenue, about a third of which came from taxes on alcoholic beverages. For moral reasons Gandhi was unwilling to link educational expansion to the consumption of liquor. If schools became financially self-supporting, the problem would not arise. There were, of course, other means than the excise on liquor for raising resources for education. In the course of his life-long campaign for the cause of mass education Gokhale had suggested a number of options, including a plea that local bodies should bear a part of the expenditure on school education and be empowered to levy a special education tax. He had also said that while expenditure on the army and the police should be restricted to the minimum that was absolutely necessary 'no state especially in these days can spend too much on an object like education'.[44] Gandhi parted company from his political mentor in proposing an altogether different route. One reason for this was an ingrained reluctance to rely on government for education, or indeed anything else, unless this became absolutely necessary for society to function. 'If we think that anything can be done only if the Government moves, we are not likely to realise our aims for ages.'[45] When, shortly after India became independent, colleagues urged him to use his influence with the Government of India to secure funding for Basic Education, Gandhi replied that 'the very move to seek Government aid would mean the end of Nayee Talim'.[46] Another reason for trying to make education self-supporting was a conviction that the quality of education mattered. The goal of primary education, as Gandhi saw it, was not simply to bring about universal literacy but to show the village masses the way to self-development. This was a truly immense task. The state simply did not have the resources for carrying it out.

> That it is the primary duty of the State to bring to its schools every boy and girl and give them proper (not perfunctory as now) education is an axiomatic truth. But in a country like India such education must largely if not wholly pay for itself.[47]

This conclusion was borne out by evidence on the American educational system.

> In America which is the richest country in the world, and where therefore perhaps there is the least need for making education self-supporting, it is the most usual thing for students to pay their way wholly or partially. If America has to model her schools and colleges so as to earn their scholastic expenses how much more necessary it must be for our schools and colleges.[48]

Inadequacy of resources and dangers of state intervention are both

negative arguments. Gandhi placed greater emphasis on the positive
virtues of his scheme. Reacting to adverse criticism of his plan by
educationists in India Gandhi remarked: 'The very idea of education
being self-supporting seems to them to rob education of all value.'[49] To
Gandhi the reverse was true. Schools, he said, must be frauds if they
cannot become self-supporting. Education to be worth its name must
be able to build up human capital from the very beginning. 'We
should be intellectual bankrupts if we cannot direct the energy of our
children so as to get from them after a year's training one anna worth of
marketable labour per hour.'[50] To Gandhi as we have seen education
was much more than human capital in the economic sense of the term.
However, his doctrine of the partnership between ethics and economics implied that a project that was ethically worthy should also be
economically viable. Accordingly he held that 'any scheme which is
sound from the educative point of view, and is efficiently managed, is
bound to be sound economically'.[51] Human labour and material, in
education as in any other enterprise, should never be used in a wasteful
and unproductive way. If they were properly used there should not,
Gandhi argued, be any difficulty in making schools pay their way. At
the same time by working for their education through productive
labour from the very beginning children would become self-reliant
and independent. The self-supporting character of school education
was not an end in itself but rather a result expected to follow from the
adoption of a scientific approach to education which sought to develop
in pupils an all-round development of their faculties.

> If such education is given, the direct result will be that it will be
> self-supporting. But the test of success is not its self-supporting
> character, but that the whole man is drawn out through the
> teaching of the handicraft in a scientific manner. In fact I will
> reject a teacher who would promise to make it self-supporting
> under any circumstances. The self-supporting part will be the
> logical corollary of the fact that the pupil has learnt the use of
> every one of the faculties.[52]

HIGHER EDUCATION

In discussing Gandhi's views on education we have so far been
concerned mostly with primary education. This corresponds to his
own priorities.

If all the collegians were all of a sudden to forget their

knowledge, the loss sustained by the sudden lapse of the memory of say a few *lakhs* of collegians would be as nothing compared to the loss that the nation has sustained and is sustaining through the ocean of darkness that surrounds three hundred millions.[53]

If he spoke about higher education at all, it was usually to express a poor opinion of it, for example: that our graduates are 'a useless lot, weak of body, without any zest for work and mere imitators';[54] that higher education in India produced 'much cry and little wool';[55] or 'that university education does not serve much purpose'.[56]

Some of Gandhi's criticisms against the prevailing system of higher education (including high school, college and university education) were presented earlier. To recapitulate, he believed that it achieved none of the true aims of education. The exclusive use of English, rather than the mother tongue, made it inevitable that the students should rely more on memory than on understanding. Indeed the system attached much more value to memorising bits and pieces of information of little use or relevance ('London is on the Thames' is an example Gandhi cites from personal experience) than to training the mind, body or character.

> The labour spent on studies is considered useless drudgery which has to be gone through that one might take the final examination, and once this is over we manage to forget as quickly as possible what we had studied.[57]

The system encouraged rote learning, inhibited intellectual growth and penalised originality. Physical education was neglected and manual dexterity held in contempt. The nature of their education, suggests Gandhi, was partly responsible for the middle classes having 'almost lost the use of their hands'.[58] The failure of the educational process to develop the students' faculties in a proper way was in Gandhi's view directly responsible for unemployment among the educated, especially among the arts students who formed the bulk of those pursuing higher studies in India: 'It is my firm conviction that the vast amount of the so-called education in arts given in our colleges is sheer waste and has resulted in unemployment among the educated classes.'[59]

These college-educated young men, noted Gandhi, were driven from pillar to post in search of jobs but they lacked useful and marketable skills. Gandhi compares them unfavourably with illiterate artisans who, at least, could earn a livelihood. On receiving education, instead of trying to improve the standards of their traditional vocations they give them up as something inherently inferior and consider it an honour to become clerks. But there were not enough clerical jobs to go round and their education had rendered them incapable of other, more useful, types of work. When an interviewer, discussing the problem of educated unemployment in India, referred to the 'overproduction of intelligence in India', Gandhi disagreed: 'The brain power has not at all increased, only the art of memorising has been stimulated, and these degrees cannot be carted to the villages. Only the brains, if there are any left, can be used.'[60]

Gandhi was prepared to concede that the foreign rulers who had imposed *pax Brittanica* on India 'have introduced education of a sort, have built schools and colleges, and built an unrivalled railway system'.[61] But while in other countries these things had brought material prosperity such was not the case in India. 'Not only the wealth of the land but even our intelligence has been drained away.'[62] This kind of education may have been suited to the requirements of a colonial economy but it had to be replaced if an independent India was to prosper.

Gandhi did not develop a Nayee Talim for the university but his views on university education are scattered throughout his writings and I shall only take up two specific issues. The first is what should determine the level and composition of a society's expenditure on higher education. Gandhi held that the relevant criterion was society's welfare rather than the specialist interests of scholars, 'I would revolutionise college education and relate it to national necessities.'[63] Accordingly, he strongly opposed any expansion of higher studies in the liberal arts in post-independence India, and suggested that the state should stop running any arts college. On the other hand he was in favour of the setting up of both colleges and universities for the study of what he considered to be socially more useful disciplines such as medicine, engineering, natural sciences and agriculture (including animal husbandry, horticulture and rural economics).

A second important question is how higher education should be financed. Gandhi's opposition to the financing of primary education by the state extended to higher education as well. Partly, this arose out of a predilection in favour of private as against state activity in general, and partly it was based on an argument from equity: 'I am not against higher education. But I am against a few *lakhs* of boys and girls receiving it at the expense of the poor taxpayer.'[64] As a general principle he proposed that 'higher education should be left to private enterprise and for meeting national requirements whether in the industries, technical arts, *belles-lettres* or fine arts'.[65] This implied a 'user pays' approach to the financing of higher education. The state should pay for the education of those whose services it would directly need while for all other branches of learning it should simply encourage private effort, including the granting of university charters liberally to 'any body of persons of proved worth and integrity, it being always understood that the universities will not cost the state anything except that it will bear the cost of running a central education department'.[66] By the same token, private industrial houses should pay for training of the engineering graduates they required. Medical colleges should be attached to certified hospitals and funded by voluntary contributions from the wealthy. Agricultural colleges should be financially self-supporting and their graduates should serve their apprenticeships on the farm rather than have to gain all their experience after graduation and at the expense of their employer.

After India gained independence the state governments came under political pressure to open new universities. Gandhi tried, unsuccessfully, to resist such claims and expressed the opinion that it was not for a democratic state to find money to set up universities. The idea that the Government should promote education by spending huge sums of money for setting up universities, he found totally unacceptable. 'If the people want them they will supply the funds.'[67]

Whatever their source of funding, universities, stated Gandhi, should practise stringent economy, avoid all pomp and splendour and try to develop strong links with the community. 'A university never needs a pile of majestic buildings and treasures of gold and silver. What it does need most of all is the intelligent backing of public opinion.'[68] The same reasoning explains his lack of enthusiasm for schemes which would help Indian students in undertaking higher and technical studies abroad. While agreeing that there was 'much to learn in foreign countries', he argued that attracting foreign scholars to India would be a more cost-efficient means of acquiring such learning than Indian students going abroad.

Gandhi claimed that he was not an enemy of higher education. 'But I am an enemy of higher education as it is given in this country.'[69] The real target of his hostility was elitism in education, even if it fostered enclaves of excellence. Higher education, he believed, could truly flourish only in a society where elementary education had become universal. 'University is at the top. A majestic top can only be sustained if there is a solid foundation.'[70] Nayee Talim was designed to provide such a foundation. For a poor country characterised by mass illiteracy and a colonial past to rush headlong into building a multitude of universities at considerable cost to the public exchequer was in his view neither efficient nor equitable. Instead he wanted facilities for higher studies to develop at a more measured pace but at the same time more in accordance with national needs.

> Under my scheme there will be more and better libraries, more and better laboratories, more and better research institutes. Under it we should have an army of chemists, engineers and other experts who will be real servants of the nation and answer the varied and growing requirements of a people who are becoming increasingly conscious of their rights and wants. And all these experts will speak not a foreign language but the language of the people.[71]

CONCLUSION

One way of looking at Gandhi's ideas on education is within the framework of his own thoughts on economics and society. What are the questions that he tries to answer? Are his answers to these mutually consistent? And are they consistent with the views that he expressed on other topics? These are the points one would then have to check. Alternatively, one could try to look at Gandhi's views on education 'from outside', from the perspectives of economics, education, psychology and so on. This would require one to compare his views on various specific issues with those held by others. In my discussion above I have sometimes adopted one approach and sometimes the other. In conclusion I shall make a few general comments on each.

There are some common elements in Gandhi's approach to social and economic issues that I have been trying to bring out in this study. That the individual is, ultimately, the relevant unit of account; that the individual's primary goal is self-realisation; that in pursuing it the individual must take the similar goal of other individuals into account, that religion is inseparable from ethics and ethics from the messy business of making choices constrained by the scarcity of resources, that in making such choices one has to rely not on established authority but on one's own conscience, and on experience gained by experimenting with truth and correcting errors – these are such common elements. Gandhi's concept of education is constituted from these just as much as his concepts of rights, inequality, industrial relations and the choice of technology. In this sense his ideas on education are entirely consistent with the rest of his thought. I should like to cite an example.

A former colleague of Gandhi's suggested to him that he should include military training as part of his educational programme for the young, for it would make them stand straight, think straight and speak straight. That Gandhi rejected the suggestion is not perhaps surprising; but he justified this not by appealing to the principle of non-violence but by an empirical argument, namely that military training did not, in fact, have the virtues claimed. Gandhi stated:

> My experience teaches me differently. I have known men in khaki rolling in gutters instead of standing straight. I have seen Dyer thinking crooked and speaking not straight but nonsense. I have known a Commander-in-Chief being unable to think at all, let alone thinking straight.[72]

Similar arguments occur frequently in Gandhi's writings. Although Gandhi had no formal knowledge of theories of education, some of his ideas have striking similarity with modern educational theory as developed, in particular, by the American philosopher and educationist, John Dewey. Gandhi shared two basic notions with Dewey: that education is a process of living, rather than only a preparation for future living; and that the 'natural development' and 'social efficiency' aims of education are inter-linked. It is the former notion that underlies Gandhi's refusal to accept drudgery as a necessary aspect of school while the second leads directly to his emphasis on the economic aspect of education at all stages. The following passage by Dewey on the economic role of education could just as well have come from Gandhi:

> Persons cannot live without means of subsistence.... If an individual is not able to earn his own living and that of the children dependent on him, he is a drag or parasite upon the activities of others.... No scheme of education can afford to neglect such basic considerations. Yet in the name of higher and more spiritual ideals, the arrangements for higher education have not only neglected them, but looked at them with scorn as beneath the level of educative concern.[73]

Dewey goes on to add that with the change from an oligarchical to a

151

democratic society, 'the significance of an education which should have as a result ability to make one's way economically in the world', should now receive more attention. In the context of a change from an autocratic, colonial society to a modern, democratic one, Gandhi made the same point.

Not only did Dewey and Gandhi set similar goals for education, they also agreed in giving crafts a central role in the school curriculum. Nayee Talim bears a family resemblance to Dewey's educational programme for American schools. Dewey, too, rejected the literary approach to education which combines 'slavish dependence upon books with real inability to use them effectively',[74] and 'turns out citizens with no sympathy for work done with the hands'.[75] He proposed instead that learning should come through activities related to the actual life of the child and that for this purpose adult occupations should form the core around which the entire curriculum was built. Where the material prosperity of a community was bound up with one or two industrial occupations, the purpose of education, he argued, would be best served by using them as the core. This would help towards integrating the school with the pupil's wider environment and the school curriculum with home life. As we have seen this was one of Gandhi's principal concerns. Dewey also regarded the practice of crafts as being necessary for practical and motor training of children, which would balance their intellectual development. He even anticipated Gandhi in recommending that reading and writing should be integrated with the child's life rather than treated merely as mechanical skills and that they should start not at the beginning of the learning process as at present but at a later stage.

While the educational reforms proposed independently by Gandhi and Dewey had much in common, the milieus in which the reforms were expected to work were vastly different. Dewey's America was an industrial society which had achieved economic progress by applying modern science and technology on a massive scale to the process of production, which was precisely the kind of economic growth that Gandhi opposed. Industrialisation, as Dewey notes, had itself endowed industrial occupations with far greater intellectual content and cultural possibilities than they used to possess.[76] In a semi-rural setting the intellectual and cultural horizons opened up by vocational education could be much more restricted than Gandhi realised.

Another renowned educationist with whom Gandhi had ideas in common is Maria Montessori. These relate to the learning process for children. The essence of Montessori's method is:

that the child must be self-motivated in order to become an active learner, one who does not merely receive a given body of knowledge as inert ideas to be memorised and repeated but who discusses for himself and is able to apply what he learns to new situations.[77]

It was the memorising of inert ideas that Gandhi saw as the most stifling feature of the colonial educational system and he tried to develop methods, and a milieu, such that the child would be an active participant in the learning process.

A more surprising ally is Mao Tse-tung. While Mao relied on organised class struggle, not *satyagraha*, for bringing about a revolutionary transformation of society, education played an important part in his concept of revolution from below; and some of his ideas on school and university education are very similar to Gandhi's. Mao deplored the overwhelming emphasis on book-learning and the neglect of practical activities that characterised traditional Chinese education. He wrote:

It takes a total of sixteen, seventeen or twenty years for one to reach the university from primary school and in this period one never has a chance to look at the five kinds of cereals, to look at how the workers do their work, how peasants till their fields, and how traders do their business.[78]

A university graduate, observes Mao, has not taken part in any practical activities or applied what he has learnt in any field of life. 'All he has is a book.'[79] Such an approach, according to Mao, cuts off the educational process from society and breeds contempt for manual labour.[80] Gandhi, as we have seen, voiced the same concerns.

Mao also, at one stage, believed like Gandhi that schools should be financially self-supporting. During the 1930s Mao singled out for praise those schools which did not depend on government for financial support and which managed to set up educational and productive facilities and to fund their own projects. He encouraged schools to undertake productive enterprises which would help them in achieving long-run financial viability.[81]

Although Gandhi cannot be said to have made any formal contribution to educational theory, or to the economics of education, he has some valuable insights to offer, especially to those concerned with problems of education in poor, developing countries with a largely rural population. Among these I regard the following as particularly relevant: first, that in allocating resources in such a country, elementary education should have priority over higher education; second, the quality and content of education, and not just its amount, matter; third, that how far in any society the external economies claimed for education are actually achieved depends on the prevailing system of education and on the social structure; and finally, that there is a case for a more significant role being played by the private sector in the provision of educational services. I should like to conclude by pointing out that Gandhi has often been depicted as an obscurantist, an enemy of science. Yet it was science that he wanted children to learn: 'I value education in the different sciences. Our children cannot have too much of chemistry and physics.'[82] What he opposed was an exclusively literary approach to education that neither helped one learn how to think for oneself nor served social needs.

8

SPECIAL TOPICS

POPULATION POLICY

This chapter is divided into two parts, each dealing with a 'special topic'. The first part discusses Gandhi's views on population policy and the second, Gandhi's 'predecessors'.

Among Gandhi's opinions regarding population policy the one which has attracted the most attention is his determined opposition to the use of contraceptive devices and it is on this that I shall focus; but I begin the discussion by considering Gandhi's position on two 'theoretical' issues that have a bearing on population policy in general.

This first is whether in arriving at a judgement on the overall level of welfare of a society, one should be concerned solely with the welfare per head of the population or should attach weight to population size as well. The second issue is when, if at all, a country can be said to be over-populated. A question that has some significance for population policy is whether in assessing the level of welfare of a society any weight should be attached to numbers as such. The utilitarian approach to population control as interpreted by Sidgwick suggests that it should. According to him:

> the point up to which, on Utilitarian principles, population ought to be encouraged to increase is not that at which average happiness is the greatest possible – as appears to be often assumed by political economists of the school of Malthus – but at which the product formed by multiplying the number of persons living into the amount of average happiness reaches its maximum.[1]

This issue has also been extensively discussed in the literature on the optimum size of population. Which side of this debate would Gandhi have been on? He would not, in any case, agree to regarding happiness as equivalent to welfare; nor would he define welfare only in terms of economic considerations. For him, as pointed out earlier, if a standard of living is thought of as a level of welfare then moral and material welfare must both be included in the reckoning. However, even if this broader definition of welfare was adopted and the difficulties involved in bringing moral and material elements into a common unit of measurement somehow resolved, the question of whether total or average welfare is the proper focus of concern would still remain relevant.

Passages occur throughout Gandhi's writings on population suggesting that for a judgement on the level of society's welfare he would be against imputing any weight to numbers as such. In an early piece, written in 1913, he deplores the fact that whenever a child is born we give thanks to God, and describes this as 'only a way of covering up our pitiable condition'.[2] And he asks: 'Of what good is it to India or the world to be swarmed over with worthless creatures, as with ants?'[3] It was the 'worthiness' of the life lived by each person, not the numbers living, that mattered. In the course of an interview in 1935, when asked if he believed in 'many children', he replied that he believed in 'no children', though he conceded that this was an ideal that could not be realised in practice.[4] On the eve of independence he declared: 'The propagation of the race rabbit-wise must undoubtedly be stopped.'[5] Clearly numbers as such held no appeal for Gandhi, whose over-riding concern was quality rather than magnitude. A related, though distinct, issue is the meaning of 'over-population'. In Gandhi's time, and ours, the concept of over-population has been linked to the Malthusian theory of population. To Malthus and his followers there is a natural tendency for the growth of numbers, which is governed by 'the passion between the sexes', to out-run that of the means of subsistence, which is limited by the supply of factors of production, especially land. 'Positive checks' such as famines are nature's way of restoring balance. Considerations of this kind still exert a powerful influence on discussions of the world 'population explosion' and on population policy in developing countries.

Some of Gandhi's writings on population growth strike a distinctly Malthusian note, for example: 'If people want to multiply like rabbits they will have also to die like rabbits.'[6] At other times he appears more sceptical. 'This little globe of ours is not a toy of yesterday. It has not suffered from the weight of over-population through its age of countless millions.'[7] Gandhi was not arguing that something that did not happen in the past cannot happen in future. In criticising a book which he thought had attacked Malthus unfairly, Gandhi notes that modern science has enormous power to save life, which could lead to a large reduction in death rates. Without a corresponding fall in birth rates an 'unbearable increase' in population would be the outcome.[8] However, Gandhi held a more optimistic view of human nature than Malthus. Human beings were rational agents and they were adaptable. They had succeeded in averting the threat of global over-population by ingenuity and self-restraint, and would continue to do so in the future. The fear of over-population sprang from the fear of securing 'reasonable comfort' for the existing population but such fear was exaggerated if not entirely misplaced.

There was another important difference between Gandhi and Malthus: Gandhi emphasised that the means of subsistence available to a society depended not only on factor-endowments but on how these factors were being utilised. Here the political element played a crucial role. 'India is today ill-equipped for taking care even of her present population, not because she is over-populated but because she is forced to foreign domination whose creed is progressive exploitation of her resources.'[9] He was making the same point on the eve of independence: the occurrence of famines cannot by itself be taken as evidence of over-population. It was simplistic to see famines in India in Malthusian perspective, i.e. as an expression of 'positive checks' undertaken by nature in order to prevent population growth from out-running the means of subsistence 'The famines of India are not a calamity descended upon us from nature but a calamity created by the rulers – whether through ignorant indifference or whether consciously or otherwise does not matter.'[10]

Gandhi adds that the prevention of drought, the principal cause of crop failure and famine, was not beyond the reach of human effort and ingenuity, which had indeed proved effective elsewhere. In colonial India, 'a sustained intelligent effort' towards this end had never been made.[11] If in free India such an effort was made, the phantom of over-population could be exorcised. Indeed, Gandhi's opinion was that given this effort 'this country is capable of supporting twice as many people as there are in it today'.[12] Not that Gandhi was in favour of doubling the population size: he would have viewed such a prospect with horror. He was simply questioning whether India was 'over-populated' in the Malthusian sense of the term. And in this, he was continuing the tradition of Indian economic nationalists who had long maintained that it was not over-population but colonial rule, and the misallocation of resources resulting from it, that kept India poverty-stricken and famine-prone. I have discussed their arguments elsewhere.[13] I shall now take up my principal topic; Gandhi's attitude to birth control.

By the 1920s the movement for controlling births by the use of contraceptive devices, which had started in some Western countries, had reached India as well. It was confined to a section of the Indian educated middle-class living in metropolitan centres. Gandhi quickly declared himself to be an opponent of the wider use of contraception. As he noted then and repeated later, artificial methods of birth control in some form or other had long been used in all societies.

> The practice of preventing progeny by means of artificial methods is not a new thing. In the past such methods were practiced secretly and they were crude. Modern society has given them a respectable place and made improvements. They have been given a philanthropic garb.[14]

Gandhi opposed the movement for birth control with much vehemence. He regarded the use of artificial methods for preventing births as morally unacceptable and he held fast to this opinion to the very end of his life though the topic itself appears less and less often in his later writing. His arguments, by and large, are much the same as those used by doctrinaire opponents of birth control, such as orthodox Catholics, elsewhere. His first argument is that the opportunity of satisfying sexual desire without the possibility of having children as a consequence would eliminate the need for self-restraint and thereby encourage reckless or immoral behaviour. 'Artificial methods are like putting a premium upon vice. They make men and women reckless.'[15] Births had to be controlled but rigid sexual self-restraint, both within and outside marriage, was the answer.

Second, sexual union was intended by God for progeny and no other purpose. Third, contraceptives are an 'unnatural interference' which contravenes the laws of nature.[16] Fourth, it is wrong to try to avoid the consequences of one's own action. 'It is a sin to bring forth unwanted children but I think it is a greater sin to avoid the consequences of one's own action.'[17] The use of contraceptives would enable people to avoid the first sin, but only at the cost of committing the second.

There are two methods of birth control to which Gandhi did not object. One is the 'safe period' method in which sexual intercourse is restricted to a period of about 10 days in a month. He gives two reason for not condemning it in the way he condemned the use of contraceptive devices: it had an element of self-control, which had to be exercised during the rest of the month; and it was open in practice 'largely only to married couples'.[18] The other method is sterilisation of males. While condemning proposals for compulsory sterilisation as inhuman Gandhi appears at one stage to have regarded voluntary sterilisation as an acceptable way of preventing births. 'Sterilisation is a sort of contraceptive and though I am against the use of contraceptives in the case of women I do not mind voluntary sterilisation in the case of man, since he is the aggressor.'[19]

However he seems to have had second thoughts about this, for in a letter written later in the same year he writes that he cannot express a definite opinion about the method but is inclined against it on the grounds that coercion was likely to arise in applying it and that it could (like other methods of contraception) cause more immorality.

While opposing the use of contraception, Gandhi continued to describe himself as a supporter of birth control. And though he calls on both men and women to control births by the exercise of self-restraint Gandhi suggests that women have a special responsibility in this matter that goes well beyond self-restraint: they should also restrain their male partners. Gandhi tried to justify this emphasis by a number of arguments. Sexual intercourse, to have any claim to legitimacy, had to be based on mutual consent. 'In my opinion sexual union to be legitimate is permissible only when both the parties desire it. I do not recognise the right of either partner to compel satisfaction.'[20] On the other hand, according to Gandhi, while both males and females were subject to sexual passion, male and female sexuality were not identical in nature. 'I do not believe that woman is prey to sexual desire to the same extent as man. It is easier for her than for man to exercise self-restraint.'[21] Furthermore, women, who had to bear the burdens of pregnancy and child-care, were more likely than men to be inclined towards a smaller family size. Gandhi suggested, that women should help towards reducing the frequency of sexual intercourse, 'by learning to say "no" to their husbands when they approached them carnally'. They should, in other words, undertake a form of non-violent non-cooperation. This was not as unrealistic as it seemed, for 'I do not suppose all husbands are brutes, and if women only knew how to resist, then all will be well'.[22] Such knowledge could be acquired. 'I hold that the right education in this country is to teach woman the art of saying no even to her husband, to teach her that it is no part of her duty to become a mere tool or doll in her husband's hands.'[23]

Suggesting that this was not realistic, Mrs Nair, a leading social worker of Cochin who had come to interview Gandhi on his views about birth control, pointed out that for a Hindu woman without income or assets of her own, to defy her 'Lord and Master' in this way might have disastrous consequences: under the law as it stood she could be denied maintenance and lose her home.[24] Again Gandhi had no answer, except to say that this could only be true of a microscopic minority of women.

Gandhi often combined rigid commitment to an abstract principle with considerable flexibility in its application. At an early stage of the debate on birth control, he had already come to believe that 'it is likely that artificial means of birth control will continue to be used. But it is necessary to create a climate of opinion in which they are regarded as undesirable'.[25] His moral arguments against birth control were designed precisely for this purpose. But he also resorted to a more pragmatic argument. 'Assuming that birth control by artificial aids is justifiable under certain conditions it seems to be utterly impracticable of application among millions.'[26] Indeed, he suggests, it may even be 'easier to induce them to practise self-control than control by contraceptives'.[27] Even if such methods gained popularity among educated middle-class people living in towns those who most needed to limit their families would not be easily reached in this way; and 'the poor women who may be obliged to bear children against their will' would find little help from campaigns for birth control.[28]

Whatever his case, Gandhi usually argued well. This cannot be said of his case against contraception, which consists not so much in the careful marshalling of facts and logic as in the reiteration of what has to be proved. Thus, for example, the argument that contraceptives invariably lead to recklessness, that as he puts it, given access to such devices, 'men and women will be living for sex alone',[29] not only lacks credibility but is inconsistent with his usual view of human nature which he credits with considerable powers of rationality and discipline. As regards the argument from artificiality, a critic pointed out that if the use of contraceptives is to be rejected on that ground, so should that of dentures and artificial limbs. To this Gandhi had no real answer, stating merely that while false teeth, too, were indeed artificial and unnatural, they served a necessary purpose which artificial methods of birth control did not – thus in effect conceding the critic's point, namely that 'artificiality' as such did not constitute a sufficient ground for rejection.[30] More serious perhaps, and certainly more typically Gandhian, is the argument that one should face up to the consequence of one's actions; but it turns entirely on how the 'action' itself is defined: one who uses contraceptive devices could well claim that he *is* facing up to the consequences of his action; namely the avoidance of births. That Gandhi himself had some doubts about his case against contraception is suggested by the fact that on occasion he assumed the role of the devil's advocate, presenting the case *for* contraception. This he did by spelling out the logic of a letter written to him by a woman who supported the wider use of artificial methods of birth control. He interprets the correspondent as saying something like the following:

> We the advocates of contraception have come on the scene only recently. You self-controllers have had the field to yourselves all these long generations, maybe thousands of years. What have you to show to your credit? Has the world learnt the lesson of self-control? What have you done to stop the misery of over-burdened families?[31]

Gandhi notes that between the supporters of contraception and himself there is common ground, for their long-run aims are similar. They do not bear him ill-will because of his advocacy of self-restraint but even wish him success in his effort, for he might perhaps save some wives from the unwanted approaches of their husbands. But they ask:

> Why should you seek to decry the methods which we employ and which take note of and make every allowance for common human weaknesses or habits and which when properly employed almost never fail to accomplish their purpose?[32]

Gandhi states his correspondent's case with sympathy and puts on record his appreciation of 'the anguish of a sister filled with compassion for the families that are always in want because of the ever-increasing number of children'.[33] He does not succeed, however, in providing an effective answer to her question. All he can say is that in settling issues of this kind a long time-horizon is called for and that one should not lose patience.

In another article written a few years later, Gandhi sets out the case for contraception in a slightly different way. What its advocates are saying, according to Gandhi, is that sexual desire is a natural instinct which it is not desirable to suppress, even if that was possible, and that the control of births by the exercise of self-restraint is difficult to practice. If a substitute for self-restraint is not prescribed, the health of innumerable women is bound to suffer through frequent pregnancies. Further, if births are not regulated, the result will be over-population.

Individual families will be pauperised, and their children will be ill-fed, ill-clothed and ill-educated. Therefore it is the duty of scientists to devise harmless and effective methods of birth control.[34] This version of the case, too, receives some sympathy from Gandhi, though he does not agree with its basic premise that to suppress the sexual instinct is either undesirable or impossible. He concludes the article by saying that the argument had failed to convince him because the benefits of contraception were outweighed by its evils. The use of contraception 'bids fair to kill the desire for self-restraint' which was too heavy a price to pay for any possible immediate gain.

Gandhi did not, however, rely on sexual restraint, whether exercised by oneself or imposed by one's partner, as the sole means of controlling births. He was, as I have noted, committed to a slower rate of population growth both in India and in the world at large, but he wanted to bring this about without relying either on coercion or on the use of 'artificial' devices of birth control. He had therefore to rely, apart from restraint in sexual behaviour, on trying to change customs and beliefs which tended to promote an increase in population. Among these is the practice of marriage. There was no reason why every person should be expected to marry yet in India this was the prevailing norm. And perhaps this explained why the incidence of marriage was so very high. In European countries celibacy commanded social respect and the proportion of the population, and in particular that of the female population, who never married was much greater. 'Spinsters among us are practically unknown except the nuns who leave no impression on the political life of the country. Whereas in Europe thousands claim celibacy as a common virtue.'[35]

A change in the prevailing belief system, especially among women, could help bring this about. 'If the mothers of India could be inclined to believe that it is sinful to train boys and girls for a married life, half the marriages in India will automatically stop.'[36] But 'every girl, every Indian girl is not born to marry. I can show many girls who are today dedicating themselves to service instead of serving a single man'.[37]

Another change which would have the effect of slowing population growth, and for which Gandhi campaigned throughout his life, was raising the age of marriage. He denounced the custom of child marriage, which was widespread in India, and claimed that the lowest age of marriage for males that was permitted by Hindu scriptures was 25 years. Gandhi's own view was that it should be revised further to 30 or so.[38]

A higher birth rate was also encouraged by social approval of a large family size as the norm: 'the superstition of larger families being an auspicious thing, and therefore desirable, still persists'.[39] However, social norms were not something fixed and unchanging: they could be changed by educating the public. Symbolically a start could be made by cutting down on the celebration of new arrivals. 'Every untimely addition to the family is ushered in amid trumpets of joy and feasting.'[40] Gandhi, on the contrary, confessed to feeling nothing but sorrow when he heard of births in this land.[41] Society had to move towards adopting a small family size as the norm and ideally the norm should be a one-child family. Gandhi even claimed to have found approval for the one-child norm in Hindu scriptures.

Gandhi's views on population policy are largely of historical interest only. While he was strongly against a large family size being the social norm, his proposed means of preventing that outcome are much the same as those proposed by Malthus. Unlike Malthus', Gandhi's writings on birth control are also marked by a horror of sex bordering on the pathological. His attitude recalls that of some of the early Christian Fathers but is totally at variance with the Hindu tradition to which Gandhi professed to belong. In that tradition *Kama* was regarded, along with *Artha*, *Dharma* and *Mokhsa* as an essential component of a virtuous and balanced life.

GANDHI'S PREDECESSORS

The special topic discussed in this part of the chapter is 'Gandhi's predecessors'. I should like to begin this discussion by pointing out that Gandhi's ideas on moral, economic and political issues were very much his own. Whenever he borrows concepts from others, whether from the *Bhagavadgita* or Buddha or Tolstoy or Ruskin or textbooks on jurisprudence, he gives them a twist that brings them into line with the thrust of his own thinking. While such borrowings helped, sometimes by extending his 'repertoire' beyond its habitual range, and more often by confirming to Gandhi himself that he was on the right track, his interpretations of the originals are often far from reliable, and the ideas even of some whom he acknowledged as his mentors – Ruskin is the most striking example – were actually not only very different from but often opposed to his own.

Second, Gandhi had a great many 'predecessors' who thought on the same lines as he did in some respect or other. The writings of the great Indian social reformers of the nineteenth century, Swami Vivekananda in particular, provide parallels to Gandhi's approach to social issues.[42] Here, however I shall consider only two – Buddha and Ruskin. Iyer remarks: 'Gandhi's moral and political insights grew out of a coherent set of concepts, the nuances of which he explored over six decades.'[43] It was the coherence of his own concepts on basic issues that enabled him to borrow from others without becoming either inconsistent or excessively eclectic. For the purpose of gaining understanding of Gandhi's social and economic thought, I would regard Buddha as his most significant 'predecessor'. The ethical approach to economic issues that marks Gandhi's writings has much in common with Buddhism.

Gandhi himself prefers to include Buddhism, along with Jainism, under the rubric of the 'Hindu' tradition. According to Gandhi, what Buddha did was to introduce a living reformation of the petrified faith that surrounded him. This was achieved through Buddha's overriding emphasis on the basic ethical values, truth and *ahimsa* and his attack both on the hierarchy of caste and on religious rites and ceremonies. 'Buddha', says Gandhi, 'fearlessly carried the war into the enemy's camp and brought down on its knees an arrogant priesthood.'[44] Eventually, Gandhi goes on, the jealousy of the Hindu priestly class succeeded in driving Buddhism away from the frontiers of India but the spirit of Buddhism was never erased. It was absorbed by Hinduism itself and its moral values lived on in the minds of the Indian people. Although, except on a few occasions, Gandhi does not explicitly acknowledge his debt to Buddhist thought, the elements of the Hindu ethic to which he most often appeals bear a Buddhist stamp. Iyer comments justly: 'Gandhi's radical reinterpretation of Hindu values in the light of the message of the Buddha was a constructive, though belated, response to the ethical impact of the early Buddhist reformation on decadent India.'[45]

Early in his political career Gandhi entered into a controversy with Tilak on the relationship of politics to ethics. Was the absolute commitment to truth and non-violence that Gandhi wished to impose on the Indian national movement really appropriate to the political arena? The Lokamanya thought not. It might be more appropriate, he suggested, for *sadhus*. But politics was a game of worldly people, not of *sadhus*. In a spirited rejoinder to Tilak, Gandhi insisted that the Buddhist maxim that non-anger wins over anger lays down an eternal principle and that this was the law not for the unworldly alone but essentially for the worldly. 'With deference to the Lokamanya, I venture to say that it betrays mental laziness to think that the world is not for *sadhus*.'[46] Ethics, according to Gandhi, was essentially a worldly enterprise and at its core was a desperate attempt to become *sadhu*. This debate has an ancient parallel in Indian political thought. According to Kautilya's *Arthasastra* each sphere of action had its own appropriate rules of conduct which represented its own morality. In politics 'reasons of state' were therefore to be regarded as binding. Buddhism on the contrary stood for the over-riding authority of moral law. While different types of activity might, indeed, be conducted by their own rules, these remained subject to the claims of ethics. 'Buddhism', notes Ghoshal, 'with its stern and unbending code of ethics stood for the unqualified supremacy of the moral law over governmental affairs.'[47] So did Gandhi. And this applied just as well to economic affairs.

Buddhism does not, however, regard economic activity as such as unethical. On the contrary it gives economic, and in particular business, enterprise an honoured place. For a proper perspective on Gandhi's economic thought, certain specific elements in the Buddhist approach to economics are especially relevant. First, a persistent theme of Buddhist texts is that the worldly and the spiritual spheres of activity are not different in kind. They are, as it were, cut from the same cloth and the conditions required for success in them have a large overlap. In the *Majjhimanikaya*, for instance, one who is successful in spiritual enterprise is likened to 'a rich and wealthy man on a long journey through the woods who should eventually emerge safe and sound without loss of goods'. Gandhi thought in much the same way. In formulating economic concepts such as *swadeshi* or trusteeship Gandhi often used a 'saintly idiom'. This, I believe, reflects not so much his religiosity as a belief that material and spiritual considerations can be described in much the same language.

Second, the general principle of economic conduct for the Buddhist layman is *appamada*, which translates roughly as paying attention and taking care. The basic virtues that this principle invokes are attention, carefulness, conscientiousness and diligence. The householder who seeks to follow the *Dhamma* must therefore work hard, avoid wasting resources, cultivate his skills, practise thrift and, without becoming possessive, take good care of his possessions. The householder who succeeds in acquiring wealth by honest means and through his own energy and effort, who does not run into debt and retains ownership of his property, who enjoys both material well-being and independence and who uses his wealth for the public good is commended by Buddha; and the wealth of such a man is described as 'wealth that has seized its opportunity, turned to merit and is fittingly made use of'. Gombrich sums up: 'Buddha *never* suggests that laymen should eschew property, he *commends* wealth which is righteously acquired by one's own effort.'[48]

Gandhi's concern with *appamada* runs through his writings on economic topics. It underlies his praise of productive power as a form of godliness: 'There is no separate species called gods in this universe, but all who have the power of production and will work for the community using that power are gods-labourers no less than capitalists.'[49] The same concern explains his emphasis on the crucial importance of personal effort. Even his own favourite project, *khaddar*, would, he said, be quite useless if it could be obtained without effort. '*Khaddar* has the greatest organising power in it because it has itself to be organised and because if affects all India. If *khaddar* rained from heaven it would be a calamity.'[50]

For the same reason, bettering one's economic condition by one's own active effort was superior to having the same outcome brought about by the state. 'It is one thing to improve the economic condition of the masses by state regulation of taxation and wholly another for them to feel that they have bettered their condition by their own sole personal effort.'[51]

The principle of *appamada* also provides a moral justification for being concerned with economic efficiency. Unlike many others who have criticised capitalist enterprise on moral grounds, Gandhi never rejected efficiency as a worthy norm. Whatever the project, be it a school or a *khadi* shop or a rural health care system or even arranging a marriage ceremony Gandhi always insisted on costs being reduced to the absolute minimum required to achieve a desired outcome. His persistent refusal despite criticism from the left, to condemn the acquisition of wealth, expresses the same spirit: 'my advice that monied men may earn their millions (honestly of course) but so as to dedicate them to the service of all, is perfectly sound'.[52]

Likewise, while condemning exploitation of workers by capitalists, he refused to condemn all businessmen as individuals: 'My relations with the rich will continue. I don't look upon the rich as wicked and upon the poor as angels.'[53] Statements of this kind are consistent with a Buddhist attitude to wealth which is in sharp contrast to that of the Christian Fathers who could see 'no possibility of acquiring great riches without resort to evil practices or inheritance from those who had resorted to them',[54] and for this reason called on all Christians to avoid seeking riches.

In commenting on scholastic economic thought Viner criticises St

Thomas, and by implication, followers of a religious approach to economics, for neglecting 'the possibility that the most socially beneficial use that individuals make of their ability and wealth is to engage in productive enterprise and to reinvest their earnings',[55] Gandhi certainly did not neglect it and indeed it is this possibility that provided him with a justification for trusteeship.

Another aspect of Buddhist thought that is relevant for an understanding of Gandhi's approach to economics concerns the assumption of self-interest. Interpreted as meaning that individuals are motivated *solely* by self-interest, it now forms the basis of the prevailing paradigm of neo-classical economics. As we have seen, Gandhi rejected this assumption. He never denied, however, the importance of self-interest as *one* of the basic motivations of individual behaviour. Buddhist teaching provides a useful corrective to the belief that forgetting one's own interest is necessarily a good thing. Buddha classifies men into four types: those who live thinking neither of their own good nor that of others, the second solely of others' good, the third solely of their own good, and the fourth both of their own good and that of others. It is the last group of men whom Buddha considers the best.[56]

Again, self-interest is not necessarily the opposite of altruism, for 'in helping oneself one helps another and in helping another one helps oneself'.[57] Disregarding the interest of others is unethical but so is disregarding one's own interest. This has economic implications. If people are, and should be, guided by self-interest alone it makes sense to adopt policies and arrange institutions in such a way that the expression of self-interest is unrestricted. Free markets will do the rest. On the Buddhist view, a more rational strategy would be to devise mechanisms of decision-making which enable self-regarding and other-regarding motivations to act in tandem. That the same view underlies many of Gandhi's recommendations on economic policy was pointed out in Chapter 2.

There are some other issues, such as those relating to the environment and the welfare of animals, on which Gandhi's pronouncements also sound a Buddhist note. Some of his ideas in this regard were discussed in Chapter 3. More directly, the doctrine of *ahimsa* led Gandhi to oppose popular movements for the abolition of landlordism which might involve violence, and also to propose drastic reductions in military and defence spending by the Government of India.

On some important issues Gandhi's ethical view differed from that of Buddhism. One such is whether charity is a virtue. Gandhi not only refused to regard charity as necessarily virtuous, some of his strongest moral criticism was directed at the indiscriminate practice of charity in India. His position was contrary to the Buddhist and Hindu view, which is that charitable donations confer merit on the donor irrespective of their consequences. The difference follows logically from the fact that the Buddhist commitment to altruism was rooted in one's feeling of sympathetic identification with other living creatures.[58] This is in essence, a form of 'self-regarding altruism'. The altruism that Gandhi favoured was, on the other hand, consequentialist in character.[59]

Again, while Gandhi's concept of *sarvodaya*, the welfare of all, is perfectly consistent with the Buddhist ethic, his principle of neighbourhood, which requires us always to give precedence to the welfare of a neighbour over that of someone who lives farther away, is not. Gandhi's was not a truly universalistic world view as Buddha's was.

The only other 'predecessor' of Gandhi whom I shall discuss is John Ruskin. Gandhi is commonly described as a disciple of Ruskin whose book *Unto This Last* he rendered into Gujrati in a series of articles under the title *Sarvodaya* (literally, the welfare of all). Gandhi pointed out at the time that he was not really attempting a translation but rather to present extracts from the book in a manner intelligible to Indians who did not know English. For this reason, he did not explain what the title of the book meant, for it could be understood only by a person who had read the Bible in English. Since, however, Gandhi took the aim of Ruskin's book to be working for the welfare of all, rather than only that of the greatest number, he chose to name it *Sarvodaya*.

That book, and particularly its first essay, 'The Roots of Honour', anticipates Gandhi in insisting on the importance of ethical considerations for economic analysis. Gandhi shared Ruskin's distrust of classical political economy with its model of 'economic man' engaged in the pursuit of individual self-interest; and he agreed with Ruskin that this provides too narrow a basis for understanding human conduct. Ruskin's belief that a purely economic model of human behaviour is necessarily mis-specified because 'the disturbing elements in the social problem . . . alter the essence of the creature under examination' finds repeated echoes in Gandhi's writings. Nevertheless the differences between Gandhi and Ruskin are far deeper than their similarities.

Gandhi and Ruskin held strikingly different views on the role of the state in social and economic life. Gandhi distrusted the state and denied that individuals owed it moral allegiance. He believed that except in certain special circumstances private enterprise was preferable both on ethical and economic grounds to state enterprise, and wanted the power and functions of the state to be restricted to a minimum. Ruskin, on the contrary, found in discipline and interference by the state the only true safeguard against national degradation and argued that 'government must have a degree of authority over the people of which we now do not so much as dream'.[60] Paternal help, should, however, accompany paternal discipline. His stern and watchful state would take care of every individual from the cradle to the grave. 'Every child must be fed, clothed and educated by the State.'[61] Even marriage would cease to be a decision by individuals and become instead a privilege conferred by the state on maidens and bachelors who were deemed to be worthy. Those who were, would – if they needed it – receive a fixed income from the state appropriate to their station in life for seven years from the date of their marriage. Likewise land would cease to be regarded as private property that could be sold or rented but would instead belong to the state which could lend any man as much land as was needful. The authority of the state was to be paternalistic but all-pervasive and the duty of individuals lay in submitting to that authority with grace and reverence. This logically implies, for instance, that there could never be a moral justification for civil disobedience.

Their opposing views on the role of the state reflect a basic conflict of moral attitudes. For Gandhi it is the individual who counts. Ruskin, on the other hand, imputes value not to the individual as such but rather to society itself, seen as an organic whole. Gandhi is committed to equality in the sense that treating people as equals is a basic value, asserts the inherent equality of all human beings and condemns any notion of hierarchy as a moral evil.[62] For Ruskin it is the inequalities among individuals and groups that are inherent and fundamental. Such inequalities, he believes, possess a permanent character and have the effect of dividing humankind into an ordered hierarchy, a ranking by merit based ultimately on blood and race. Ruskin claims to have observed such a hierarchy in nature, believes it to be sanctified by Holy Writ, and his vision of the ideal social order is based on it. The concept of hierarchy provides Ruskin with a ready-made theory of government.

My continual aim has been to show the eternal superiority of some men to others, sometimes even of one man to all others and to show also the advisability of appointing such persons or person to guide, lead, or on occasion even to compel or subdue their inferiors according to their own better knowledge and wiser will.[63]

But why should superiority, assuming it exists, be eternal, i.e. permanent? Ruskin, like many others, found the answer in race and lineage. Accordingly he argued that governing was a privilege that should be reserved for gentlemen. Ruskin's definition of a gentleman, the natural-born ruler of any society, was stated explicitly in racial terms: 'Its primal, literal and perpetual meaning is a man of pure race, well-bred in the sense that a horse or dog is well-bred.'[64] Between the well-bred and ill-bred 'human creature' there was as much difference as between a wolfhound and the vilest mongrel-cur.[65] This inequality was permanent and unalterable. Education could not provide a remedy. Ruskin was indeed a great believer in education but he saw it not as a leveller, but on the contrary as a reinforcer of existing inequalities in rank, merit and capacity. Education that tried to enhance the self-esteem of the disadvantaged was false education. 'And true education is a deadly cold thing, with a Gorgon's head on her shield, and makes you every day think worse of yourself.'[66]

Government by superior creatures was part of the natural order of things, but in Ruskin's England it was under threat: 'The so-called higher classes being generally of. purer race than the lower have retained the true idea and the convictions associated with it but are unable to speak them out.'[67] It was government by people of these higher classes, government by gentlemen, that Ruskin's 'socialism' wanted to restore. Parliamentary democracy he held in contempt: 'of all puppet-shows in the Satanic Carnival of the earth the most contemptible puppet-show is a Parliament with a mob pulling the strings'.[68] But even if there had to be a parliament it was 'wrong to compose our Parliament in great part of infidels and Papists, gamblers and debtors'.[69] Proposals that were being debated at the time for extension of the franchise filled Ruskin with horror and he was equally opposed to Catholic emancipation and votes for working men. Gandhi believed in universal suffrage.

The racial argument also provides a rationale for empire. Ruskin, a racist in the traditional sense of the term, believed that certain races were intrinsically superior to others. The 'English race', a race mingled of the best northern blood, was the highest race of all and this provided a moral basis for their establishing imperial rule over people of other breeds.

> England must found colonies as fast and far as she is able . . . seizing every piece of fruitful waste she can set her foot on, and there teaching these her colonists that their chief virtue is fidelity to their country and their first aim to advance the power of England by land and sea.[70]

Ruskin saw clearly that the imperial enterprise would require considerable resources to be used for military rather than peaceful purposes but he regarded this as entirely proper, provided only that the cultivation of the arts was maintained as well. A paternalistic state must discipline the masses into the arts of war as well as those of peace. Indeed he believed that the arts of peace *require* war: 'all the pure and noble arts of peace are founded on war; no great art ever yet rose on earth, but among a nation of soldiers'.[71] There is no place for *ahimsa* in Ruskin's moral world, and his cult of race, war and empire reminds one of Rudyard Kipling or Winston Churchill rather than Gandhi. In particular, the notion of the unity of war and peace was quite unacceptable to Gandhi, who expressed surprise that 'there are intelligent men who talk and gullible men who subscribe to the talk, of the "humanising influence" of war'.[72]

Clearly Ruskin's world outlook was not only very different from but in some respect directly opposed to Gandhi's. As Bondurant has observed, 'Gandhi did not share the more conservative views of Ruskin which held the common man inferior, erected an aristocratic hierarchy and denied the masses any political control on grounds of incompetence.'[73] Ruskin did not consider the masses of men as ends in themselves; rather he treated them as means to the ends of others. Gandhi, on the other hand, believed in the worth of the individual and considered the individual's welfare the ultimate social goal. Given such basic differences between them, why has Gandhi so often been regarded as a disciple of Ruskin?

The principal reason is that Gandhi himself, in his autobiography, acknowledges Ruskin as a mentor. Describing *Unto This Last*, which he read through the night on a train journey from Johannesburg to Durban, as a formative influence, Gandhi professes to have discovered some of his deepest convictions reflected in this 'great book' of Ruskin's which made him transform his life. However, this dramatic account of his debt to Ruskin appears highly exaggerated. Woodcock suggests that: 'from a principle of humility that made him reluctant to accept all the credit for his achievements',[74] Gandhi tended to exaggerate the influence of others on his thought, and also that because he was not a widely read man, the minor works of such writers as Ruskin and Tolstoy assumed greater importance for him than perhaps they really had. Moreover, much of what Gandhi claims to have discovered in Ruskin's 'great book' was simply not there. According to Gandhi, the essence of *Unto This Last* consists in three maxims:

1 That the good of the individual is contained in the good of all.
2 That a lawyer's work has the same value as a barber's in as much as all have the same right of earning their livelihood from their work.
3 That a life of labour, i.e. the life of the tiller of the soil and the handicraftsman, is the life worth living.

Maxim 2 is not stated directly by Ruskin. The concept of uniform wages, it is true, is implicit in the title of the book itself, which is borrowed from the Bible: in the parable of the vineyard labourers the householder pays a full day's wage to those hired at the eleventh hour, over-riding objections from the other workmen. However, Lee rightly warns against this being misconstrued as a plea for a living wage (which Gandhi himself was wont to make), or a fixed remuneration for all, even in the same job. It was rather a call for a fixed payment for work of a certain grade.[75] A bad workman would not, argues Ruskin, be able to undercut the good one, for he would not be able to work at that job at all. (Ruskin seems to be assuming a given aggregate demand for labour and a highly elastic labour supply.) All that can safely be asserted is that Ruskin wanted industrial wages to be just, as he thought those in the professions already were.

Whether Ruskin's book teaches maxim 3 is even more dubious. Fitch writes: 'The idea that manual occupations are degrading is constant with Ruskin and one of the primary aims of his society is to keep the dirty work and its moral effects to a minimum.'[76]

While maxim 1 is part of Ruskin's message in *Unto This Last*, it can be interpreted in two distinct ways: that individuals should be motivated by altruism rather than mere self-interest or that individuals exist for society rather than the other way round. Ruskin asserted both these propositions: Gandhi accepted the first but not the second.

Though Gandhi, for the most part, derived from Ruskin's book ideas that he either already held or was struggling with, it did have an important effect insofar as it provoked him to think through in a more systematic way the nature of the relationship between ethics and economics. There is no indication that Gandhi ever studied the works of Ruskin taken as a whole nor that he was aware of Ruskin's racist views. Such views, however, including a belief in the importance of 'breeding' in people as well as animals, were a part of the intellectual baggage carried by the British ruling elite in India[77] and to these Gandhi did occasionally refer in his political writings. Lee sums up Ruskin's 'moral' critique of political economy as follows: 'In place of "Liberty" and "Anarchy" was set order, hierarchy, obedience and place. All anarchy is the forerunner of poverty and all prosperity begins in obedience.'[78]

But as between obedience and anarchy, Gandhi's sympathies were with the latter. Lee points out further that it was the concept of an organic status-based society founded on authority that gave Ruskin a platform from which he could launch into contemporary liberalism and its ideological basis, political economy.[79] Gandhi too was a critic of classical political economy but his outlook was even farther away from Ruskin's than it was from Adam Smith's.

9

THE LEGACY OF GANDHI

This chapter is concerned with the impact of Gandhi's economic ideas and their long-run relevance. It will be brief, for much of what I have to say has been anticipated in previous chapters, in the course of my discussion of Gandhi's ideas on individual topics. The chapter consists of four sections. The first section considers the impact of Gandhian ideas on Indian economic policy. The relationship of economics with ethics is discussed in the second, and Gandhi's contributions to the concept of rural development in the third. The last section discusses some methodological issues.

THE IMPACT OF GANDHI ON INDIAN ECONOMIC POLICY

I shall begin by considering the impact of Gandhi's ideas on economic policy in India. Briefly, their impact was very limited. Shortly after India gained independence, a correspondent wrote to Gandhi complaining that although he had argued all his life in favour of 'moral' economic policies, now that the British power had quit and the Indian National Congress was governing India, Gandhi had become strangely silent. 'You write nothing against the unmoral economics of India,'[1] complained the correspondent. People had started believing that Gandhi was behind the economic policies being followed by the Congress government. Gandhi's reply was an admission of failure.

Those who are in charge of the government are my fellow-workers . . . If I have failed to convince them of the soundness and feasibility of the economics referred to by the correspondent, how should I expect to convince others? They do not feel that they would be able to carry the people of India with them in the prosecution of what may be summed up as the '*khadi* economics' and to renovate the villages of India through village industries.[2]

Gandhi's insight that his erstwhile fellow-workers who were now in charge of the Government did not believe in Gandhian economic policies and had no wish to put them into practice was entirely correct. So was his view that the people at large had grave doubts about their feasibility. Economists in India had always been sceptical about the Gandhian approach. In his early years of public life, Gandhi himself had sometimes shared their misgivings. 'This may prove wrong. Economists may tell us in the future that we were mistaken.'[3] Later, he came to distrust their advice, as is clear from a letter he wrote to a group of economists who wished to meet him. 'Do not tell me *ex cathedra* that the whole thing is doomed to failure, as some economists have done before. Such condemnation would not impress me.'[4]

The doubts were not confined to economists alone. A Christian missionary friend of Gandhi's who was sympathetic to his moral approach to economics had asked him: 'Can you put back the hands of the clock and induce people to take to your *khadi* and make them work on a mere pittance?'[5] At the time, Gandhi remarked that this friend 'did not know his India'.[6] Time has shown that, perhaps on this matter at least, his friend knew 'his India' better than Gandhi himself.

Gandhi had always insisted that truly ethical policies must be practicable, they should not involve continuing economic loss. A solution based on village industries could avoid such loss only by reducing costs or if there was a switch in consumers' preferences towards their products. The prevailing technology of rural industries did not allow any significant cost reduction. That would require the use of mechanical techniques of production, which was precisely what the Gandhian strategy was designed to avoid. And moral suasion, as Gandhi himself came to realise towards the end of his life, was not a reliable means of bringing about changes in consumers' preferences.

Gandhian economics came to be identified with the spinning wheel, and more generally, with village industry. But experience in India and elsewhere amply demonstrates that village industry is not an adequate answer to rural unemployment and mass poverty. Gandhi's position on technology does not, however, have to be interpreted so narrowly. The logic of that position, as I have argued in Chapter 4, could be expressed in terms of the relative factor-intensity argument. Gandhi's insights into the problem of choice of techniques in labour-abundant, capital-short economies continue to be relevant.

ETHICS AND ECONOMICS

In his lectures on ethics and economics, Amartya Sen argues that 'the nature of modern economics has been substantially impoverished by the distance that has grown between economics and ethics'.[7]

Gandhi's writings on economic topics over six decades can be seen as a lengthy effort to bridge that distance. That economic questions have an ethical dimension is not only a matter of common knowledge, it is also recognised in public debate on issues relating to economic policy. This dimension fails, however, to get reflected in the literature of economics which is restricted to what Sen has called the 'engineering approach', characterised by concern with primarily logistic issues rather than with ultimate ends. The failure has led not only to a trivialisation of the analysis of important social issues but also to a perception on the part of the public, and policy-makers, that theoretical economic analysis is not particularly relevant to the real world.

Taking the ethical aspect of economic behavior into account may help both towards enriching the quality of economic analysis and expanding its scope. However, it will not necessarily make it any easier to reach agreement on questions of policy, for, as Gandhi so clearly recognised, different ethical principles are involved in even the simplest actions and these principles may clash. Nevertheless, a Gandhian approach to the linking of economics and ethics could be useful in a number of ways.

First, formal and explicit recognition that ethical considerations of various kinds do influence the action of economic agents in varying degree, depending on circumstances, could help re-establish the links between normative and positive economics which have been severed by the prevailing neo-classical orthodoxy. A broader-based and more credible foundation for economic policy could be provided thereby.

Second, Gandhi's ethical stance builds a bridge between the two principal contending schools in current ethical theory, consequentialism and deontology. According to Gandhi, as was noted in Chapter 1, there is no wall of separation between means and ends, between an action and its outcome. Consequences may, therefore, attach to actions as such, as well as to the outcomes they may help to bring about. Indeed, from a moral point of view consequences may be attributed to the means adopted, i.e. the action performed, in a more direct and immediate sense than to outcomes achieved, for the outcome may depend not only on the agent's action but on those of other people as well for 'we have always control over our means but not over the end'.[8] Hence the individual is more capable of determining what is a feasible set of actions at any given time than of predicting what the consequences of those actions will be. But certain actions – the practice of untouchability, for example – may have an infinitely high degree of moral evil attached to them. While the argument maintains a consequentialist format, it does take care of core deontological concerns.[9]

Third, Gandhi was also much ahead of his time in pointing out that not all kinds of preference-satisfaction necessarily contributed to human welfare. Both for explaining observed behaviour and prescribing policy the concept of preference-satisfaction was more complex than economists allowed. What passes for preferences may simply be habits, often bad habits, picked up from the social milieu and, once adopted, carried on without considering alternatives or reflecting on consequences. A legacy of social history need not necessarily represent an adequate basis for individual or social choice. Economic development consisted not in satisfying such preferences to a greater and greater extent but in trying to change them. Indeed, according to Gandhi this was the central task confronting those who wanted to bring about a transformation of rural society.

> We have got to be ideal villagers, not these villagers with their queer ideas, or absence of ideas, about sanitation and giving no thought to how they eat and what they eat. Let us not, like most of them, cook anyhow, eat anyhow, live anyhow. Let us show them the ideal diet. Let us not go by mere likes and dislikes but get at the root of those likes and dislikes. Don't rest content with simply saying 'The food disagrees with me.' Find out the reasons why it disagrees . . . We have to teach them [villagers] how to economise in time, health and money.[10]

Last, Gandhi is concerned not only with what ethics can do for economics but also with what economics can do for ethics. The latter concern, which is quite unusual among moralist critics of the economic approach, leads him to suggest that if a project, however good it may be from an ethical point of view, requires continuing economic loss, it is unsound and should be avoided. Many of the projects usually recommended by religious lobbies surely fit that description.

GANDHI AND RURAL DEVELOPMENT

Gandhi's writings, especially those relating to his Constructive Programme, contain some valuable insights into the development process in a rural economy. One such insight is the need for decentralisation. With the decline and fall of the communist economic order the notion of planning for development has come into disrepute. The traditional nineteenth-century doctrine that *laissez-faire* offers the only way out of the poverty trap for rural societies, is rapidly becoming once again the 'received opinion' in development economics.

Those with direct experience of life and labour in village societies may find neither option satisfactory. The experience of less developed countries shows clearly enough that centralised state planning simply does not work. Yet the hazards of market failure have not vanished. Gandhi argued that a limited degree of decentralised planning was both possible and desirable, and explicitly dissociated himself from the view that the core of planning was centralisation. 'I must dissent from the view that the core of planning is centralisation. Why should not decentralisation lend itself to planning as well as centralisation?'[11]

As we have seen Gandhi's over-riding concern was the decentralisation of production, which was to be achieved through village industries. He was also opposed to centralised state control of the distribution of foodgrains or other necessary items, and spoke out against price-control and rationing which were being used as techniques of food planning in independent India. '"Control" is a vicious thing. It is responsible for much of the corruption that is rampant today.'[12] There were, he believed, enough cereals, pulses and oil-seeds in the villages of India. Growers did not understand the artificial control of prices, said Gandhi, and they naturally refused willingly to part with their stock at a price much lower than they commanded in the open market. This made price-control economically inefficient. The moral consequences were bad too for controls bred corruption and fraud. The risk of a temporary price rise in the wake of de-control seemed to Gandhi a lesser evil. His prediction that controls would breed corruption, in India as elsewhere, proved to be accurate. But they also bring out how his concept of the unity of ethics and economics worked in practice. In certain circumstances, for example during a famine, the law of supply and demand could serve as a 'devilish law' but Gandhi was in favour of using it as a basis for economic policy if circumstances warranted it, that is if ethical and economic considerations pointed in the same direction.

Second, Gandhi was much concerned with self-respect, a concept that is missing from the literature of development economics. For Gandhi as for Rawls it was the most important 'primary good'.[13] Concern for self-respect forms a common thread running through Gandhi's plea for the limitation of wants, his doctrine of bread-labour, his reservations about charity as a virtue and his insistence on cleanliness as an important element in one's standard of living. Three-quarters of the Indian people lived in villages, but the villagers no longer had the self-respect they had once enjoyed. Foreign rule, unclean and insanitary living conditions and habits, recurrent famines, endemic semi-starvation, enforced idleness for a third of the year, the inhuman practice of untouchability, all these had seriously eroded their human dignity and self-respect. Economic development was a means of bringing self-respect to the individuals who lived in villages and thereby to village society as a whole. It was not just a matter of money: 'You cannot bring a model village in being by the magic wand of money.'[14] Such a perspective implies that bundles of goods and services can no longer be regarded as the only constituent elements of economic development. Goods and services *are* important. Their availability up to a basic minimum is essential for self-respect, but a sense of independence is important too. The mechanism by which the consumption of goods and services by villagers is ensured is also important, not just the level of consumption alone. For this reason Gandhi disapproved of bureaucratic devices of a paternalistic welfare state, even if they were meant to benefit villagers. These were not, he thought, conducive to the long-term goals of self-respect and self-reliance, but instead made village people passive recipients of state charity. Gandhi did not live to see the enormous expansion in local, national and sometimes international bureaucracy in developing countries, purportedly in pursuit of the 'basic needs strategy' often acclaimed by development economists, but because he regarded self-respect as the most basic need of all he would probably have disapproved. And though much progress has been achieved in techniques of feeding the hungry by private, state and international agencies, few donors have seen fit to remember Gandhi's anguished cry: 'What kind of an arrogant servant of the poor was this who rides in comfort in a car between rows of people eating?'[15]

The attainment of self-respect is a goal of production as well as consumption activities. It is, Gandhi believed, an important issue in work motivation. Ranade and his followers had described economic development as a process of learning-by-doing, but how well or how fast people actually learned depended on the nature of their motivation. A major problem of 'command economies' is how to motivate people to work. Self-respect arising from a sense of participation in village level work activity could provide one such motivation. That required building up a practical framework for decision-making which was village-based, which sought to increase mutual trust and consultation and to keep caste and class conflicts to a minimum. This was what Gandhi meant by decentralised planning and it represented an approach rather than a programme. 'I cannot speak with either the definiteness or the confidence of a Stalin or a Hitler as I have no cut and dried programme which I can impose on the villagers.'[16] But one might ask, why should *planning* even if it is decentralised, be necessary at all? This is where Gandhi's thesis that rural development requires changing preferences comes in. The workings of the market can only reflect existing preferences (and incomes). But if the existing preferences of villagers, for example in respect of sanitation and health practices, reflect bad habits, increasing their incomes could make matters worse. It is their preferences that will have to be changed, and they can only do it themselves – but they will require help. External agencies can provide such help. In Gandhi's Constructive Programme his village workers drawn from the national movement were meant to play this part.

> He will not go out as a patron saint of the villages, he will have to go in humility with a broomstick in his hand. There is a Trinity of Evil – insanitation, poverty and idleness – that you will have to be faced with and you will fight them with broomsticks, quinine and castor oil and if you will believe me, with the spinning wheel.[17]

Of the three it was insanitation that was, according to Gandhi, the most formidable evil. Most of the diseases prevalent in rural society, in India or elsewhere, were directly or indirectly the result of insanitary habits. It was widely believed, said Gandhi, that insanitation was caused by poverty and that if economic conditions improve, sanitation was bound to improve as well, but this, he thought, was just not true. Poverty, he suggested, played a relatively small part in causing insanitary conditions. The latter, in his view, were the product of bad habits handed down from generation to

generation. Again the only effective remedy was education, together
with appropriate legislation, particularly at the level of municipalities.

SOME METHODOLOGICAL ISSUES

For contemporary critics of the methodology of modern, neo-
classical economics there is an important lesson to be learned from
Gandhi's writings: that to be an effective critic of a theory it is not
necessary to neglect its positive elements. Those who criticise
modern economic analysis for its narrow focus do have a point.
But they weaken their case by failing to recognise its many positive
aspects – among them its focus on the individual and its analytical
rigour – and falling back instead either on out-moded Marxist
dogma or the confused jargon of holism. Often, those who criticise
the economic approach for either a religious or a humanistic reason,
do so from a holistic point of view.

Human behaviour, they hold, constitutes a single organic whole:
because every aspect of human behaviour is tied inextricably to every
other, the analysis of any one aspect, such as the economic, is
impossible. Behaviour can only be observed or understood as a whole.
While the method of abstraction may indeed be applicable to the
natural sciences, it is, they argue, out of place in the discussion of social
or economic behaviour. Accordingly, a recent study which applauds
Gandhi as one of the pioneers of 'humanistic economics' states:
'Humanistic economics does not mix with scientific abstractions.
Dry calculations and mathematical abstractions should be avoided
and instead, men, women and their social institutions should be
studied.'[18]

If the method of abstraction does not apply, there cannot then be
any such thing as economic analysis. That was not, however, Gandhi's
view. He remained committed to the validity of analytical reasoning
based on abstraction. Those aspects of reality that were not of central
importance to the phenomenon being discussed could be abstracted
from and hence in effect be treated as 'disturbing factors'. Deductive
reasoning applied to a set of postulates was, he held, just as applicable
in social sciences as in mathematics and the natural sciences. Gandhi's
writings contain numerous references to Euclid, Galileo and Newton
whose approaches to problem-solving he held out as models for those
trying either to understand human behaviour or find solutions for
social problems. The essence of the scientific method is in Gandhi's

judgement trying to work out solutions to problems for oneself rather than taking someone else's word for it.

> A person who is scientifically inclined does not take the truth of anything for granted; he tries to prove it himself. In this way he develops his own intellect and also obtains knowledge of the potentialities of things.[19]

Scientists who came after, obtained great results *because* they followed this method and a *khadi* worker, suggests Gandhi, should adopt it too. There was a difference. Newton and Galileo were interested in following a scientific quest rather than in serving the masses but a *khadi* worker's concern was to find a solution to the problems of poverty and hunger. But this made it *more* necessary, not less, that the *khadi* worker too should follow the method of science.[20] The scientific method also involved the use of abstract definitions and concepts.

An example that Gandhi was fond of giving was that although Euclid's straight line might not be capable of being drawn on a blackboard, the impossibility of the task could not be permitted to alter the definition. That Gandhi criticised standard economic analysis for failing to take ethical considerations into account has sometimes been taken as indicating that he was against relying on deductive reasoning in economics. Not so. The problem with the economic model, as Gandhi saw it, was *not* that it abstracted from *some* aspects of reality but rather that the ethical aspects that it was abstracting from were central to the phenomena under study and that *these* could not properly be treated as disturbing factors. In choosing assumptions any set of postulates was *not* as good as any other: experience and intuition had a vital role to play. Nevertheless, if more appropriate assumptions were made and deductive reasoning rigorously applied conclusions that were both valid and relevant could be reached. And Gandhi never ceased to believe that such a 'new kind of economics' could indeed be developed.

Another philosophical position that Gandhi shared with standard economic theory is his firm commitment to methodological individualism. In both economics and ethics it is the individual who is, for Gandhi, the relevant unit of account. It is individuals, not groups, who can reason, have moral sense and exercise choice. Gandhi had little sympathy with the holistic notion that 'society' is ontologically prior to 'the individual' (i.e. that a society can exist in a way unrelated to the existence of individual members of it); or that social choice need not necessarily depend on choices by individuals making up the society. He consistently attacked collectivist theories of state and society. 'If the individual ceases to count what is left of society?'[21] That one can be a determined enemy of the inequality and injustice that are characteristic of societies driven by 'possessive individualism' without giving up a commitment to the individual is a valuable part of the legacy of Gandhi. His is a theory of non-possessive individualism.

NOTES

1 INTRODUCTION

1 J. J. Anjaria, 'The Gandhian Approach to Indian Economics', *Indian Journal of Economics*, 1941–42, volume 22, p. 357.
2 Ibid., p. 357.
3 *The Hindu*, 21 December 1931; *The Collected Works of Mahatma Gandhi*, 90 volumes, New Delhi, Government of India, Publications Division, 1958–84 (hereafter CW), 48, p. 353.
4 Speech at Gandhi Seva Sangh Meeting, 5 March 1936; CW 62, p. 241.
5 *Harijan*, 1 February 1948; CW 90, p. 480.
6 *Harijan Sevak*, 15 September 1946; CW 85, p. 267.
7 *Harijan*, 28 July 1946; CW 85, p. 33.
8 CW 10, p. 7.
9 Ibid.
10 Louis Fischer, *The Life of Mahatma Gandhi*, London, Cape, 1951, p. 466.
11 *Navajivan*, 8 August 1926; CW 31, p. 277.
12 Anjaria, op. cit., p. 358.
13 B. R. Nanda, *Gandhi and his Critics*, Delhi, Oxford University Press, 1985, p. 145.
14 Ibid.
15 *Amrita Bazar Patrika*, 5 January 1946; CW 82, p. 334.
16 *Harijan*, 29 March 1935; CW 60, p. 355.
17 Ibid., p. 355.
18 W. H. Morris-Jones, 'Mahatma Gandhi, Political Philosopher?', *Political Studies*, 1960, volume 8, p. 18.
19 *Harijan*, 3 October 1936; CW 63, p. 341.
20 *Navajivan*, 28 June 1925; CW 27, p. 308.
21 *Young India*, 6 October 1921; CW 21, p. 246.
22 *Young India*, 3 October 1929; CW 41, p. 496, italics added.
23 *Harijan*, 28 November 1936; CW 64, p. 85.
24 *Young India*, 21 July 1920; CW 18, p.73.
25 *Young India*, 5 March 1925; CW 26, p. 226.
26 *Young India*, 26 February 1925; CW 26, p. 202.

27 *Harijan*, 30 May 1936; CW 62, p. 388.
28 *Navajivan*, 19 June 1927; CW 34, p. 23.
29 W. H. Morris-Jones, op. cit., p. 18.
30 *Young India*, 13 October 1921; CW 21, p. 290.
31 *Young India*, 27 October 1921; CW 21, p. 357.
32 *Harijan*, 21 September 1934; CW 58, p. 353.
33 *Navajivan*, 8 August 1926; CW 31, p. 276.
34 *Navajivan*, 29 May 1927; CW 33, p. 392.
35 *Navajivan*, 22 September 1929; CW 41, pp. 449–50; *The Bombay Chronicle*, 15 November 1932; CW 51, p. 428; and Gandhi to Prabhashankar Pattani, 5 January 1933; CW 52, p. 373.
36 *Navajivan*, 8 September 1929; CW 41, p. 365.
37 An up-to-date account of the state of the debate will be found in Philip Pettit (ed.) *Consequentialism*, Aldershot, Dartworth, 1993. I have also found Anthony Quinton, *Utilitarian Ethics*, London, Duckworth, 1989, useful.
38 Gandhi to Jal A. P. Naoroji, 4 June 1932; CW 50, p. 14.
39 Quoted in Raghavan Iyer, *The Moral and Political Writings of Mahatma Gandhi*, Oxford, Clarendon Press, 1986, volume 3, p. 410.
40 See Bhikhu Parekh, *Bentham's Political Thought*, London, Croom Helm, 1973, especially pp. 16–17.
41 Samuel Scheffter, *The Rejection of Consequentialism*, Oxford, Clarendon Press, 1982, p. 10.
42 Speech at Prayer Meeting, 28 June 1947; CW 88, p. 231.
43 *Indian Opinion*, 19 January 1907; CW 6, p. 285.
44 *Harijan*, 8 June 1947; CW 88, p. 59.
45 See for example; CW 14, pp. 515–16; CW 37, p. 270; and *Nanda*, op. cit., p. 146.
46 *Young India*, 5 November 1925; CW 28, p. 434.
47 Robert Nozick, *Anarchy, State and Utopia*, Oxford, Blackwell, 1947, p. 166.
48 *Navajivan*, 22 September 1929; CW 41, p. 449.
49 *Young India*, 13 September 1928; CW 37, p. 270.
50 Gandhi to Premabehn Kantak, 21 June 1935; CW 61, p. 183.

2 PREFERENCE, UTILITY AND WELFARE

1 *Harijan*, 28 July 1946; CW 85, pp. 32–33.
2 *Harijan*, 1 February, 1942; CW 73, p. 93.
3 Brian Barry, *Political Argument*, London, Routledge and Kegan Paul, 1965, p. 38.
4 Ibid., pp. 40–41.
5 *Navajivan*, 1 March 1925; CW 26, pp.175–76.
6 *Hind Swaraj*; CW 10, p. 37.
7 *Indian Opinion*, 29 May 1909; CW 9, p. 277.
8 *Harijan*, 1 February 1942; CW 73, p. 94.
9 Quoted in R. Iyer (ed.) *The Moral and Political Writings of Mahatma Gandhi*, Oxford, Clarendon Press, 1986, volume 3, p. 446.

NOTES

10 Gandhi to Krishna Chandra, 14 May 1936; CW 62, p. 403.
11 *Harijan*, 11 May 1935; CW 60, p. 464.
12 *Harijan*, 2 November 1935; CW 62, p. 59.
13 Quoted in Iyer (ed.), op. cit., volume 1, p. 384.
14 Leo Tolstoy, *What I Believe, Works*, translated by A. Maude, London, Oxford University Press, 1933, volume 11, p. 472.
15 Speech at Muir College Economic Society, 22 December 1916; CW 13, p. 315.
16 *Harijan*, 12 February 1938; CW 66, p. 355.
17 Speech at Muir College Economic Society, 22 December 1916; CW 13, p. 315.
18 Gandhi to Jamnadas Gandhi, 17 March 1914; CW 12, p. 389.
19 Speech at Muir College Economic Society, 22 December 1916; CW 13, p. 312.
20 Ibid.
21 Ibid.
22 Gandhi to W. B. Stover, 16 June 1927; CW 34, p. 9.
23 Ibid.
24 See also in this connection Chapter 3, pp. 47–48.
25 Gandhi to Jamnadas Gandhi, 17 March 1914; CW 12, p. 387.
26 *Young India*, 8 December 1921; CW 21, p. 546.
27 Quoted in B. N. Ganguli, *Gandhi's Social Philosophy*, Delhi, Vikas, 1973, p. 50.
28 *Navajivan*, 15 December 1929; CW 42, p. 282.
29 *Harijan*, 12 February 1938; CW 66, p. 355.
30 *The Hindu*, 26 January 1946; CW 83, p. 27.
31 *Harijan*, 25 August 1946; CW 85, p. 97.
32 *The Hindu*, 26 January 1946; CW 83, p. 27.
33 *Young India*, 14 June 1928; CW 36, p. 400.
34 *Harijan*, 22 August 1936; CW 63, p. 233.
35 *Young India*, 20 August 1919; CW 16, p. 30.
36 Ibid., p. 30; also CW 26, p. 278.
37 *Young India*, 20 August 1919; CW 16, p. 30.
38 *Harijan*, 23 March 1947; CW 87, p. 26.
39 *Harijan*, 1 March 1935; CW 60, p. 254.
40 Ibid.
41 *Young India*, 20 May 1919; CW 16, p. 30.
42 *Navajivan*, 1 March 1925; CW 26, p. 173.
43 *Young India*, 15 November 1925; CW 28, p. 428.
44 *Young India*, 30 May 1929; CW 40, p. 435.
45 Ibid.
46 *Harijan*, 10 August; CW 58, p. 294.
47 *Harijan*, 18 April 1936; CW 62, p. 324.
48 *Young India*, 12 March 1925; CW 26, p. 279.
49 Presidential Address at Belgaum Congress, 26 December 1924; CW 25, p. 475.
50 Ibid.
51 *Young India*, 12 March 1925; CW 26, p. 278.
52 Ibid.

53 *Young India*, 1 September 1921; CW 21, pp. 42–43.
54 *Harijan*, 24 December 1938; CW 68, p. 188.
55 Interview by Alice Schalek, 20 March 1928; CW 36, p. 128.
56 *Young India*, 10 December 1919; CW 16, p. 336.
57 Gandhi's Presidential Address at Belgaum Congress, 26 December 1924; CW 25, p. 475.
58 *Harijan*, 12 February 1938; CW 66, p. 354.
59 *The Hindu*, 26 January 1946; CW 83, pp. 26–27.
60 *Harijan*, 1 March 1935; CW 60, p. 256.
61 Ibid.
62 *Harijan*, 18 April 1936; CW 62, p. 324.
63 Ibid.
64 *Young India*, 3 November 1921; CW 21, p. 391; and *Navajivan*, 2 August 1925; CW 28, p. 11.
65 *The Hindu*, 23 March 1925; CW 26, p. 350. Also *Harijan*, 5 October 1934; CW 59, p. 129.
66 *Harijan*, 6 July 1935; CW 61, p. 232.
67 *Young India*, 11 November 1926; CW 32, pp. 23–24.
68 *Young India*, 10 December 1919; CW 16, p. 336.
69 *Harijan*, 16 December 1939; CW 71, p. 28.
70 *Young India*, 17 June 1926; CW 31, p. 11.
71 *Navajivan*, 30 August 1925; CW 28, p. 135.
72 Gandhi to Bagala Prasanna Guha Roy, 11 April 1926; CW 30, p. 275.
73 *Young India*, 27 May 1926; CW 30, p. 454.
74 Gandhi to Nagardas Lallubhai, 30 April 1926; CW 30, p. 386.
75 Ibid.
76 *Young India*, 27 May 1926; CW 30, p. 454.
77 *Young India*, 12 January 1922; CW 22, p. 160.
78 *Young India*, 22 September 1920; CW 18, p. 276.
79 *Young India*, 11 November 1926; CW 32, p. 26.
80 Ibid.
81 *Young India*, 22 May 1924; CW 24, p. 101.
82 *Navajivan*, 22 February; CW 26, p. 186.
83 *Young India*, 11 November 1926; CW 32, p. 25.
84 *Navajivan*, 11 January 1925; CW 25, p. 578.
85 *Young India*, 17 July 1924; CW 24, p. 406.
86 *Young India*, 11 November 1926; CW 32, p. 25.
87 *Young India*, 17 July 1924; CW 24, p. 406.
88 *Navajivan*, 11 January 1925; CW 25, p. 578.
89 *Young India*, 22 May 1924; CW 24, p. 101.
90 *Young India*, 18 November 1926; CW 32, p. 60.
91 *The Hindu*, 9 March 1925; CW 26, p. 245.
92 *Khadi Jagat*, August 1941; CW 74, p. 279.
93 *Harijan*, 26 August 1939; CW 70, p. 104.
94 Ibid., p. 205.
95 See Ajit Dasgupta, *Growth, Development and Welfare*, Oxford, Blackwell, 1988.
96 Speech to Businessmen, Karachi, 8 July 1934; CW 58, p. 152.
97 Gandhi to Brijkrishna Chandiwala, 4 June 1934; CW 58, p. 56.

98 Gandhi to Raja Gopala Krishnaiyya, 2 July 1934; CW 58, p. 141.
99 *Navajivan*, 22 November 1925; CW 28, p. 468.
100 *Navajivan*, 3 February 1929; CW 38, p. 430.
101 Presidential Address at Belgaum Congress, 26 December 1924; CW 25, p. 485.
102 *Navajivan*, 24 April 1921; CW 20, p. 33.
103 Gandhi to Maganlal Gandhi, 15 November 1917; CW 14, pp. 90–91.
104 *Navajivan*, 2 August 1925; CW 28, p. 15.
105 *Navajivan*, 2 August 1925; CW 28, p. 7.
106 Ibid.
107 *Forward*, 1 August 1925; CW 27, p. 465.
108 *Bombay Chronicle*, 31 July 1921; CW 20, p. 449.
109 Ibid.
110 *Harijan*, 2 November 1935; CW 62, p. 88.
111 *Navajivan*, 2 August 1925; CW 28, p. 8.
112 Gandhi to Lilian Edger, 6 July 1927; CW 34, p. 118.
113 *Harijan*, 8 June 1940; CW 72, p. 137.
114 *Young India*, 15 September 1927; CW 34, p. 480.
115 *Harijan*, 7 December 1935; CW 62, p. 166.
116 Speech on the Birth Anniversary of Tolstoy, 10 September 1928; CW 37, p. 265.
117 Draft Constitution for the Ashram; CW 13, p. 94.
118 Speech at International Sanatorium, 9 December 1931; CW 48, p. 415.
119 *Young India*, 11 August 1927; CW 34, p. 319.
120 *The Hindu*, 23 March 1925; CW 26, p. 380.
121 *Harijan*, 29 June 1935; CW 61, p. 211.
122 *Navajivan*, 16 September 1928; CW 37, p. 268.
123 'History of the *Satyagraha* Ashram', 11 July 1932; CW 50, p. 216.
124 *Hindi Navajivan*, 6 February 1930; CW 42, p. 458.
125 Speech at 'Kaliparaj' Conference, Vedchi, 18 January 1925; CW 26, p. 19.
126 Convocation Address at Punjab Qaumi Vidyapith, Lahore, 6 December 1924; CW 25, p. 404.
127 Advice to students, Patna, 28 April 1947; CW 87, p. 379.
128 *Young India*, 14 June 1928; CW 36, p. 400.
129 *Navajivan*, 3 July 1927; CW 34, p. 99.
130 *Harijan*, 16 May 1936; CW 62, p. 368.
131 *Harijan*, 8 March 1935; CW 60, p. 266.
132 *Harijan*, 16 May 1936; CW 62, p. 368.
133 *Harijan*, 12 February 1938; CW 66, p. 355.
134 *Harijan*, 8 March 1935; CW 60, p. 267.
135 *Young India*, 15 October 1925; CW 28, p. 339.
136 See for example, Thomas Schwartz, 'Human Welfare: What It is Not', in H. B. Miller and W. H. Williams (eds) *The Limits of Utilitarianism*, University of Minnesota Press, 1982, especially pp. 195–99.
137 Dan W. Brock, *Life and Death*, Cambridge, Cambridge University Press, 1993, p. 29.

3 RIGHTS

1 *Taking Rights Seriously*, London, Duckworth, 1977.
2 Ibid., p. 184.
3 Ronald J. Tercheck, 'Gandhi and Moral Autonomy', *Gandhi Marg*, January–March 1992, volume 13, no. 4, p. 454.
4 *Young India*, 8 January 1925; CW 25, p. 564.
5 *Harijan*, 27 May 1939; CW 69, p. 50.
6 *Harijan*, 13 October 1940; CW 73, pp. 89–90.
7 Ibid., p. 90.
8 Gandhi to Julian Huxley, before 17 October 1947; CW 89, p. 348.
9 Speech at Prayer Meeting, 29 June 1947; CW 88, p. 238.
10 *Young India*, 26 March 1931; CW 45, p. 339.
11 *The Hindu*, 16 August 1920; CW 18, p. 165.
12 *The Hindu*, 16 August 1920; CW 18, p. 165.
13 Ibid.
14 Speech at Prayer Meeting, 28 June 1947; CW 88, pp. 230–31.
15 Speech at Prayer Meeting, 29 June 1947; CW 88, p. 238.
16 *Harijan*, 1 May 1937; CW 65, p. 159.
17 Ibid.
18 Joan Bondurant, *Conquest of Violence*, revised edn, Berkeley and Los Angeles, University of California Press, 1965, p. 167.
19 *Navajivan*, 31 May 1931; CW 46, pp. 257–58.
20 Ibid., p. 257.
21 Ibid., p. 258.
22 *Harijan*, 3 April 1937; CW 65, p. 48.
23 *Young India*, 20 October 1927; CW 35, p. 99.
24 CW 45, p. 370, footnote 1.
25 CW 45, p. 373.
26 *Harijan*, 17 April 1937; CW 65, p. 79.
27 Gandhi to S. Krishna Aiyar, 27 January 1933; CW 53, p. 165.
28 A Letter, 15 January 1933; CW 53, p. 59.
29 Gandhi to S. D. Nadkarni, 27 January 1933; CW 53, p. 164.
30 Alan R. White, 'Rights and Claims', in M. A. Stewart (ed.) *Law, Morality and Rights*, Dordrecht, Reidel, 1983, p. 159.
31 Ibid., p. 157.
32 Bosanquet, *Philosophical Theory of the State*, fourth edn, London, Macmillan, 1958, p. 188.
33 Ibid., p. 191.
34 Ibid., p. 195.
35 Ibid., p. 190.
36 Bondurant, op. cit., p. 168.
37 *Navajivan*, 7 September 1919; CW 16, p. 93.
38 *Young India*, 5 January 1922; CW 22, p. 142.
39 *Navajivan*, 7 September 1919; CW 16, p. 93.
40 *Young India*, 5 January 1922; CW 22, p. 143.
41 Bosanquet, op. cit., p. 199.
42 Bondurant, op. cit., p. 162.
43 CW 16, p. 441.

44 Ibid., p. 442.
45 *A Theory of Justice*, London, Oxford University Press, 1973, p. 364.
46 *Navajivan*, 2 August 1925, quoted in Raghavan Iyer (ed.) *The Moral and Political Writings of Mahatma Gandhi*, Oxford, Clarendon Press, 1987, volume 3, p. 101.
47 I have examined this argument elsewhere; see my *Growth, Development and Welfare*, Oxford, Blackwell, 1988, pp.72–84.
48 Charles Fried, *Right and Wrong*, Cambridge, Mass., Harvard University Press, 1978, p. 113.
49 CW 58, p. 37.
50 Bondurant, op. cit., pp. 162–63.
51 *Harijan*, 13 April 1935; CW 60, p. 417.
52 Pyarelal, *Mahatma Gandhi*, Ahmedabad, Navajivan Press, 1965, volume 1, p. 315.
53 *Young India*, 8 December 1927, quoted in Iyer, op. cit., volume 1, p. 504.
54 *Young India*, 6 October 1921; CW 21, p. 248.
55 Ibid.
56 Gandhi to Jawaharla Nehru, 25 April 1925, *A Bunch of Old Letters*, London, Asia Publishing House, 1960, p. 43.
57 See e.g. *Young India*, 13 September 1928; CW 37, p. 270; Gandhi to Bhagawanji Purushottom, 24 October 1926; CW 31, p. 529.
58 *Anarchy, State and Utopia*, Oxford, Blackwell, 1980, pp. 39–40.
59 See, for example, Norman P. Barry, *An Introduction to Modern Political Theory*, London, Macmillan, 1981, p. 188.
60 See Amartya Sen, 'Rights and Agency', *Philosophy and Public Affairs*, 1981, volume 11, pp. 3–28; see also, Ajit Dasgupta, op. cit., pp. 79–82.
61 'Analysis of Right', in Eugene Kamenka and Alice Erh-Soon Tay (eds) *Human Rights*, London, Edward Arnold, 1978, p. 85.
62 Ibid., p. 86.

4 INDUSTRIALISATION, TECHNOLOGY AND THE SCALE OF PRODUCTION

1 *Essays on Indian Economics*, Bombay, Thacker, 1899, p. 29.
2 Ibid., p. 30.
3 See, for example, *Selected Works of Jawaharlal Nehru*, New Delhi, Orient Longman, 1973, volume 5, p. 512.
4 Gandhi's speech at Subjects Committee Meeting of the AICC, 24 October 1934; CW 59, p. 225.
5 22 September 1931, CW 48, p. 48.
6 Quoted in *Selected Works of Jawaharlal Nehru*, op. cit., 5, p. 510, fn 3.
7 M. N. Roy and Evelyn Roy, quoted in Dennis Dalton, *Mahatma Gandhi, Non-violent Power in Action*, New York, Columbia University Press, 1993, p. 83.
8 See for example M. N. Roy, *India's Message, Fragments from Prisoner's Diary*, Calcutta, Renaissance Publishers, 1950.

9 CW 10, p. 58.
10 Ibid.
11 *Bombay Chronicle*, 31 July 1921; CW 20, p. 449.
12 CW 10, p. 59.
13 Ibid.
14 Ibid., p. 60.
15 *Harijanbandhu*, 15 October 1933; CW, 56, p. 94.
16 Gandhi to Sam Higginbottom, 11 November 1934; CW 59, p. 324.
17 Gandhi to M. Visvesvarayya, 23 November 1934; CW 59, p. 388.
18 *Harijan*, 30 November 1934; CW 59, p. 413.
19 *Harijan*, 23 March 1947; CW 87, p. 26.
20 Talk with Manu Gandhi, 21 April 1947; CW 87, p. 326.
21 Talk with Visitors, 26 June 1947; CW 88, p. 213.
22 *Harijan*, 2 November 1934; CW 48, p. 166.
23 Ibid.
24 *Young India*, 17 September 1925; CW 28, pp. 188–89.
25 CW 48, p. 166.
26 *Harijan*, 2 November 1934; CW 48, p. 166.
27 *Young India*, 13 and 20 November 1924; CW 25, p. 251.
28 Ibid.
29 Talk with Manu Gandhi, 10 April 1947; CW 87, p. 249.
30 *Harijan*, 27 January 1940; CW 71, p. 130.
31 *Harijan*, 29 July 1940; CW 73, pp. 29–30.
32 *Harijan*, 2 November 1934; CW 48, p. 163.
33 *Young India*, 12 November 1931; CW 48, p. 224.
34 *Harijan*, 8 October 1931; CW 48, p. 47.
35 *Harijan*, 11 May 1935; CW 61, p. 46; see also CW 71, pp. 79–80.
36 *Young India*, 11 August 1927; CW 34, p. 261.
37 *Harijan*, 29 September 1940; CW 73, p. 29.
38 *Young India*, 20 December 1928; CW 38, p. 243.
39 *Young India*, 12 November 1931; CW 48, p. 225.
40 Gandhi to Giri Raj, 4 October 1929; CW 41, p. 511.
41 Gandhi to M. Visvesvarayya, 10 December 1934; CW 59, p. 435.
42 Discussion with J. F. Horrabin and others, 3 December 1931; CW 48, p. 385.
43 Gandhi to Giri Raj, 4 October 1929; CW 41, p. 511.
44 *Harijan*, 15 September 1946; CW 85, p. 239.
45 Talk with Socialists, 27 May 1947; CW 88, p. 16.
46 *Harijan*, 2 November 1931; CW 48, p. 164.
47 *Harijan*, 22 June 1935; CW 61, p. 187.
48 *Harijan*, 27 January 1940; CW 71, p. 130.
49 *Navajivan*, 19 June 1927; CW 34, p. 26.
50 Discussion with J. F. Horrabin and others, 3 December 1931; CW 48, p. 385.
51 *Harijan*, 2 November 1934; CW 48, p. 166.
52 Talk with Rajendra Prasad, 27 June 1947; CW 88, p. 221.
53 Talk with Socialists, 27 May 1947; CW 88, p. 17.
54 Talk with Manu Gandhi, 10 April 1947; CW 87, p. 249.
55 *Young India*, 13 and 20 November 1924; CW 25, p. 255.

56 *Harijan*, 22 June 1935; CW 61, p. 187.

57 *Harijan*, 28 July 1946; CW 85, pp. 33–34.

58 *Harijan*, 7 December 1935; CW 62, p. 166.

59 Talk with Manu Gandhi, 10 April 1947; CW 87, p. 249.

60 A. P. Thirlwall, *Growth and Development*, fifth edn, Basingstoke, Macmillan, 1994, especially pp. 180–81, 232–35 and 244. The argument, it is true, neglects the possibility that more capital-intensive techniques could stimulate the growth-rate by diverting income towards those with a higher propensity to save. However, Gandhi was not interested in growth as such.

61 *Harijan*, 1 February 1942; CW 73, p. 94.

62 See Ajit Dasgupta, *Growth, Development and Welfare*, Oxford, Blackwell, 1988, especially Chapter 5.

63 P. J. Cain and A. G. Hopkins, 'The Political Economy of British Expansion Overseas, 1750–1914', *Economic History Review*, volume 33, 1980, p. 479.

64 'The Imperialism of Free Trade', reprinted in W. R. Louis (ed.) *Imperialism, the Robinson and Gallager Controversy*, New York, 1976, p. 58.

65 Speech at Subjects Committee Meeting, AICC, 24 October 1934; CW 59, p. 225.

66 B. R. Nanda, *Gandhi and His Critics*, Delhi, Oxford University Press, 1993, p. 129.

67 *The Hindu*, 21 December 1931; CW 48, p. 353.

68 Sherry Twerkle, *Computers and the Human Spirit*, London, Granada, 1984, p. 172.

69 Herbert Simon, 'The Social Impact of Computers', in Tom Forester (ed.) *The Microelectronics Revolution*, Oxford, Blackwell, 1980, pp. 430–31.

70 'A Note on Gandhi', in Dr Sarvapalli Radhakrishnan (ed.) *Mahatma Gandhi*, Bombay, Jaico Publishing House, 1994, p. 329.

5 INEQUALITY

1 For an exposition and a critique of the notion see Bernard Williams, 'The Idea of Equality', in Peter Laslett and W. R. Runciman (eds) *Philosophy, Politics and Society*, Oxford, Blackwell, 1962, pp. 110–31.

2 *Young India*, 11 August 1927; CW 34, p. 314.

3 Ibid., pp. 314–15.

4 Gandhi to Nehru, 2 May 1933, *A Bunch of Old Letters*, London, Asia Publishing House, 1960, p. 113.

5 Quoted in Joan V. Bondurant, *Conquest of Violence*, revised edn, Berkeley and Los Angeles, University of California Press, 1965, pp. 168–69.

6 Williams, in Laslett and Runciman, op. cit., p. 115.

7 John Rawls, *A Theory of Justice*, New York, Oxford University Press, 1973, p. 100.

8   Larry S. Temkin, *Inequality*, New York and Oxford, Oxford University Press, 1993.
9   Ronald Dworkin, *Taking Rights Seriously*, London, Duckworth, 1977, p. 227.
10 M. K. Gandhi, *Constructive Programme*, second edn, Ahmedabad, Navajivan Publishers, 1945, pp. 20–21.
11 Gandhi to Lord Irwin, *Young India*, 12 March 1930; CW 43, p. 5.
12 *Young India*, 30 June 1927; CW 34, p. 79.
13 Ibid., p. 79.
14 *The Hindu*, 26 January 1946; CW 83, p. 27.
15 Simon Kuznets, *Modern Economic Growth*, New Haven, Yale University Press, 1966.
16 *Harijan*, 13 March 1937; CW 64, p. 421.
17 Gandhi to Amrit Kaur, 26 April 1935; CW 61, p. 3.
18 *Navajivan*, 25 September 1921; CW 21, p. 199.
19 *Harijan*, 20 June 1936; CW 63, p. 33.
20 *Harijan*, 20 April 1935; CW 60, p. 440.
21 Ibid.
22 *Harijan*, 4 July 1936; CW 63, p. 44.
23 *Young India*, 20 October 1927; CW 35, p. 115.
24 Speech at Gandhi Seva Sangh Meeting, Hudli, 20 April 1937; CW 65, p. 136.
25 E.g. CW 29, p. 400; CW 35, p. 146.
26 *Harijan*, 4 July 1936; CW 63, p. 50.
27 *Young India*, 30 December 1926; CW 32, p. 476.
28 *Young India*, 29 July 1926; CW 31, p. 213.
29 *Young India*, 22 September 1927; CW 34, pp. 550–51.
30 *Young India*, 14 May 1935; CW 27, p. 15.
31 *Young India*, 6 October 1921; CW 21, pp. 245–50.
32 *The Hindu*, 1 December 1927; CW 35, p. 327.
33 *Young India*, 20 October 1927; CW 35, p. 99.
34 Speech at Public Meeting, Hyderabad, 6 April 1929; CW 40, p. 208.
35 Bhikhu Parekh, 'Gandhi and the Logic of Reformist Discourse', in Bhikhu Parekh and Thomas Panham (eds) *Political Discourse*, New Delhi, Sage, 1987, p. 284.
36 *Harijan*, 18 July 1936; CW 63, p. 154.
37 *Harijan*, 28 September 1934; CW 59, p. 91.
38 *Young India*, 29 July 1926; CW 31, p. 214.
39 See Parekh, op. cit., p. 284.
40 *Harijan*, 16 November 1935; CW 62, p. 121.
41 *Harijan*, 22 August 1936; CW 63, p. 232.
42 Ibid.
43 *Young India*, 30 December 1926; CW 32, p. 442.
44 *Young India*, 29 July 1926; CW 31, p. 212.
45 *Navajivan*, 21 August 1921; CW 21, p. 2.
46 *Young India*, 16 May 1929; CW 40, p. 382.
47 *Harijanbandhu*, 7 August 1938; CW 67, p. 230.
48 *Harijan*, 25 July 1936; CW 63, p. 172.

49 *Young India*, 22 September 1927, quoted in Bondurant, op. cit., p. 169.
50 T. Scanlon, 'Nozick on Rights, Liberty and Property', *Philosophy and Public Affairs*, 1976, volume 6, pp. 9–10.
51 John Rawls, *A Theory of Justice*, New York, Oxford University Press, 1973, p. 102.
52 See, for example, Antony Copley, *Gandhi, Against the Tide*, Oxford, Blackwell, 1987, p. 87.
53 See, for example, 'The Caste System', *Young India*, 8 December 1920; CW 19, pp. 83–85.
54 B. R. Nanda, *Gandhi and His Critics*, Delhi, Oxford University Press, 1985, p. 26.
55 *Harijan*, 1 August 1936; CW 63, p. 190.
56 See, for example, Gandhi to Dr M. S. Kelkar, 16 June 1927; CW 34, p. 10. Also *Navajivan*, 2 October 1921; CW 21, p. 233.
57 Answers to questions at Gandhi Seva Sangh Meeting, 6 May 1939; CW 69, p. 220.
58 Bhikhu Parekh, *Colonialism, Tradition and Reform, An Analysis of Gandhi's Political Discourse*, New Delhi, Sage, 1989, p. 229.
59 Quoted in Nanda, op. cit., p. 26.
60 *The Hindu*, 6 October 1927; CW 35, p. 81.
61 Ibid.
62 Gandhi to David B. Hart, 21 September 1934; CW 59, p. 45.
63 *Harijan*, 13 March 1937; CW 64, p. 421.
64 Jitendra Nath Mohanty, *Reason and Tradition in Indian Thought*, Oxford, Clarendon Press, 1992, especially Chapter 9.
65 Quoted in Raghavan Iyer (ed.) *The Moral and Political Writings of Mahatma Gandhi*, Oxford, Clarendon Press, 1986, volume 2, p. 262.
66 Mohanty, op. cit., p. 275.
67 *Young India*, 21 July 1921; CW 20, p. 409.
68 *Harijan*, 24 February 1940; CW 71, p. 207.
69 Madhu Kishawar, 'Gandhi on Women', *Economic and Political Weekly*, volume 20, Part I, No. 40, 5 October 1985, Part II, No. 41, 12 October 1985.
70 *Harijan*, 2 May, 1936; CW. 62, p. 363.
71 Speech at Women's Meeting, Bombay, 8 May 1919; CW 15, p. 290.
72 *Hindi Navajivan*, 11 July 1929; CW 41, p. 179.
73 *Young India*, 14 January 1932; CW 48, p. 424.
74 See *Navajivan*, 6 April 1930; CW 43, p. 191.
75 Kishawar, op. cit., Part I, p. 1697.
76 *Harijan*, 21 April 1946; CW 83, p. 399.
77 *Young India*, 21 July 1921; CW 20, p. 411.
78 *Young India*, 21 July 1921; CW 20, p. 411.
79 CW 30, p. 365.
80 *Young India*, 23 September 1926; CW 31, p. 443.
81 *Young India*, 3 February 1927; CW 33, pp. 44–45.
82 Ibid., p. 45.
83 *Harijan*, 23 May 1936; CW 62, p. 435.
84 *Young India*, 21 May 1931; CW 46, p. 75.

85   Speech at D. J. S. College Hall, Karachi, 5 February 1929; CW 39, p. 416.
86   *Young India,* 3 June 1926; CW 30, p. 365.
87   *Young India,* 3 October 1929; CW 41, p. 494.
88   Ibid.
89   Ibid.
90   *Hindi Navajivan,* 8 August 1929; CW 41, p. 269.
91   *Young India,* 17 October 1929; CW 42, pp. 4–5.
92   Ibid., p. 5.
93   *The Hindu,* 29 October 1944; CW 78, p. 238.
94   *The Daily Herald,* 28 September 1931; CW 48, p. 80.
95   *Harijan,* 7 April 1946; CW 83, p. 338.
96   Ibid.
97   Ibid.
98   *Young India,* 25 November 1926; CW 32, pp. 89–90.
99   *Young India,* 21 May 1931; CW 46, p. 75.
100 *Young India,* 19 August 1926; CW 31, p. 314; and *Young India,* 23 September 1926; CW 31, p. 443.
101 *Narajivan,* 10 July 1927; CW 34, p. 142.
102 Ibid.
103 *Harijan,* 8 June 1940; CW 72, p. 137.
104 Ibid.
105 *The Daily Herald,* 28 September 1931; CW 48, p. 80.
106 Ibid., p. 80.
107 *Navajivan,* 2 June 1929; CW 41, p. 7.
108 *Harijan,* 12 October 1934; CW 59, p. 147.
109 *Harijan,* 24 February 1940; CW 71, p. 20.
110 *Harijan,* 16 March1940, quoted in Iyer, op.cit., volume 1, p. 62.
111 *Harijan,* 2 December 1939; CW 70, p. 381.
112 *Harijan,* 24 February 1940; CW 71, pp. 206–9.
113 Madhu Kishawar, 'Gandhi on Women', *Economic and Political Weekly,* volume 20, Part I, No. 40, 5 October 1985, p. 1701.
114 Constructive Programme, Its Meaning and Place, 13 December 1941; CW 75, p. 155.
115 Quoted in D. G. Tendulkar, *Mahatma,* Bombay, V. K. Iharevi and Tendulkar, 1952, volume 6, p. 376.
116 *Harijanbandhu,* 20 December 1936; CW 63, p. 421.
117 *Harijan,* 12 October 1934; CW 59, p. 147.
118 Gandhi to Manilal and Sushila Gandhi, 20 June 1927; CW 34, p. 32.
119 *Harijan,* 24 February 1940; CW 71, p. 208.
120 Quoted, Sophia Wadia, 'The Path of *Satyagraha*', in S. Radhakrishnan (ed.) *Mahatma Gandhi,* Bombay, Jaico Publishing House, 1966, p. 247.
121 Constructive Programme, Its Meaning and Place, 13 December 1941; CW 75, p. 155.
122 Pushpa Joshi, *Gandhi on Women,* Ahmedabad, Navajivan Publishing House, 1988, Foreword by Ella R. Bhatt, pp. VII–VIII.
123 *Young India,* 17 October 1929; CW 42, p. 5.
124 Ibid .

125 *Young India*, 23 May 1929; CW 40, p. 417.

126 Ibid., p. 417.

127 Ibid., p. 418.

128 Answers to Questions, 31 May 1935; CW 61, p. 124.

129 *Harijan*, 24 February 1940; CW 71, p. 207.

130 *Young India*, 16 April 1925; CW 26, p. 516.

131 *Hindusthan Times*, 28 December 1938; CW 68, p. 230.

132 Andre Beteille, *Society and Politics in India*, London, Athlone Press, 1991, p. 238.

133 S. G. Sardesai, 'Gandhi and the CPI', in M. B. Rao (ed.) *The Mahatma, A Marxist Symposium*, Bombay, People's Publishing House, 1969, p. 48.

134 Kishawar, op. cit., Part II, p. 1699.

135 Rolf Dahrendorf, 'On the Origin of Social Inequality', in Laslett and Runciman, op. cit., p. 94.

136 *Bombay Chronicle*, 19 May 1939; CW 69, p. 63.

6 THE THEORY OF TRUSTEESHIP

1 Speech at Gandhi Seva Sangh Meeting, 6 May 1939; CW 69, p. 219.

2 See *The Hindu*, 7 September 1945; CW 81, p. 210.

3 *Harijan*, 16 December 1939; CW 71, p. 28.

4 *Harijan*, 25 August 1940; CW 72, p. 400.

5 Ibid.

6 *Harijan*, 16 December 1939; CW 71, p. 28.

7 *Harijan*, 22 February 1948; CW 90, pp. 521–22.

8 CW 69, p. 219.

9 Interview to N. K. Bose, 9–10 November 1934; CW 59, p. 318.

10 *Harijan*, 20 February 1937; CW 64, p. 385.

11 Ibid., pp. 384–85.

12 *Labour Monthly*, March 1932; CW 48, p. 244.

13 *Harijan*, 1 March 1942; CW 75, p. 357.

14 *Bombay Chronicle*, 13 April 1945; CW 79, p. 367.

15 Ibid.

16 *Harijan Sevak*, 22 February 1942; CW 75, p. 312.

17 *Labour Monthly*, March 1932; CW 48, p. 241.

18 CW 76, Appendix I, p. 420.

19 *Bombay Chronicle*, 13 April 1995; CW 79, p. 366.

20 Talk with Manu Gandhi, 15 April 1947; CW 87, p. 284.

21 *Harijan*, 25 August 1940; CW 72, p. 401.

22 *The Hindu*, 7 September 1945; CW 81, p. 210.

23 Geeta Abrol, 'Gandhian Doctrine of Trusteeship and Its Relevance to Modern Times', in J. S. Mathur (ed.) *Gandhian Thought and Contemporary Society*, Bombay, Bharatiya Vidya Bhavan, 1974, p. 147.

24 Interview by Margaret Bourke-White, 29 January 1948; CW 90, p. 521.

25 H. A. J. Ford and W. A. Lee, *Principles of the Law of Trusts*, second edn, Sydney, The Law Book Company Limited, 1990, p. 3.

26 Parker and Mellows, *The Modern Law of Trusts*, sixth edn, ed. by A. J. Oakeley, London, Sweet and Maxwell, 1994, p. 9.
27 Quoted in Ford and Lee, op. cit., p. 391.
28 Ibid.
29 Speech at opening of crèche, Ahmedabad, 1 May 1928; CW 36, p. 289.
30 *Young India*, 16 February 1921; CW 19, p. 365.
31 Speech at opening of crèche, Ahmedabad, 1 May 1928; CW 36, p. 289.
32 Ibid.
33 *Harijan*, 27 April 1940; CW 72, p. 17.
34 *Young India*, 5 December 1929; CW 42, p. 239.
35 Ibid.
36 *Young India*, 28 May 1931; CW 46, pp. 234–35.
37 *Young India*, 5 December 1929; CW 42, p. 240.
38 Speech at Zamindars' meeting, Nainital, 23 May 1931; CW 46, p. 204.
39 *Young India*, 28 May 1931; CW 46, p. 234.
40 D. G. Tendulkar, *Mahatma*, New Delhi, Government of India Publications, 1965, volume 6, p. 364.
41 Ibid., p. 366.
42 Ibid., p. 367.
43 *Harijan*, 28 April 1946; CW 84, p. 51.
44 Talk with Zamindars, 18 April 1947; CW 87, p. 304.
45 Letter to a Zamindar, 3 September 1946; CW 85, p. 254.
46 See Birendranath Ganguli, *Gandhi's Social Philosophy*, Delhi, Vikas, 1973, for the former view; and M. L. Dantwala, *Gandhism Reconsidered*, second edn, Bombay, Padma Publications, July, 1945, for the latter.
47 Dantwala, op. cit., p. 32.
48 *Harijan*, 16 February 1947; CW 86, p. 424.
49 Hiren Mukherjee, *Gandhi, A Study*, New Delhi, People's Publishing House, 1960, p. 113.
50 Francine Frankel, *India's Political Economy 1947–1977*, Princeton, Princeton University Press, 1978, p. 39.
51 Ibid., pp. 39–40.
52 Ibid., p. 40.
53 *Young India*, 5 December 1927; CW 42, p. 239.
54 Discussion with Students, 21 July 1934; CW 58, p. 217.
55 Ibid., p. 218.

7 EDUCATION

1 *Indian Opinion*, 20 November 1909; CW 9, p. 458.
2 Quoted in D. P. Sinha, *The Education Policy of the East India Company in Bengal to 1854*, Calcutta, Punthi Pustak, 1964, p. 199.
3 Sir Pendrel Moon, *The British Conquest and Dominion of India*, London, Duckworth, 1990, p. 466.
4 D. P. Singhal, *A History of the Indian People*, London, Methuen, 1983, p. 276.

5   Ajit Dasgupta, *A History of Indian Economic Thought*, London and New York, Routledge, 1993, Chapter 7, and references cited there.
6   Moon, op. cit., p. 821.
7   Phyllis Deane, *The First Industrial Revolution*, Cambridge, Cambridge University Press, 1967, p. 150.
8   Ajit Dasgupta, op. cit., pp.123–27.
9   *Speeches and Writings of G. K. Gokhale*, vols 1–3, Bombay, Asia Publishing House, 1962–67, volume 3, p. 125.
10 Quoted in B. R. Nanda, *Gokhale*, Delhi, Oxford University Press, 1977, p. 393.
11 Rahgavan Iyer (ed.) *The Moral and Political Writings of Mahatma Gandhi*, Oxford, Clarendon Press, 1986, volume 1, p. 129.
12 Speech at Surat Reception; CW 13, p. 195.
13 CW 14, p. 34.
14 *Navajivan Education Supplement*, 28 February 1926; CW 30, p. 58.
15 Ibid.
16 *Harijan*, 31 July 1937; CW 65, p. 450.
17 *Harijan*, 8 May 1937; CW 65, p. 74.
18 *Harijan*, 10 March 1946; CW 83, p. 208.
19 *Navajivan Education Supplement*, 28 February 1926; CW 30, p. 59.
20 *Harijan*, 8 May 1937; CW 65, p. 73.
21 *Young India*, 1 September 1921; CW 21, pp. 39–40.
22 *Harijan*, 7 May 1937; CW 67, p. 46.
23 *Satdharma Pracharak*, 24 March 1917; CW 13, p. 359.
24 *Harijan*, 29 September 1946; Iyer, op. cit., volume 2, p. 454.
25 *Harijan*, 9 October 1937; CW 66, p. 168.
26 Quoted in D. G. Tendulkar, *Mahatma*, op. cit., 1952, p. 228.
27 Convocation Address at Gujrat Vidyapith, Ahmedabad, 14 January 1925; CW 25, pp. 583–84. See also *Navajivan*, 27 October 1929; CW 42, p. 52.
28 *Harijan*, 2 October 1937; CW 66, p. 194.
29 Ibid.
30 *Navajivan*, 23 September 1928; CW 37, p. 301.
31 *Harijan Sevak*, 8 July 1939; CW 69, p. 205.
32 Quoted in Tendulkar, op. cit., volume 4, p. 245.
33 *Harijan*, 31 July 1937; CW 65, p. 450.
34 *Harijan*, 31 July 1937; CW 65, p. 451.
35 *Navajivan*, 23 September 1928; CW 37, p. 302.
36 Ibid.
37 CW 13, p. 264.
38 Tendulkar, op. cit., volume 4, p. 245.
39 Foreword to *Basic National Education*, 28 May 1938; CW 67, p. 99.
40 Tendulkar, op. cit., volume 4, p. 241.
41 Ibid., p. 245.
42 *Young India*, 1 September 1921; CW 21, p. 39.
43 *Young India*, 2 August 1928; CW 37, p. 111.
44 Speeches and Writings of G. K. Gokhale, volumes 1–3, Bombay, Asia Publishing House, 1962–67, volume 3, p. 136.

45 Speech at Second Gujrat Educational Conference, 20 October 1917; CW 14, p. 34.
46 *Harijan Savak*, 9 November 1947; CW 87, p. 328.
47 *Young India*, 11 July 1929; CW 41, p. 173.
48 *Young India*, 2 August 1928; CW 37, pp. 111–12.
49 *Harijan*, 11 September 1937; CW 66, p. 124.
50 Ibid.
51 *Harijan*, 6 April 1940; CW 71, p. 381.
52 *Harijan*, 11 June 1938; CW 67, p. 115.
53 *Harijan*, 31 July 1937; CW 65, p. 451.
54 Speech at Second Gujrat Educational Conference, 20 October 1917; CW 14, p. 14.
55 *Harijan*, 9 March 1940; CW 71, p. 304.
56 Talk with Workers, 19 April 1947; CW 87, p. 309.
57 *Samalochak*, October 1916; CW 13, p. 298.
58 *The Hindu*, 19 March 1925; CW 26, p. 301.
59 *Harijan*, 9 July 1938; CW 67, p. 159.
60 Tendulkar, op. cit., volume 4, p. 241.
61 *Harijan*, 3 July 1937; CW 65, p. 359.
62 Ibid.
63 *Harijan*, 31 July 1937; CW 65, p. 451.
64 *Harijan*, 9 March 1940; CW 71, p. 304.
65 Tendulkar, op. cit., volume 4, p. 242.
66 Ibid.
67 *Harijan*, 2 November 1947; CW 89, p. 403.
68 Ibid.
69 *Harijan*, 9 July 1938; CW 67, p. 163.
70 *Harijan*, 2 November 1947; CW 89, p. 402.
71 *Harijan*, 9 July 1938; CW 67, p. 163.
72 *Young India*, 19 December 1929; CW 42, p. 291.
73 John Dewey, *Democracy and Education*, New York, Macmillan, 1951, p. 139.
74 John Dewey, *Education Today*, London, Allen and Unwin, 1941, p. 30.
75 John Dewey, *Schools of Tomorrow*, New York, Macmillan, 1915, p. 315.
76 John Dewey, *Democracy and Education*, op. cit., p. 367.
77 Rita Kramer, *Maria Montessori*, Oxford, Blackwell, 1976, p. 377.
78 Quoted in John N. Hopkins, *Mao Tse-Tung and Education*, Hamden, Conn., Linnet Books, 1974, p. 76.
79 Ibid., p. 86.
80 Ibid., p. 111.
81 See Hopkins, op. cit., p. 86.
82 *Young India*, 12 March 1925; CW 26, p. 276.

8 SPECIAL TOPICS

1 H. Sidgwick, *The Methods of Ethics*, London, Macmillan, 1930, pp. 415–16.
2 *Indian Opinion*, 26 April 1913; CW 12, p. 48.

3 Ibid.
4 *Harijan*, 7 September 1935; CW 61, p. 394.
5 *Harijan*, 31 March 1946; CW 83, p. 287.
6 Interview by Mrs C. Kuttan Nair, 8 January 1935; CW 60, p. 68.
7 *Harijan*, 14 September 1935; CW 61, p. 417.
8 Gandhi to M. J. Kanetkar, 5 February 1935; CW 60, p. 176.
9 *Young India*, 13 October 1920; CW 18, p. 346.
10 *Harijan*, 31 March 1946; CW 83, p. 286.
11 Ibid.
12 *Young India*, 2 April 1925; CW 26, p. 450.
13 *A History of Indian Economic Thought*, London and New York, Routledge, 1993, especially Chapter 7 on Famines and Famine Policy.
14 'Key to Health', 12 December 1942; CW 77, p. 24.
15 *Young India*, 12 March 1925; CW 26, p. 280
16 Interview by Mrs C. Kuttan Nair, 8 January 1935; CW 60, p. 68.
17 *Harijan*, 7 September 1935; CW 61, p. 394.
18 *Harijan*, 25 January 1935; CW 62, p. 160; and *Harijan*, 14 March 1935; CW 62, p. 261.
19 Interview by Mrs C. Kuttan Nair, 8 January 1935; CW 60, pp. 68–69.
20 *Young India*, 26 April 1928; CW 36, p. 265.
21 *Harijan*, 2 May 1936; CW 62, p. 363.
22 *Harijan*, 25 January 1936; CW 62, p. 157.
23 *Harijan*, 2 May 1936; CW 62, p. 363.
24 Interview by Mrs C. Kuttan Nair, 8 January 1935; CW 60, p. 69.
25 Gandhi to Mathurdas Trikumji, 8 September 1932; CW 51, p. 30.
26 *Harijan*, 14 September 1935; CW 61, p. 417.
27 Ibid.
28 *Harijan*, 28 March 1936; CW 62, p. 296.
29 Interview by Mrs C. Kuttan Nair, 8 January 1935; CW 60, p. 67.
30 *Young India*, 2 April, 1925; CW 26, p. 453.
31 *Harijan*, 30 May 1936; CW 62, p. 458.
32 Ibid.
33 Ibid.
34 'Key to Health', 12 December 1942; CW 77, p. 24.
35 *Young India*, 13 October 1920; CW 18, p. 348.
36 Ibid., p. 347.
37 *The Hindu*, 2 December 1927; CW 35, p. 34.
38 *Indian Opinion*, 26 April 1913; CW 12, p. 49; and *Young India*, 13 October 1920; CW 18, p. 347.
39 *Young India*, 2 April 1925; CW 26, p. 450.
40 *Young India*, 13 October 1920; CW 18, p. 347.
41 Ibid., p. 346.
42 See B. N. Ganguli, *Gandhi's Social Philosophy*, Delhi, Vikas, 1973.
43 Raghavan Iyer (ed.) *The Moral and Political Writings of Mahatma Gandhi*, Oxford, Clarendon Press, 1986, volume 1, Introduction, p. 3.
44 Iyer, ibid., p. 44.
45 Iyer, ibid., volume 1, Introduction, p. 9.
46 *Young India*, 14 January 1920; CW 16, p. 491.

47 U. N. Ghoshal, *A History of Indian Political Ideas*, Madras, Oxford University Press, 1966, p. 66.
48 Richard Gombrich, *Theravada Buddhism*, London, Routledge, 1988, p. 78.
49 *Harijan*, 25 June 1938; CW 67, p. 135.
50 S. Saklatvala and M. K. Gandhi, *Is India Different? The Class Struggle in India*, London, Communist Party of Great Britain, 1927, p. 23.
51 *Harijan*, 15 May 1937; CW 65, p. 199.
52 *Harijan*, 5 May 1938; CW 67, p. 135.
53 Gandhi to Premadbehn Kantak, 21 June 1935; CW 61, p. 184.
54 Jacob Viner, 'Religious Thought and Economic Society', *History of Political Economy*, 1978, volume 10, p. 27.
55 Viner, ibid., pp. 62–63
56 *Anguttara-nikaya*, ii, 95; also iii, 12–14.
57 *Samynttaruikaya*, v, 169
58 *Dighanikaya*, Pali Text Society edn, section iii, pp. 152, 190, 192.
59 See our discussion in Chapter 2.
60 E. T. Cook and A. Wedderburn (eds) *The Works of John Ruskin*, 39 volumes, London, Allen (1903–12), volume 10, pp. 239–40.
61 Ibid., p. 240
62 See Chapter 5.
63 Clive Wilmer (ed.) *Unto This Last and Other Writings by John Ruskin*, London, Penguin Books, 1985, p. 202.
64 Cook and Wedderburn, op. cit., volume 7, p. 343.
65 Ibid.
66 Quoted in Raymond E. Fitch, *The Poison Sky*, Ohio, Ohio University Press, 1964, p. 479.
67 Cook and Wedderburn, op. cit., volume 7, p. 343.
68 Ibid., volume 12, p. 552.
69 Ibid., p. 553.
70 Ruskin's Inaugural Lecture as Slade Professor at Oxford University, quoted in Quentin Bell, *Ruskin*, London, Hogarth Press, 1978, p. 134.
71 John Ruskin, *The Crown of Wild Olive*, London, George Allen, 1893, p. 116.
72 Young India, 11 August 1927; CW 34, p. 318.
73 Joan V. Bondurant, *Conquest of Violence*, revised edn, Berkeley and Los Angeles, University of California Press, 1965, p.156.
74 George Woodcock, *Gandhi*, London Fontana/Collins, 1972, p. 25.
75 Alan Lee, 'Ruskin and Political Economy: *Unto This Last*', in Robert Hewison, *New Approaches to Ruskin*, London, Routledge and Kegan Paul, 1974, p. 78.
76 Fitch, op. cit., p. 402.
77 See Christine Bolt, 'Race and the Victorians', in C. C. Eldridge (ed.) *British Imperialism in the Nineteenth Century*, London, Macmillan, 1984, especially pp. 140–41.
78 Lee, op. cit., p.75.
79 Lee, op. cit., p. 76.

9 THE LEGACY OF GANDHI

1 *Harijan*, 14 September 1947; CW 89, p. 144.
2 Ibid., p. 145.
3 *Navajivan*, 7 September 1924; CW 25, p. 60.
4 Discussion with Economists, 30 December 1938; CW 68, p. 258.
5 *Young India*, 15 September 1927; CW 34, p. 453.
6 Ibid.
7 Amartya Sen, *On Ethics and Economics*, Oxford, Blackwell, 1987, p. 7.
8 Quoted in D. G. Tendulkar, *Mahatma*, op. cit., p. 366.
9 Buddhism too provides a synthesis of deontological and consequentialist ethics, though in a different way from Gandhi's: see Paul
Lucardie, 'A Stage in Moral Development', in Lincoln Allison (ed.)
The Utilitarian Response, London, Sage, 1990, pp. 69–70.
10 *Harijan*, 1 March 1935; CW 60, pp. 251–52.
11 *The Hindu*, 23 June, 1945; CW 80, p. 352.
12 Speech at AICC meeting, 15 November 1947; CW 90, p. 43.
13 John Rawls, *A Theory of Justice*, New York, Oxford University Press,
1973, pp. 440–46.
14 *Harijan*, 30 November 1935; CW 62, p. 146.
15 *Navajivan*, 2 August 1925; CW 28, p. 7.
16 *Harijan*, 5 December 1936; CW 64, p. 71.
17 *Young India*, 17 September 1925; CW 28, p. 109.
18 Mark Lutz, 'History and Basic Principles', in Paul Elkens and Manfred
Max-Neef, *Real Life Economics*, London, Routledge, 1992, p. 106.
19 *Khadi Jagat*, August 1941; CW 74, p. 278.
20 Ibid., pp. 278–79.
21 *Harijan*, 1 February 1942; CW 73, p. 93.

INDEX

cows: ill-treatment of 61; protection of 7, 61–2; *see also* animal rights

Dahrendorf, R. 117
Dantwala, M. L. 129–30
de-industrialisation (ruralisation) 64–5, 178–81
deontology 8–12, 176–7
deti-leti 107
Devdasis 97
Dewey, J. 151–2
dharma 11, 102
Digambar Jains 49–50
disability 34
dowry system 106–7
duty 45–50; and rights 45–50, 53–6, 63
Dworkin, R. 44–5, 90–91
Dyer, General 98

economic growth: balanced 65–6; and ethical preference 14–17; and inequality 92–3; moral consequences 17–18; stages 66
education 132–54; aims 136–40; Brahmanas 136, 141; and bread-labour 39; colonial system 132–4, 138; curriculum 142; economic aspects 138–9; English 138; handicrafts 140–42; higher 139, 146–50; military training 151; by mothers 111, 113; Nayee Talim (New Education) 140–43; primary 133–5, 139–40; reading 142; Ruskin's views 170; self-supporting schools 143–6; spiritual 136–7; villages 133–4, 137, 143; vocational 140–43; Wardha Conference (1937) 139–40, 143
egoism 30
electricity 77

Elementary Education Bill (1911) 134–5
Environmental Fund (Canada) 124
equality: as respect 88–91; right to 46–8, 53; *see also* inequality
ethical preference 13–14; and economic growth 14–17; for *khaddar* 28; and labour 36; and Swadeshi movement 21–30; and welfare 13–14, 41–3
ethics: and economics 6–7, 176–7; ethical theory 7–12; and religion 4
Euclid 2, 181, 182
euthanasia 12

famine 157
fiduciary law 124–5
Fischer, L. 3
Fitch, R. E. 172
food: bread-labour doctrine 36–43, 47, 102; cheap for the poor 33–4; foreign aid 35; giving to the poor (*sadavarta*) 32–5; preferences 16
Ford, H. A. J. 123
Ford, Henry 77
foreign aid 35
Frankel, F. 130–31
Fried, C. 59

Galileo 181, 182
Gallagher, J. 83
gender inequality 104–17
Ghoshal, U. N. 165
Gokhale, G. K. 27, 67, 134–5, 145
Gombrich, R. 165–6
government: Ruskin's theory 169–70; self-government *see swaraj*
growth *see* economic growth

Hague Convention of the Laws Applicable to Trusts 123–4
hand-spinning 25–30

happiness 8–9; and welfare 15
Harijan (newspaper) 2, 96
Harijans *see* untouchables
Hind Swaraj 3, 7, 68–9, 77
Hinduism 4–5, 103–4; and
  Buddhism 164
Hopkins, A. G. 83
hospitals 20
Hunter, Lord 57–8
Huxley, A. 67, 86
Huxley, J. 46, 53

ideal-regarding principles 14
illiteracy 134
imported goods 21–30
Indian National Congress:
  commitment to
  industrialisation 67; economic
  policy 174–5; Swadeshi
  Movement *see* Swadeshi
  Movement; and untouchability
  100
individualism 13, 45
industrial relations 125–6
Industrial Revolution 65, 74–5
industrialisation 17, 64–87;
  barriers to 66; capitalism 73–4,
  81–2, 120–21; as cause of
  unemployment 70–72, 82;
  characteristics of machinery 71,
  81; English economic
  imperialism 75; factor
  substitution 76; foreign
  markets 74–5, 82–4; Gandhi's
  objections to 66–76; heavy
  industry 76; helpful vs
  unhelpful machines 79–80;
  and the individual 85–6;
  Marxist views 67–8; mass
  production 74; and military
  power 75–6; quality of life 85;
  Ranade on 64–8; villages 73,
  78; women's labour 110–11
inequality 88–117; and caste 93,
  100–104; deserved vs
  underserved 90, 96; economic

91–3; excluded groups 90;
  gender inequality 104–17;
  Ruskin's views 169–70;
  superiority 89, 170;
  untouchables 93–104; *see also*
  equality
inheritance laws 108, 110
intellect 41
Irwin, Lord 91
Islamic law 5
Iyer, R. 164

Jains 5–6; Digambar 49–50
Japan 18, 24
Jesus 5; animal rights 61
journalism 2

Kant, I. 45
karma 96
Kasturba Gandhi National
  Memorial Fund 121
Kautilya 165
kelavani 136
khaddar 21, 25–30, 42–3, 166
Kipling, Rudyard 171
Kishawar, M. 105, 112
Koran 5
Kshatriyas 93, 102, 131
Kuznets, S. 93

labour: bonded 52; bread-labour
  doctrine 36–43, 47, 102;
  division of 38; forced 49;
  industrial relations 125–6; and
  the intellect 41; intra-family
  38–9; underutilisation 70–71;
  unemployment *see*
  unemployment; and welfare
  36–43; women's 110–11;
  workers' rights 48; working
  hours 40
land *see* agriculture
landlords: forced labour 49;
  trusteeship 126–9, 130–31
law of trusts 123–5
Lee, A. 172, 173
Lee, W. A. 123